hawkeye

ALL-NEW HAWKEYE

D1119359

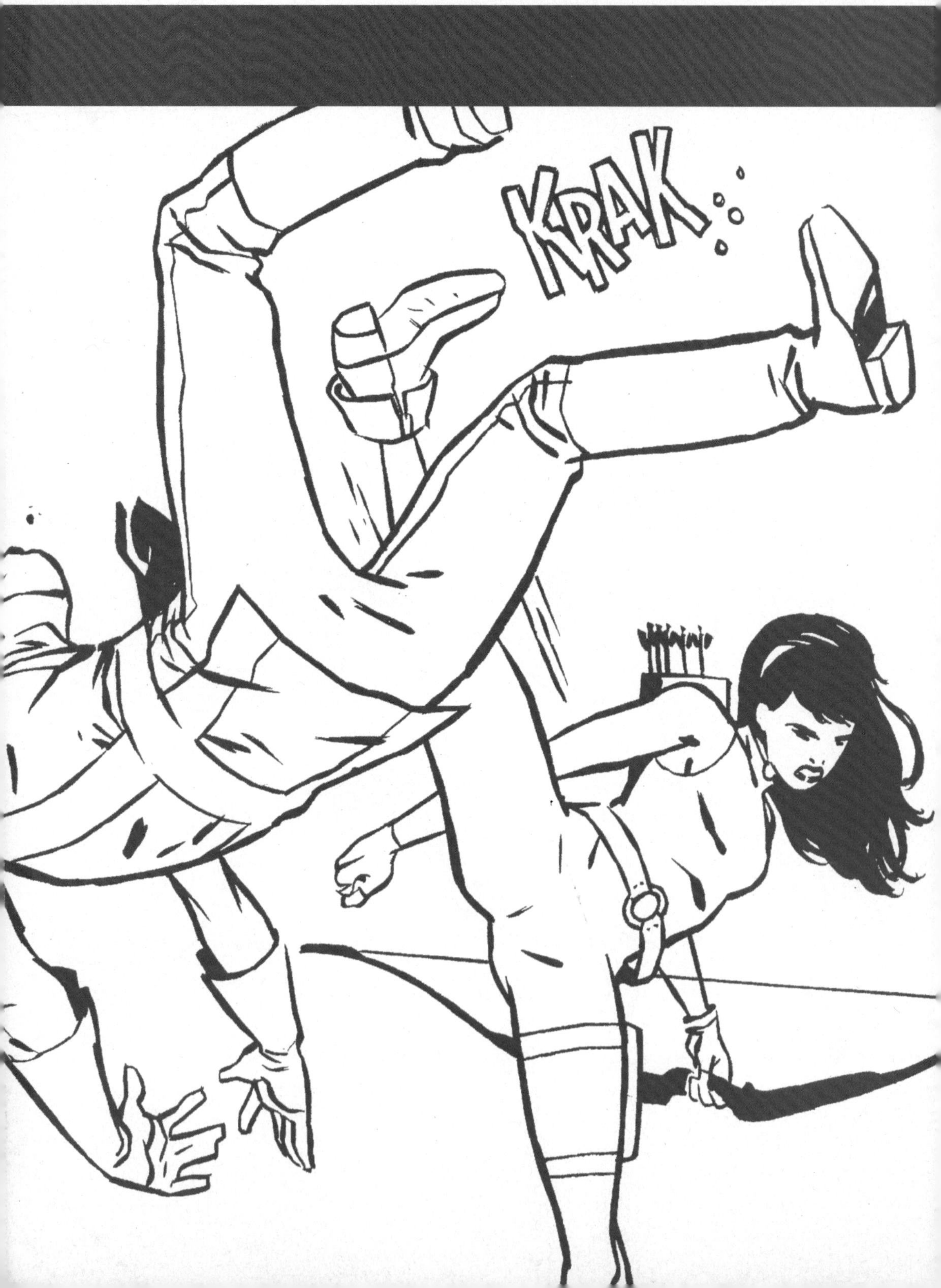
KRAK

hawkeye

ALL-NEW HAWKEYE

JEFF LEMIRE
WRITER

RAMÓN PÉREZ
ARTIST

IAN HERRING with RAMÓN PÉREZ
COLOR ARTISTS

VC's JOE SABINO
LETTERER

RAMÓN PÉREZ
COVER ART

DEVIN LEWIS
ASSISTANT EDITOR

SANA AMANAT
EDITOR

COLLECTION EDITOR: **JENNIFER GRÜNWALD** • ASSISTANT EDITOR: **SARAH BRUNSTAD**
ASSOCIATE MANAGING EDITOR: **ALEX STARBUCK** • EDITOR, SPECIAL PROJECTS: **MARK D. BEAZLEY**
SENIOR EDITOR, SPECIAL PROJECTS: **JEFF YOUNGQUIST** • SVP PRINT, SALES & MARKETING: **DAVID GABRIEL**
BOOK DESIGNER: **ADAM DEL RE**

EDITOR IN CHIEF: **AXEL ALONSO** • CHIEF CREATIVE OFFICER: **JOE QUESADA**
PUBLISHER: **DAN BUCKLEY** • EXECUTIVE PRODUCER: **ALAN FINE**

HAWKEYE VOL. 5: ALL-NEW HAWKEYE. Contains material originally published in magazine form as ALL-NEW HAWKEYE #1-5. First printing 2015. ISBN# 978-0-7851-9403-3. Published by MARVEL WORLDWIDE, INC., a subsidiary of MARVEL ENTERTAINMENT, LLC. OFFICE OF PUBLICATION: 135 West 50th Street, New York, NY 10020. Copyright © 2015 MARVEL No similarity between any of the names, characters, persons, and/or institutions in this magazine with those of any living or dead person or institution is intended, and any such similarity which may exist is purely coincidental. **Printed in Canada.** ALAN FINE, President, Marvel Entertainment; DAN BUCKLEY, President, TV, Publishing and Brand Management; JOE QUESADA, Chief Creative Officer; TOM BREVOORT, SVP of Publishing; DAVID BOGART, SVP of Operations & Procurement, Publishing; C.B. CEBULSKI, VP of International Development & Brand Management; DAVID GABRIEL, SVP Print, Sales & Marketing; JIM O'KEEFE, VP of Operations & Logistics; DAN CARR, Executive Director of Publishing Technology; SUSAN CRESPI, Editorial Operations Manager; ALEX MORALES, Publishing Operations Manager; STAN LEE, Chairman Emeritus. For information regarding advertising in Marvel Comics or on Marvel.com, please contact Jonathan Rheingold, VP of Custom Solutions & Ad Sales, at jrheingold@marvel.com. For Marvel subscription inquiries, please call 800-217-9158. **Manufactured between 9/11/2015 and 10/19/2015 by SOLISCO PRINTERS, SCOTT, QC, CANADA.**
10 9 8 7 6 5 4 3 2 1

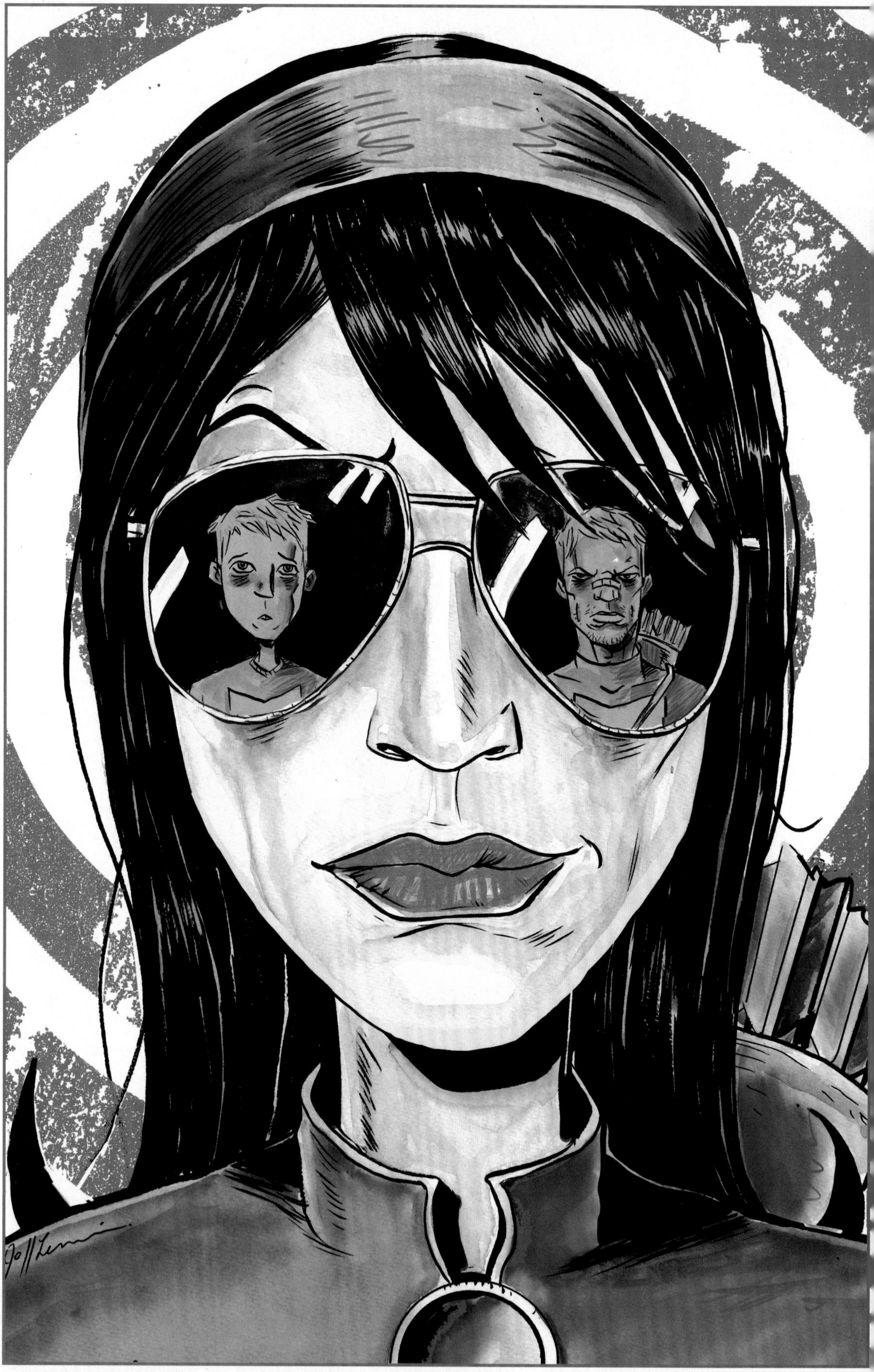

ALL-NEW HAWKEYE #1 VARIANT BY **JEFF LEMIRE**

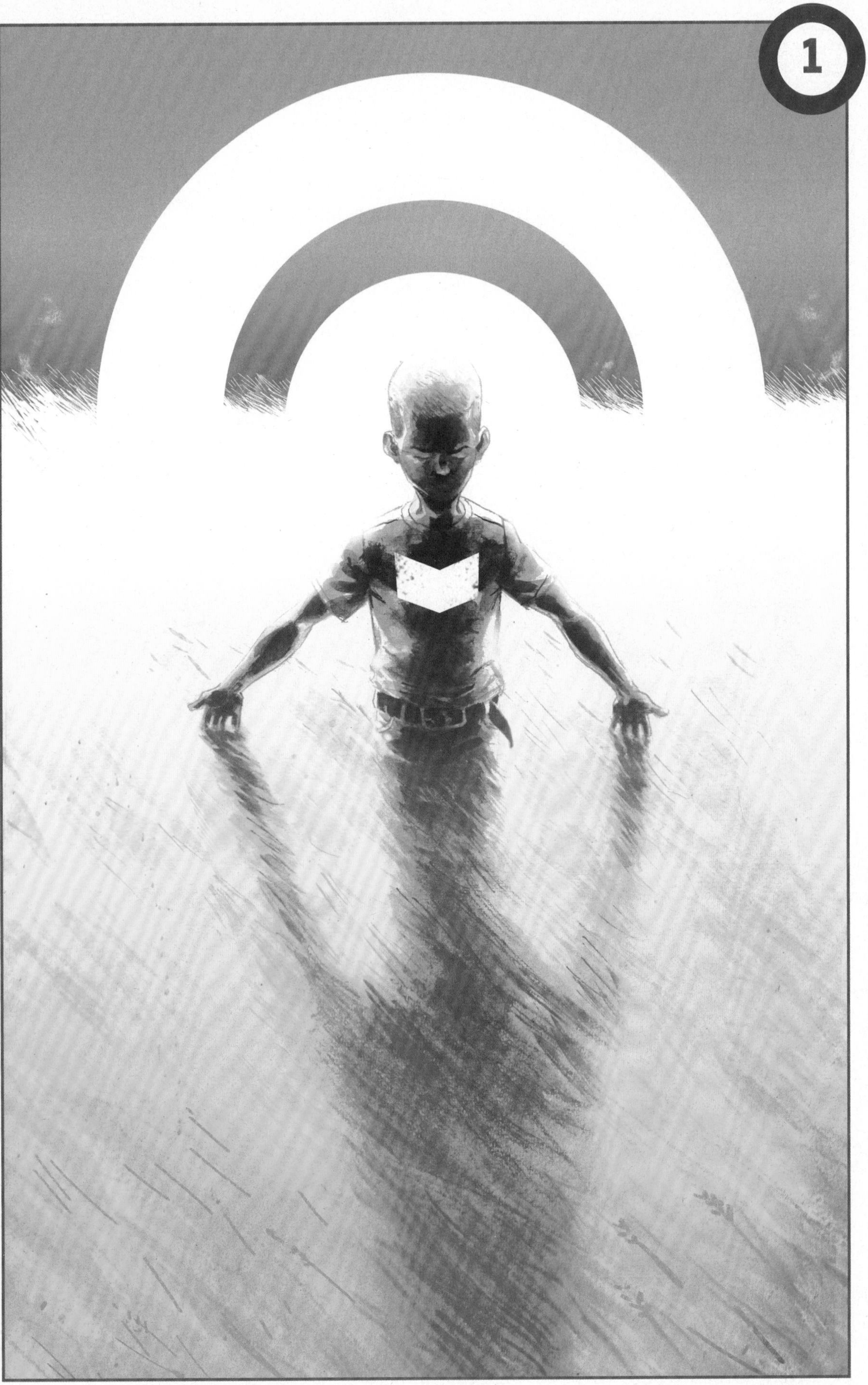
1

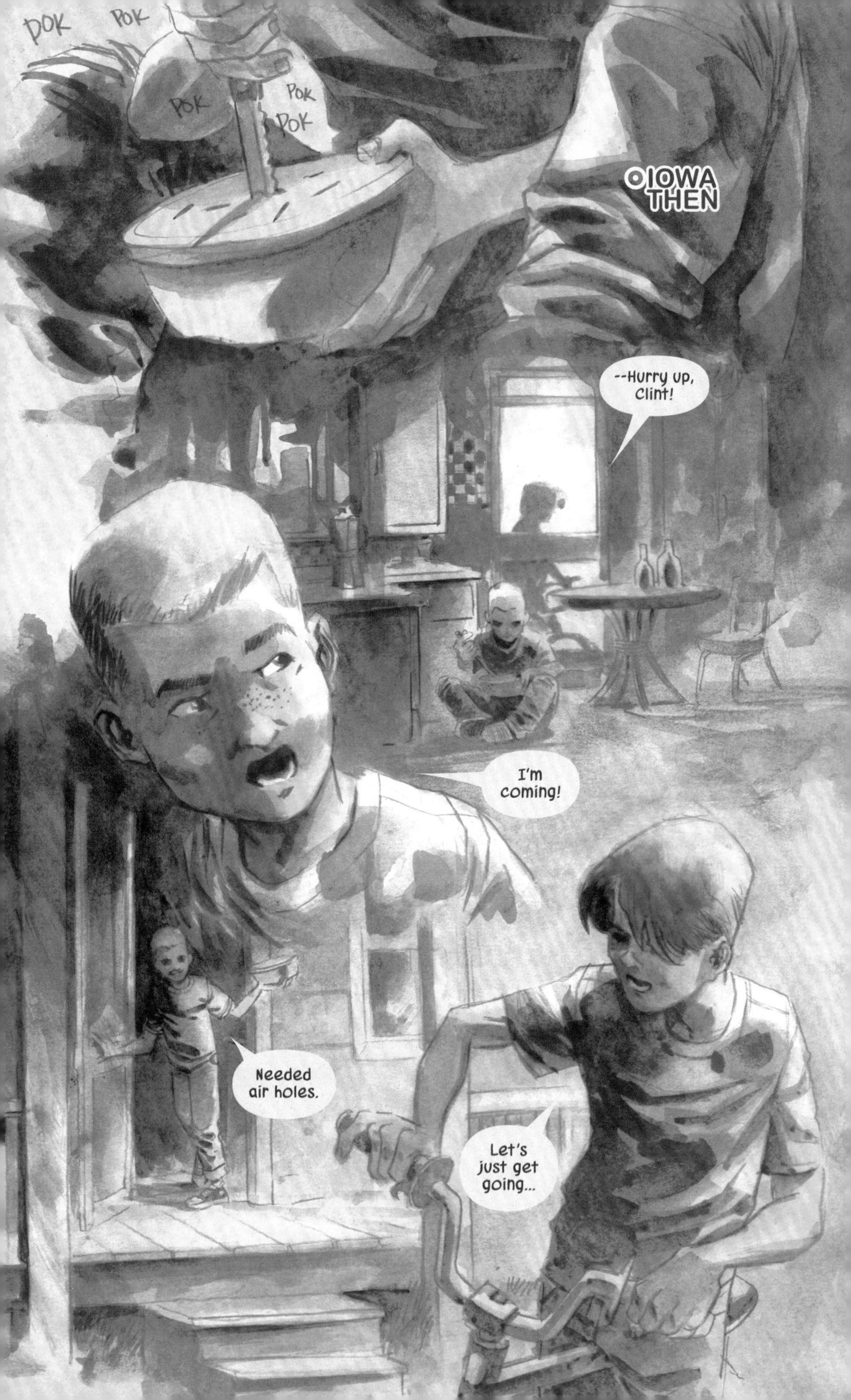
DOK POK
POK POK POK
IOWA THEN
--Hurry up, Clint!
I'm coming!
Needed air holes.
Let's just get going...

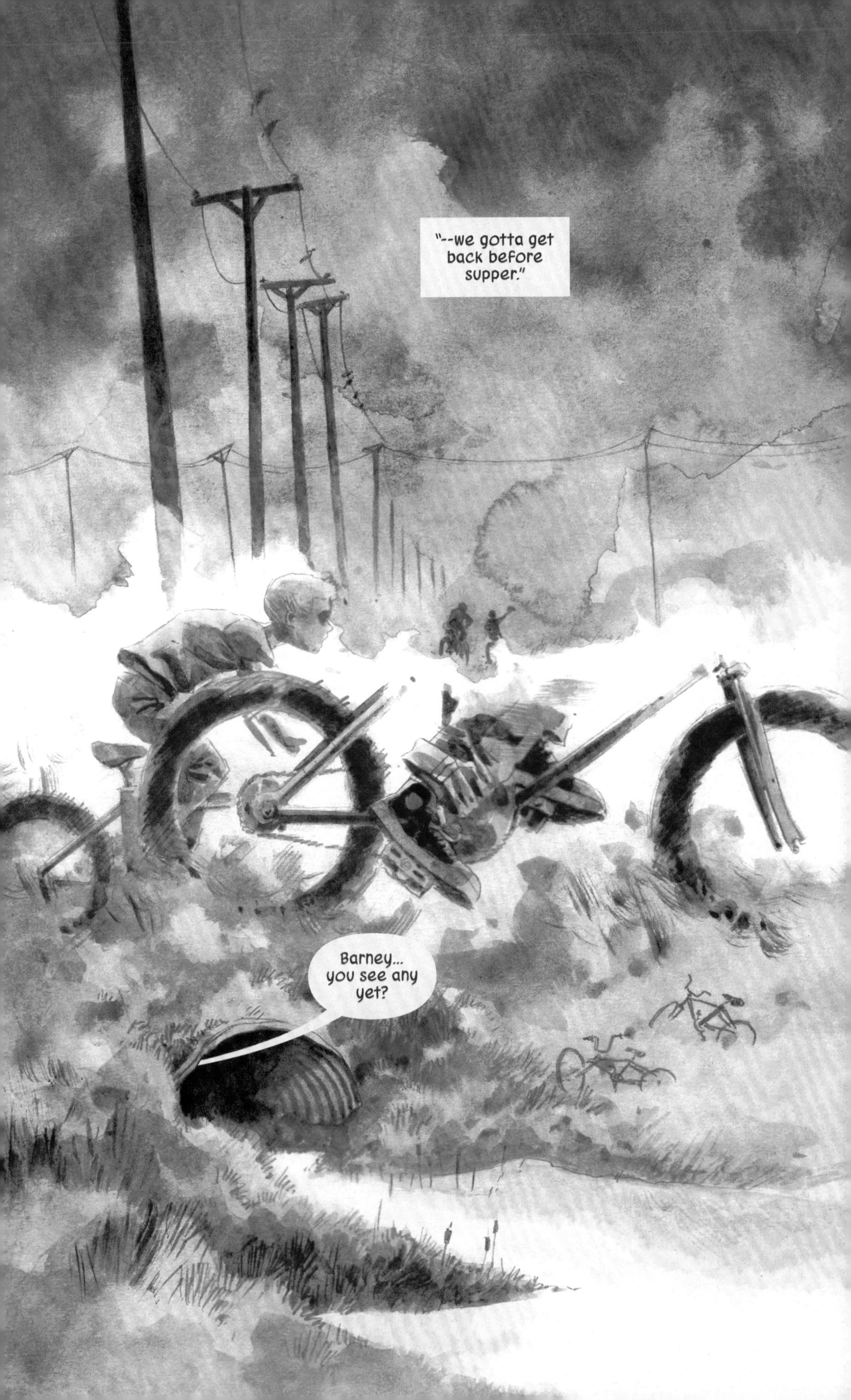
"--we gotta get back before supper."
Barney... you see any yet?

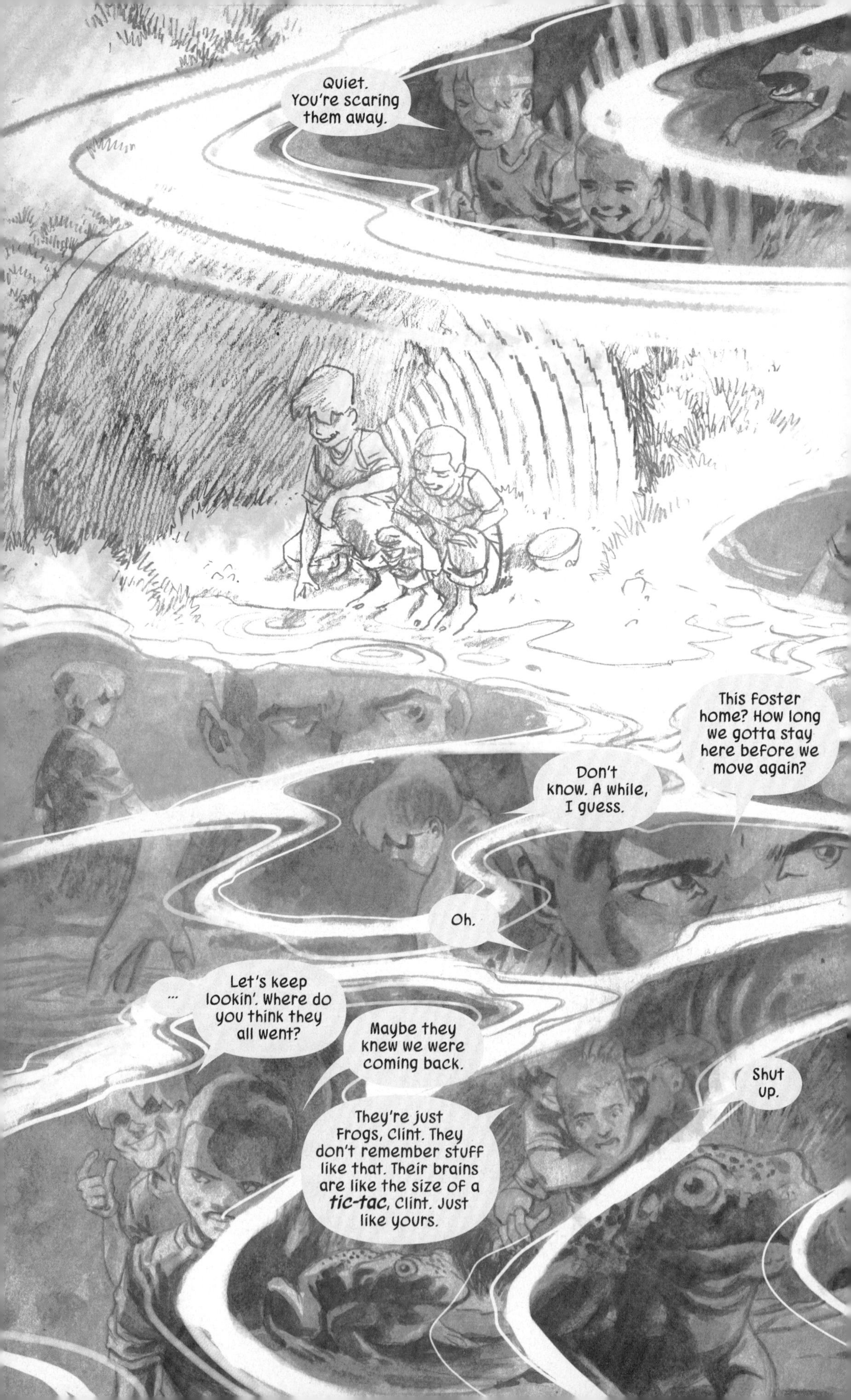
Quiet. You're scaring them away.
This foster home? How long we gotta stay here before we move again?
Don't know. A while, I guess.
Oh.
...
Let's keep lookin'. Where do you think they all went?
Maybe they knew we were coming back.
They're just frogs, Clint. They don't remember stuff like that. Their brains are like the size of a *tic-tac*, Clint. Just like yours.
Shut up.

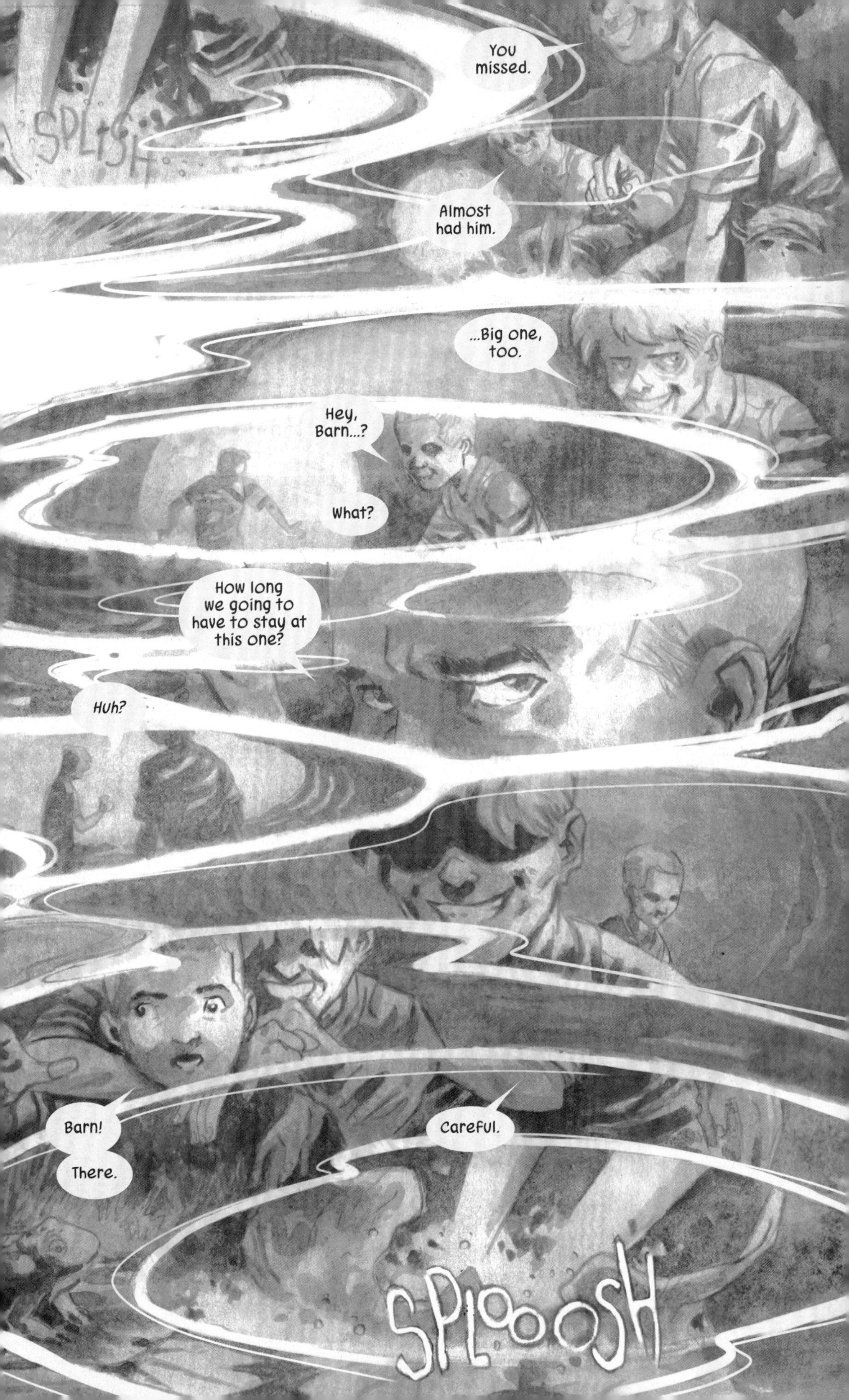
SPLISH
You missed.
Almost had him.
...Big one, too.
Hey, Barn...?
What?
How long we going to have to stay at this one?
Huh?
Barn!
There.
Careful.
SPLOOOSH

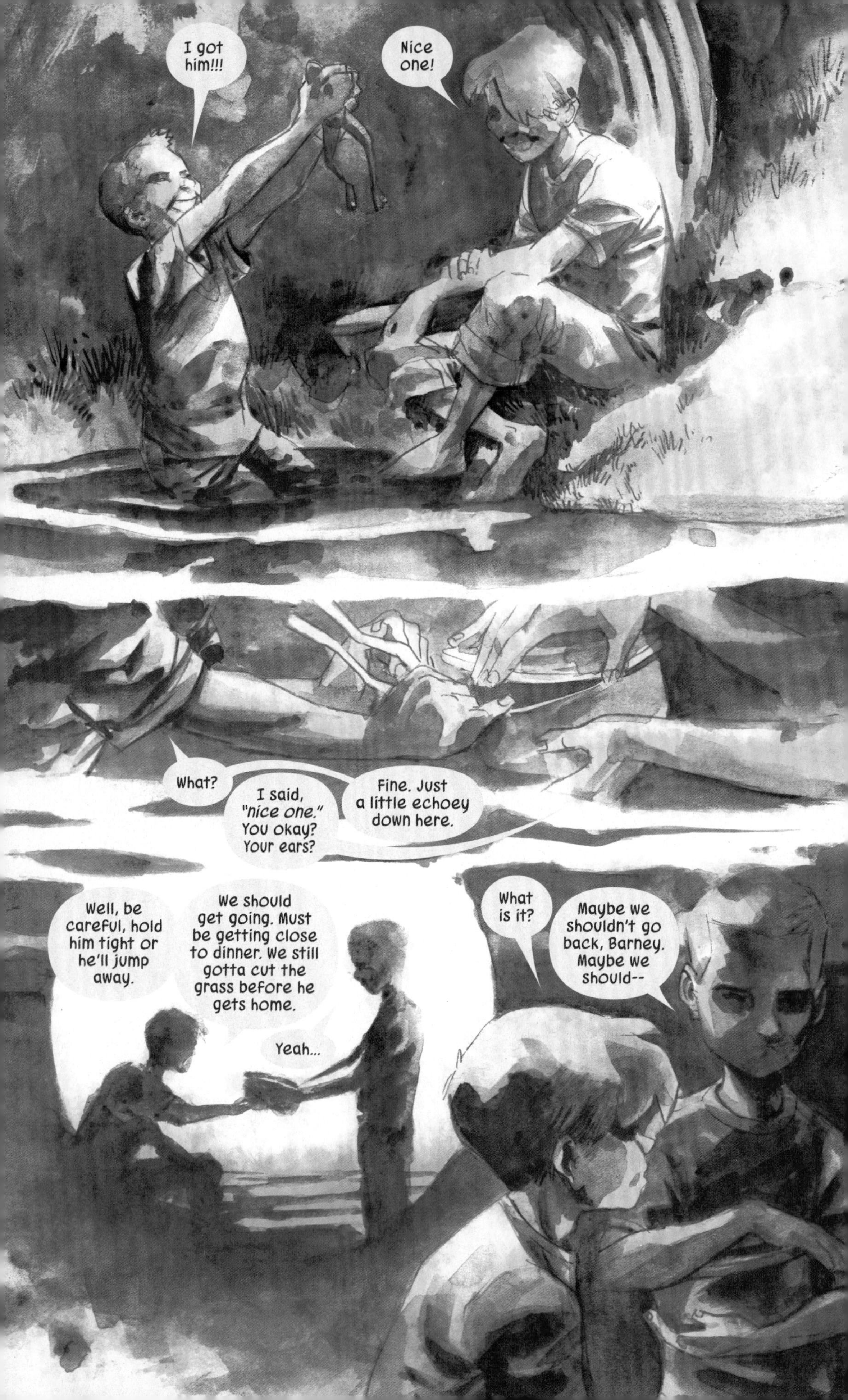
I got him!!!
Nice one!
What?
I said, "nice one." You okay? Your ears?
Fine. Just a little echoey down here.
Well, be careful, hold him tight or he'll jump away.
We should get going. Must be getting close to dinner. We still gotta cut the grass before he gets home.
Yeah...
What is it?
Maybe we shouldn't go back, Barney. Maybe we should--

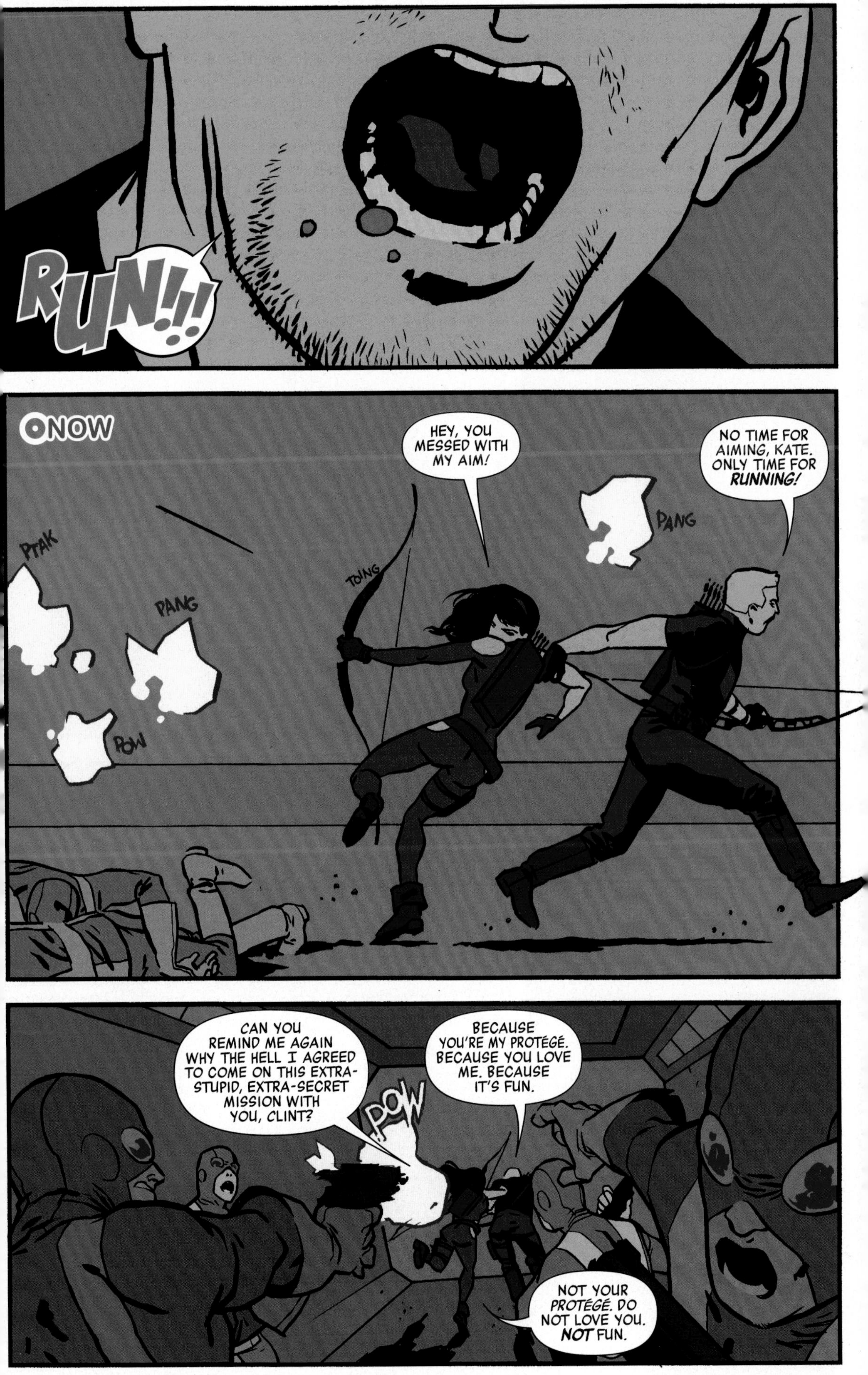
RUN!!!
NOW
HEY, YOU MESSED WITH MY AIM!
NO TIME FOR AIMING, KATE. ONLY TIME FOR ***RUNNING!***
PTAK
PANG
POW
TOING
PANG
CAN YOU REMIND ME AGAIN WHY THE HELL I AGREED TO COME ON THIS EXTRA-STUPID, EXTRA-SECRET MISSION WITH YOU, CLINT?
POW
BECAUSE YOU'RE MY PROTÉGÉ. BECAUSE YOU LOVE ME. BECAUSE IT'S FUN.
NOT YOUR *PROTÉGÉ.* DO NOT LOVE YOU. ***NOT*** FUN.

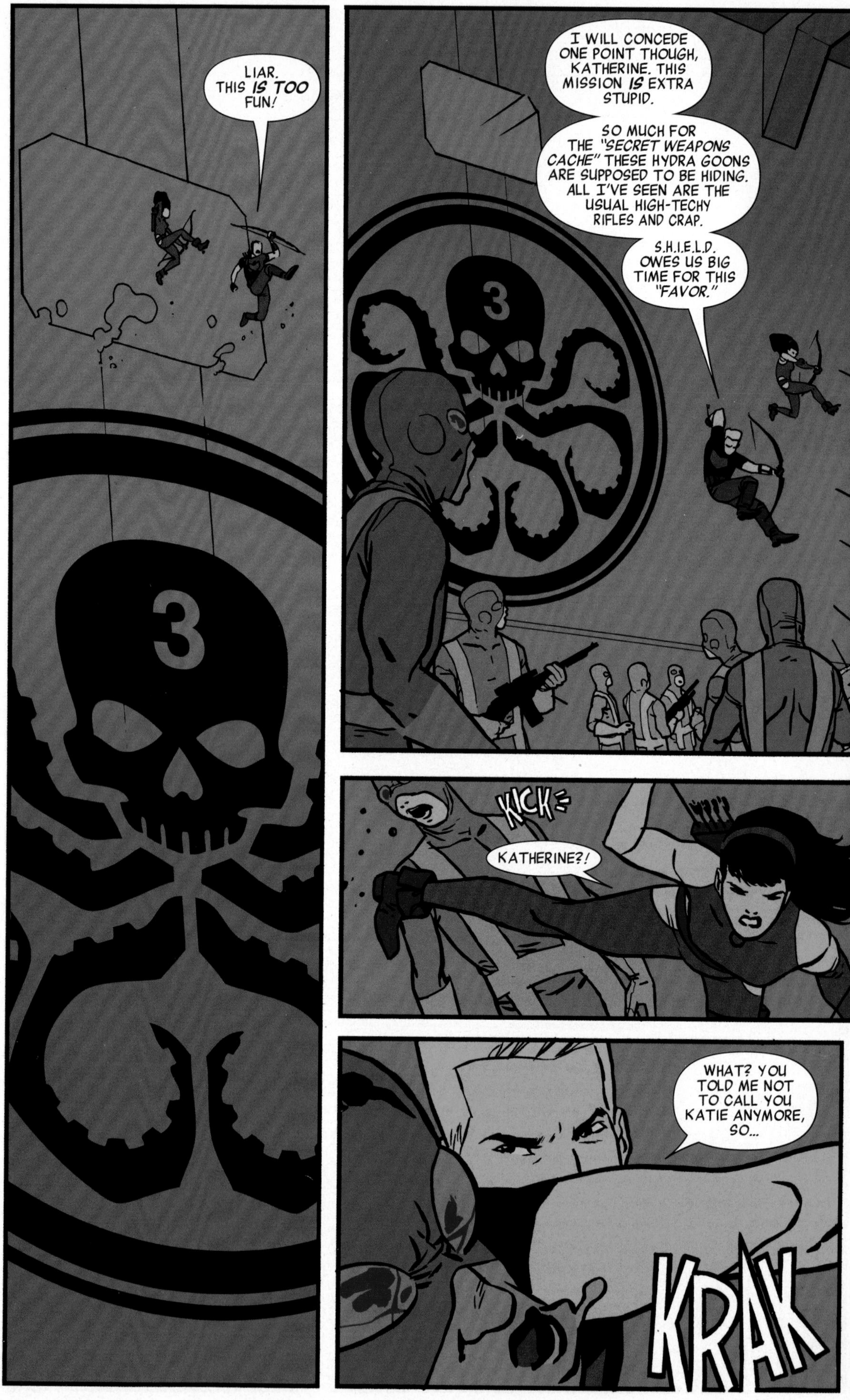
LIAR. THIS IS TOO FUN!
I WILL CONCEDE ONE POINT THOUGH, KATHERINE. THIS MISSION IS EXTRA STUPID.
SO MUCH FOR THE "SECRET WEAPONS CACHE" THESE HYDRA GOONS ARE SUPPOSED TO BE HIDING. ALL I'VE SEEN ARE THE USUAL HIGH-TECHY RIFLES AND CRAP.
S.H.I.E.L.D. OWES US BIG TIME FOR THIS "FAVOR."
3
3
KICK
KATHERINE?!
WHAT? YOU TOLD ME NOT TO CALL YOU KATIE ANYMORE, SO...
KRAK

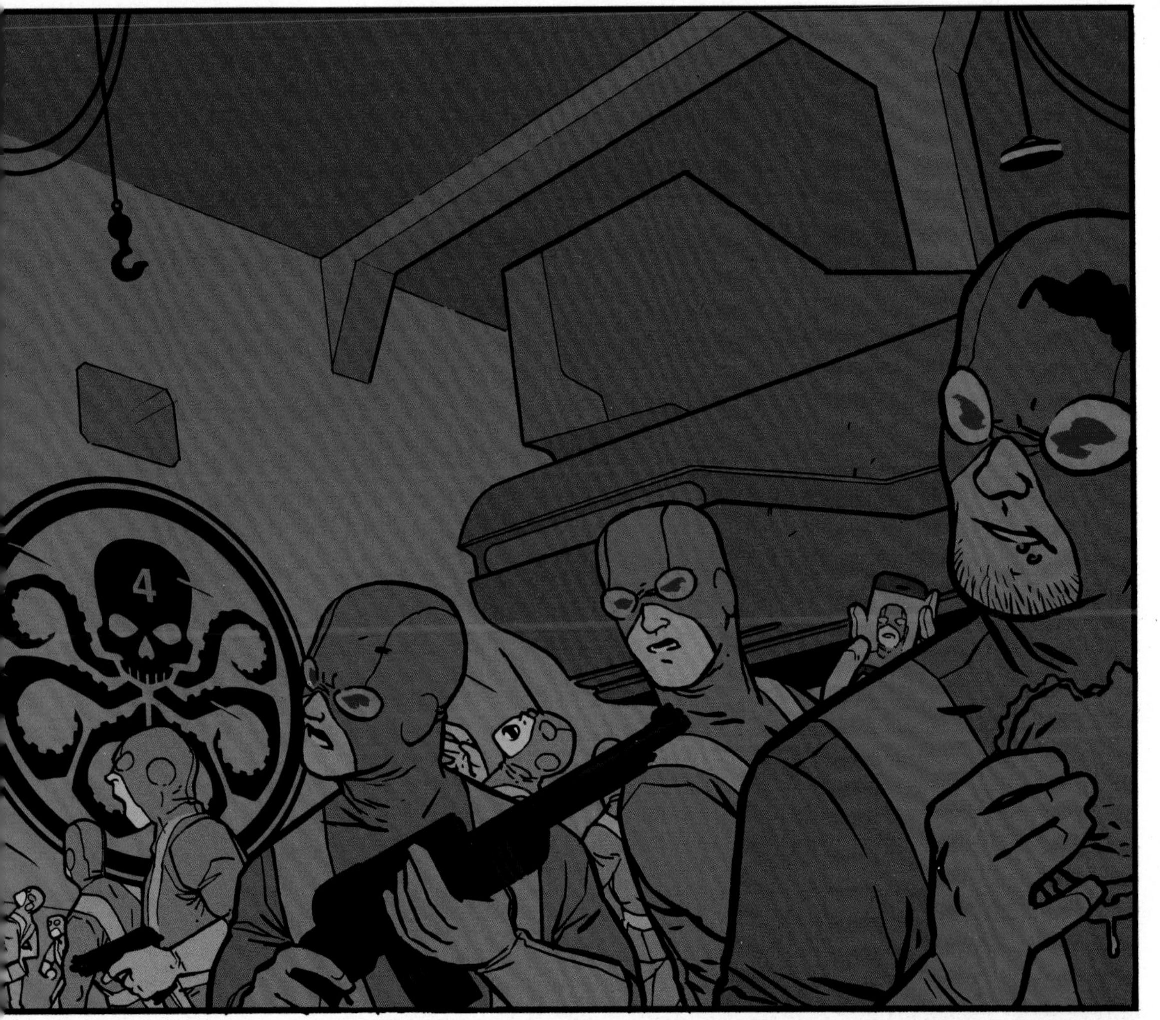

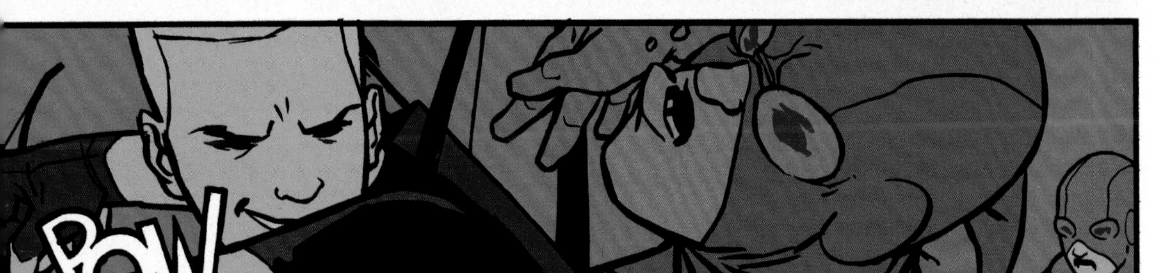
POW

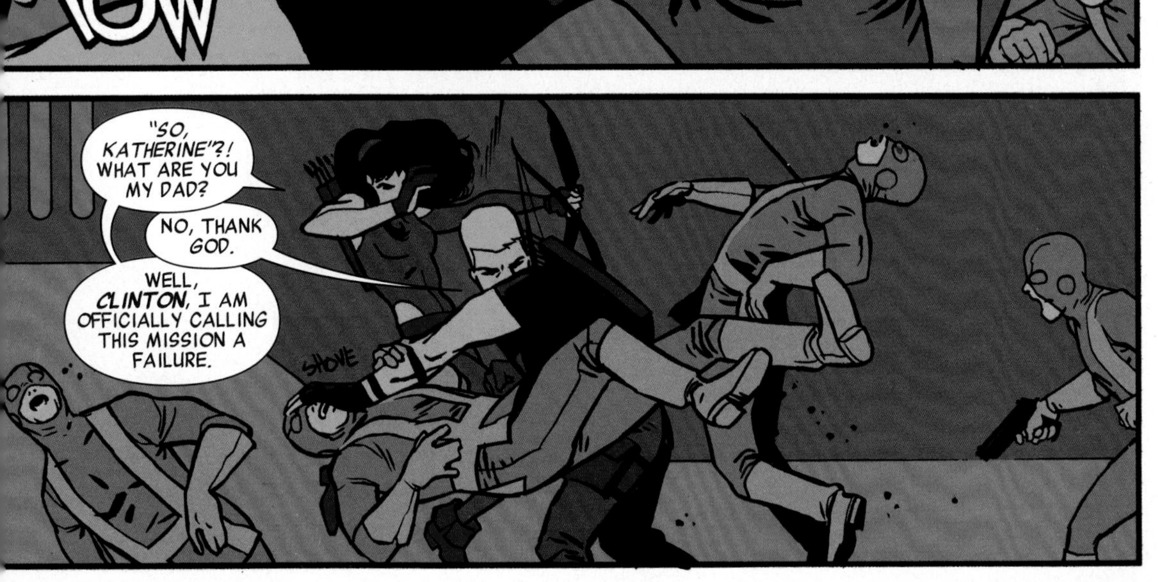
"SO, KATHERINE"?! WHAT ARE YOU MY DAD?
NO, THANK GOD.
WELL, **CLINTON**, I AM OFFICIALLY CALLING THIS MISSION A FAILURE.
SHOVE

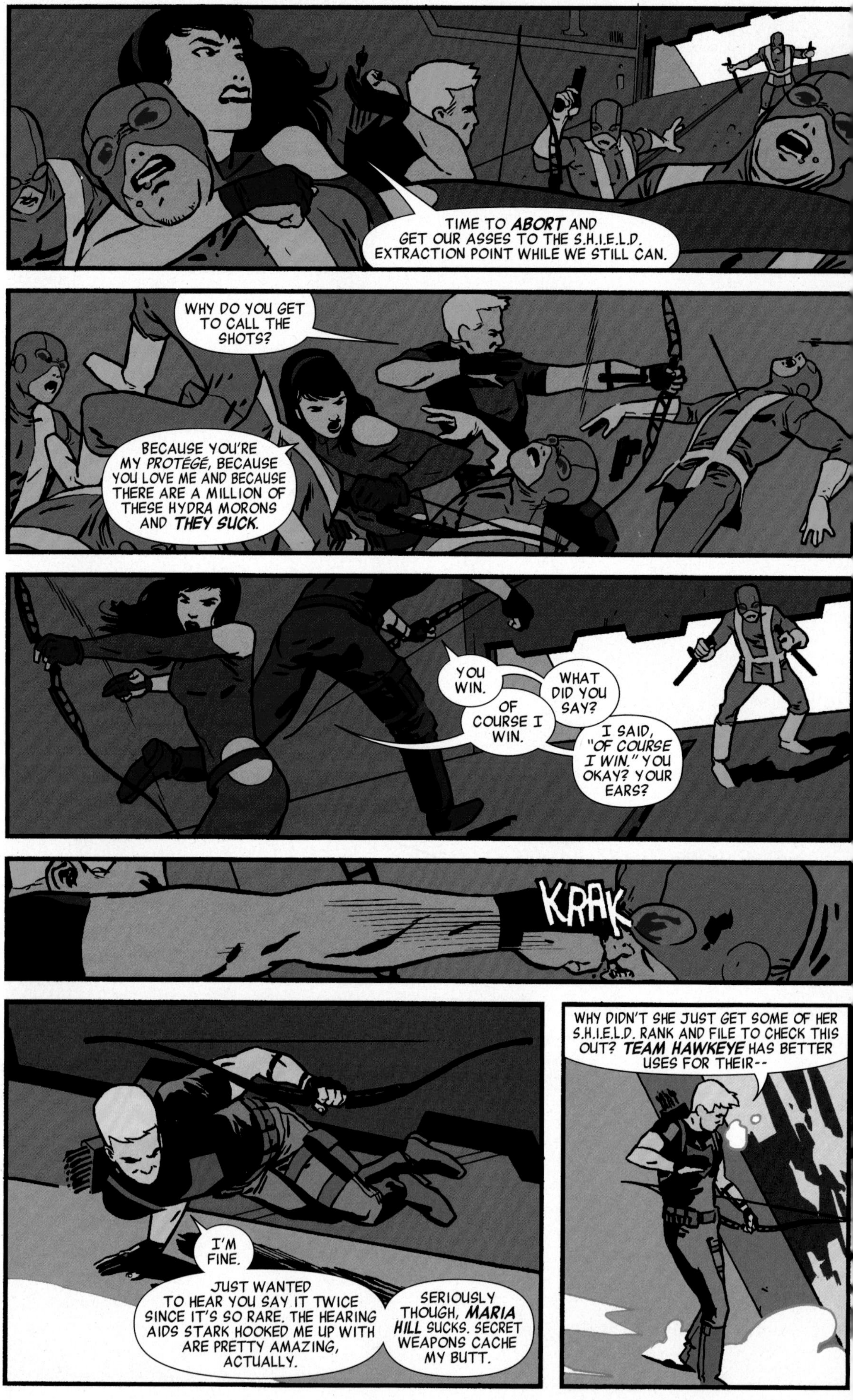
TIME TO ABORT AND GET OUR ASSES TO THE S.H.I.E.L.D. EXTRACTION POINT WHILE WE STILL CAN.
WHY DO YOU GET TO CALL THE SHOTS?
BECAUSE YOU'RE MY PROTÉGÉ, BECAUSE YOU LOVE ME AND BECAUSE THERE ARE A MILLION OF THESE HYDRA MORONS AND THEY SUCK.
YOU WIN.
OF COURSE I WIN.
WHAT DID YOU SAY?
I SAID, "OF COURSE I WIN." YOU OKAY? YOUR EARS?
KRAK
I'M FINE.
JUST WANTED TO HEAR YOU SAY IT TWICE SINCE IT'S SO RARE. THE HEARING AIDS STARK HOOKED ME UP WITH ARE PRETTY AMAZING, ACTUALLY.
SERIOUSLY THOUGH, MARIA HILL SUCKS. SECRET WEAPONS CACHE MY BUTT.
WHY DIDN'T SHE JUST GET SOME OF HER S.H.I.E.L.D. RANK AND FILE TO CHECK THIS OUT? TEAM HAWKEYE HAS BETTER USES FOR THEIR--

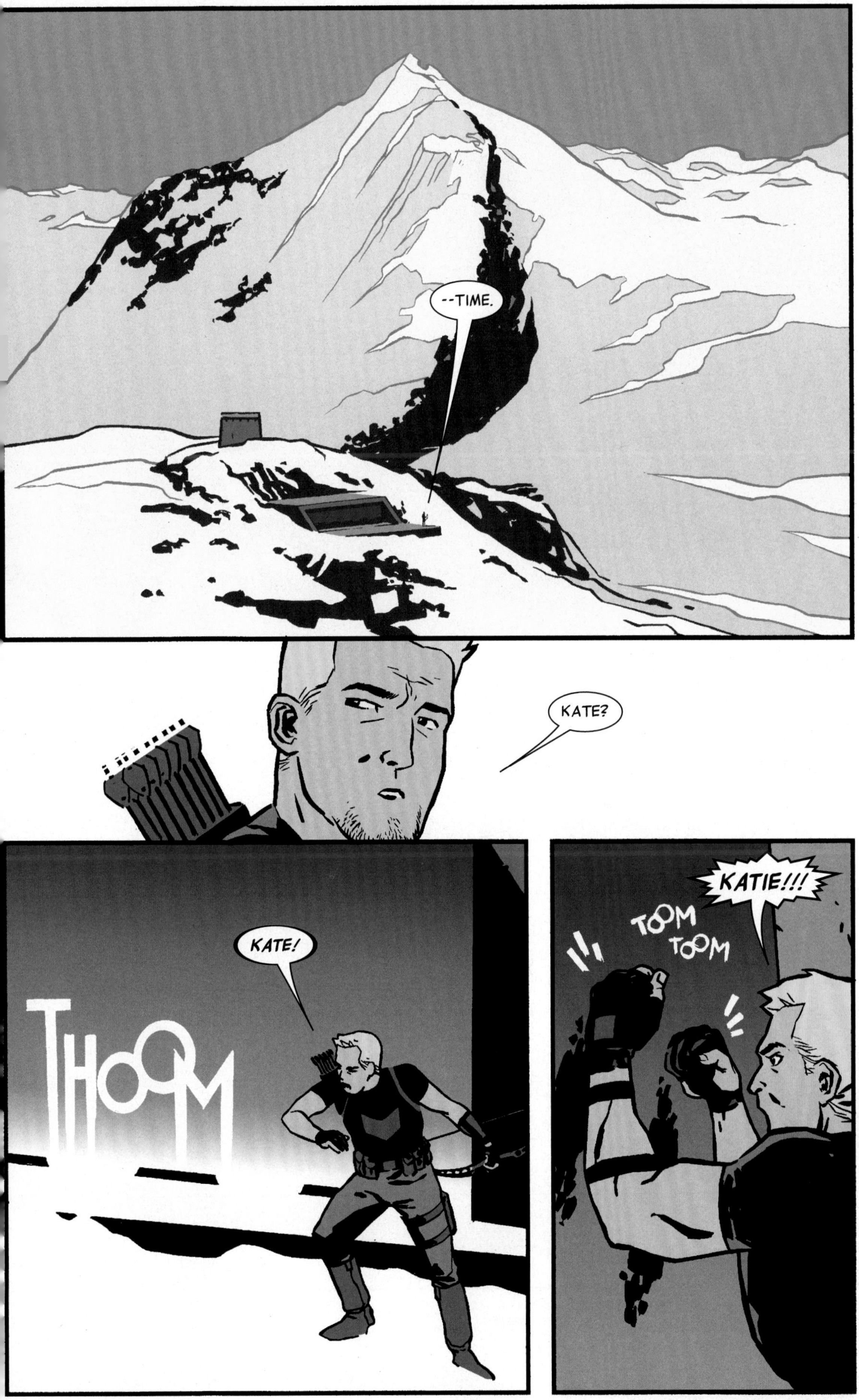
--TIME.
KATE?
KATE!
THOOM
KATIE!!!
TOOM
TOOM

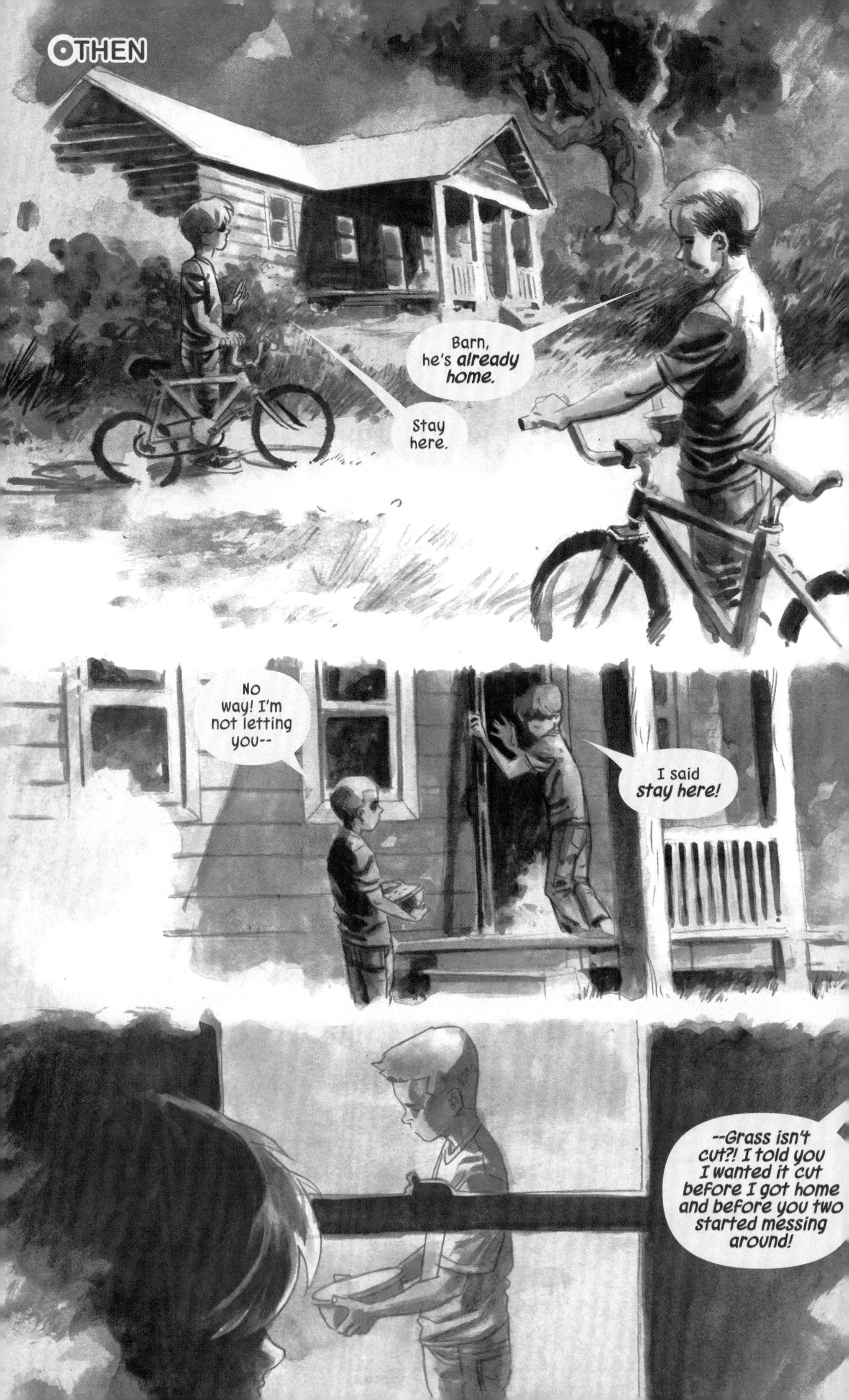
THEN
Barn, he's *already* *home.*
Stay here.
No way! I'm not letting you--
I said *stay here!*
--Grass isn't cut?! I told you I wanted it cut before I got home and before you two started messing around!

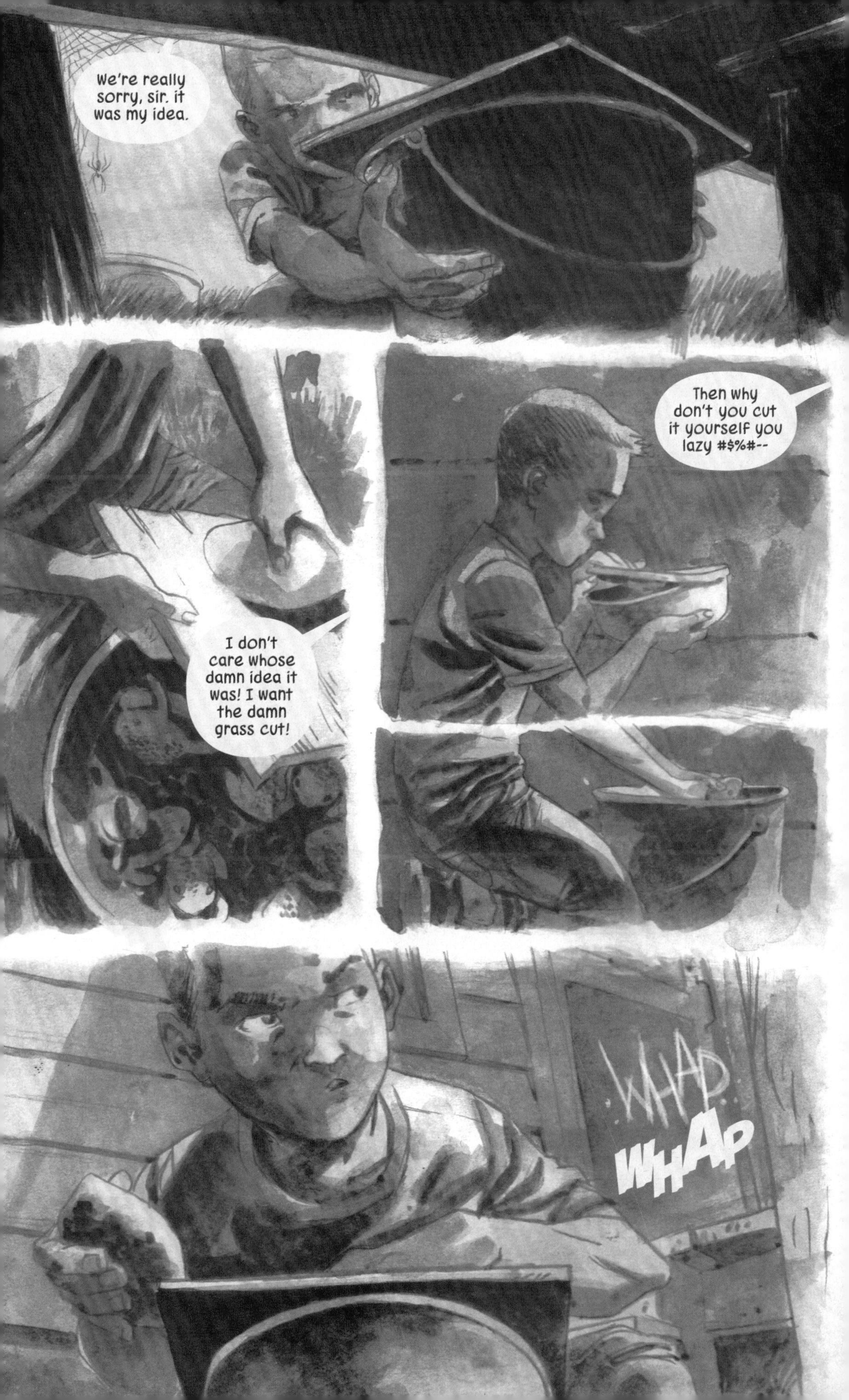
We're really sorry, sir. it was my idea.
I don't care whose damn idea it was! I want the damn grass cut!
Then why don't you cut it yourself you lazy #$%#--
WHAP
WHAP

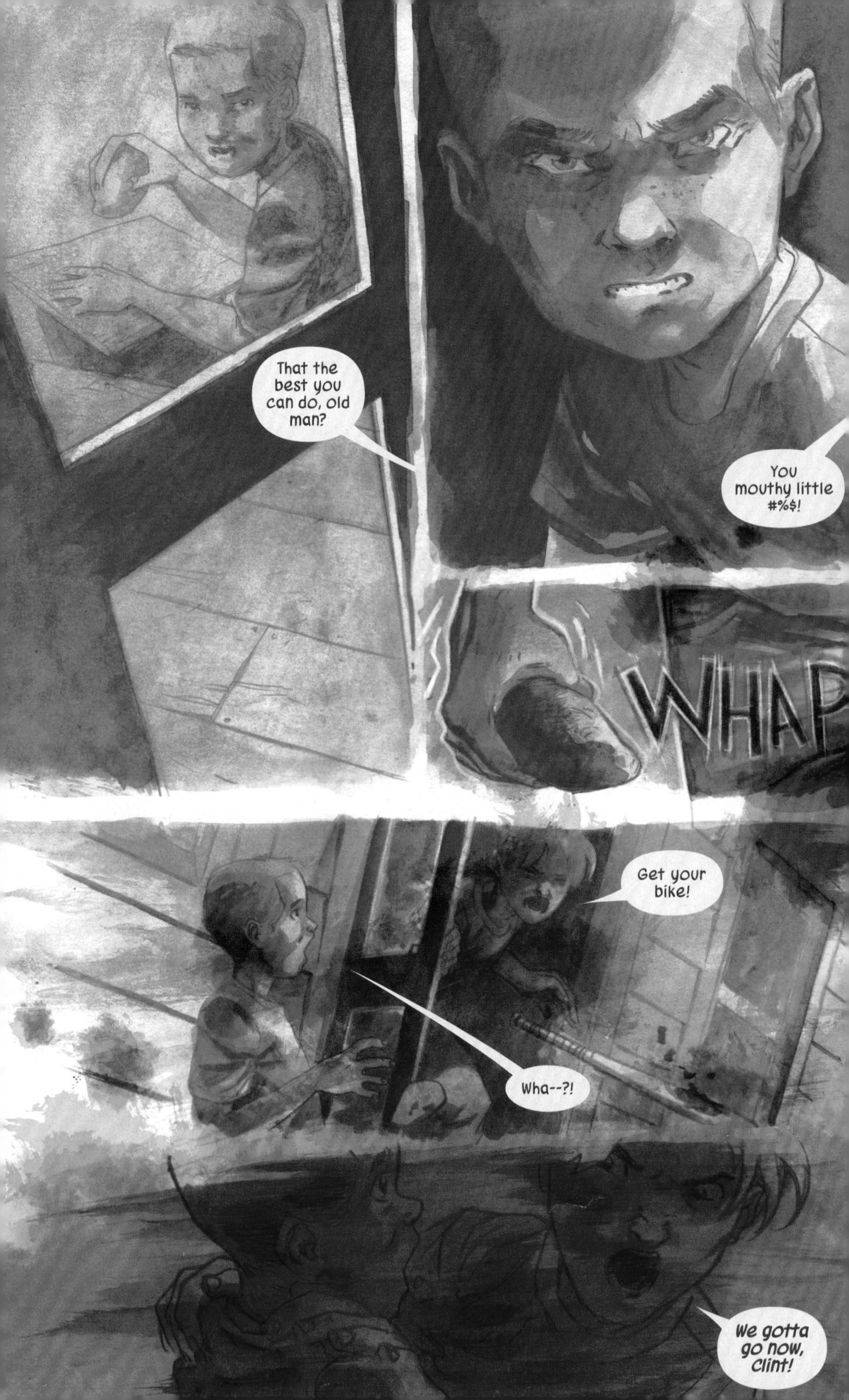
That the best you can do, old man?
You mouthy little #%$!
WHAP
Get your bike!
Wha--?!
We gotta go now, Clint!

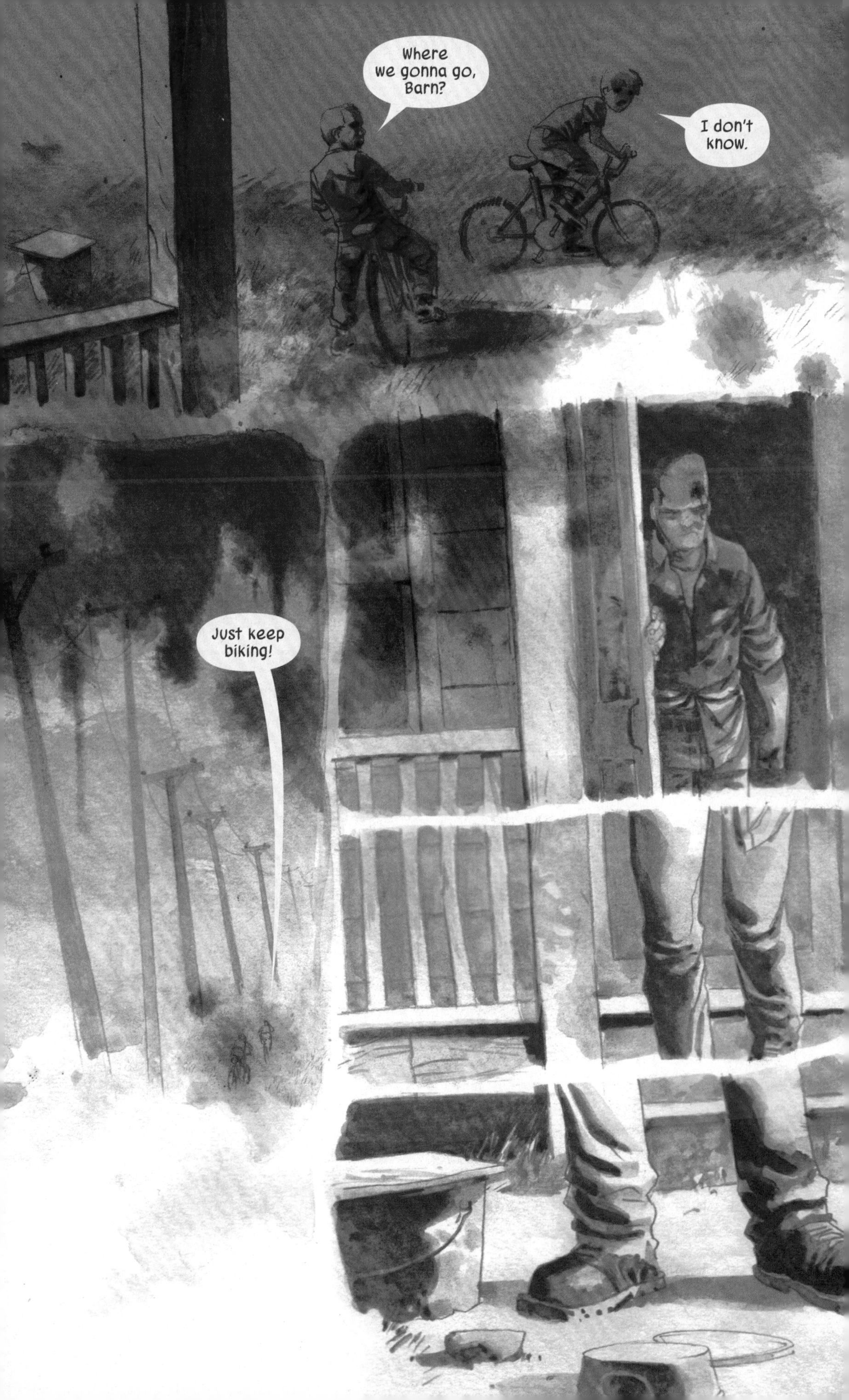
Where we gonna go, Barn?
I don't know.
Just keep biking!

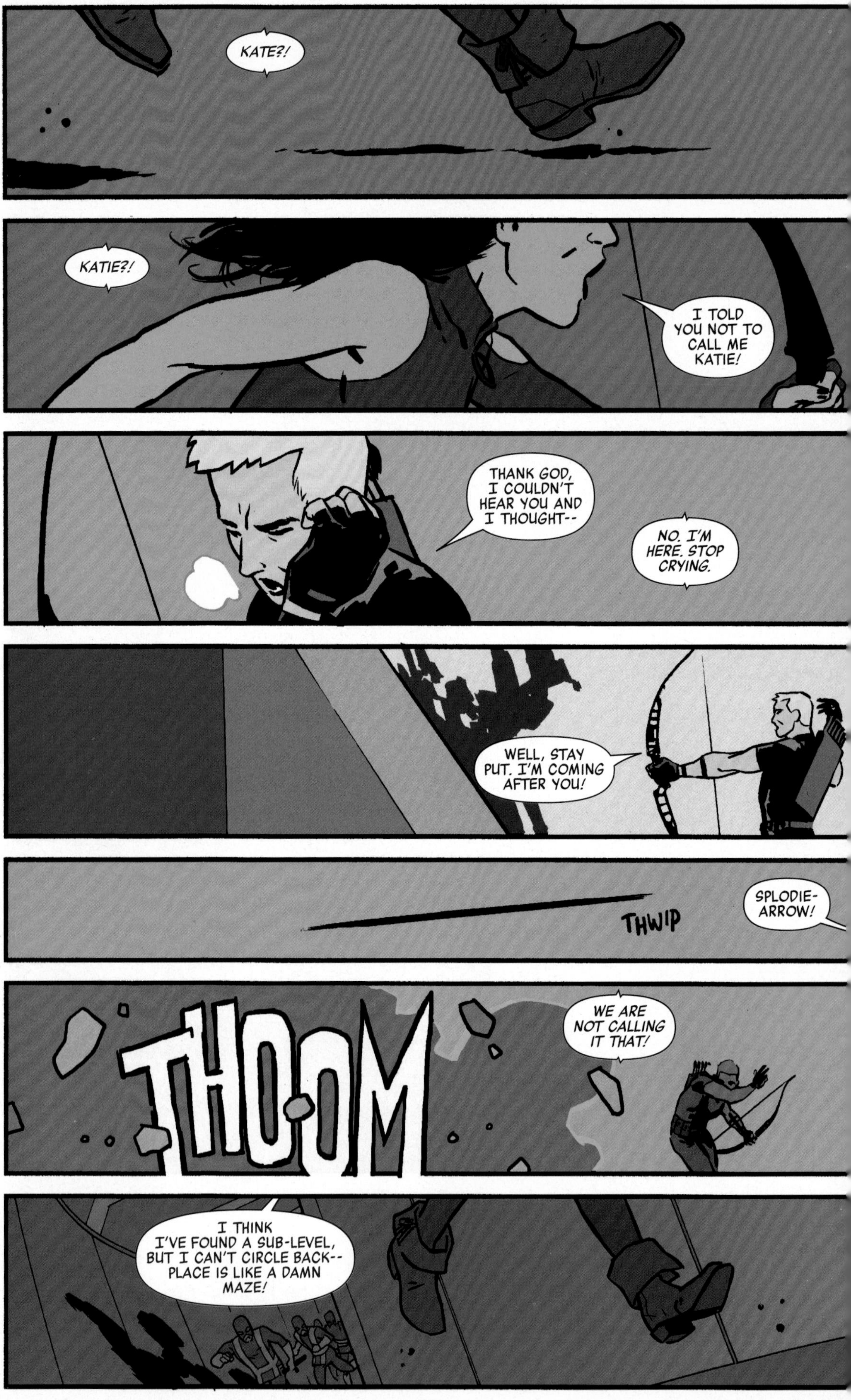
KATE?!
KATIE?!
I TOLD YOU NOT TO CALL ME KATIE!
THANK GOD, I COULDN'T HEAR YOU AND I THOUGHT--
NO. I'M HERE. STOP CRYING.
WELL, STAY PUT. I'M COMING AFTER YOU!
THWIP
SPLODIE-ARROW!
THOOM
WE ARE NOT CALLING IT THAT!
I THINK I'VE FOUND A SUB-LEVEL, BUT I CAN'T CIRCLE BACK-- PLACE IS LIKE A DAMN MAZE!

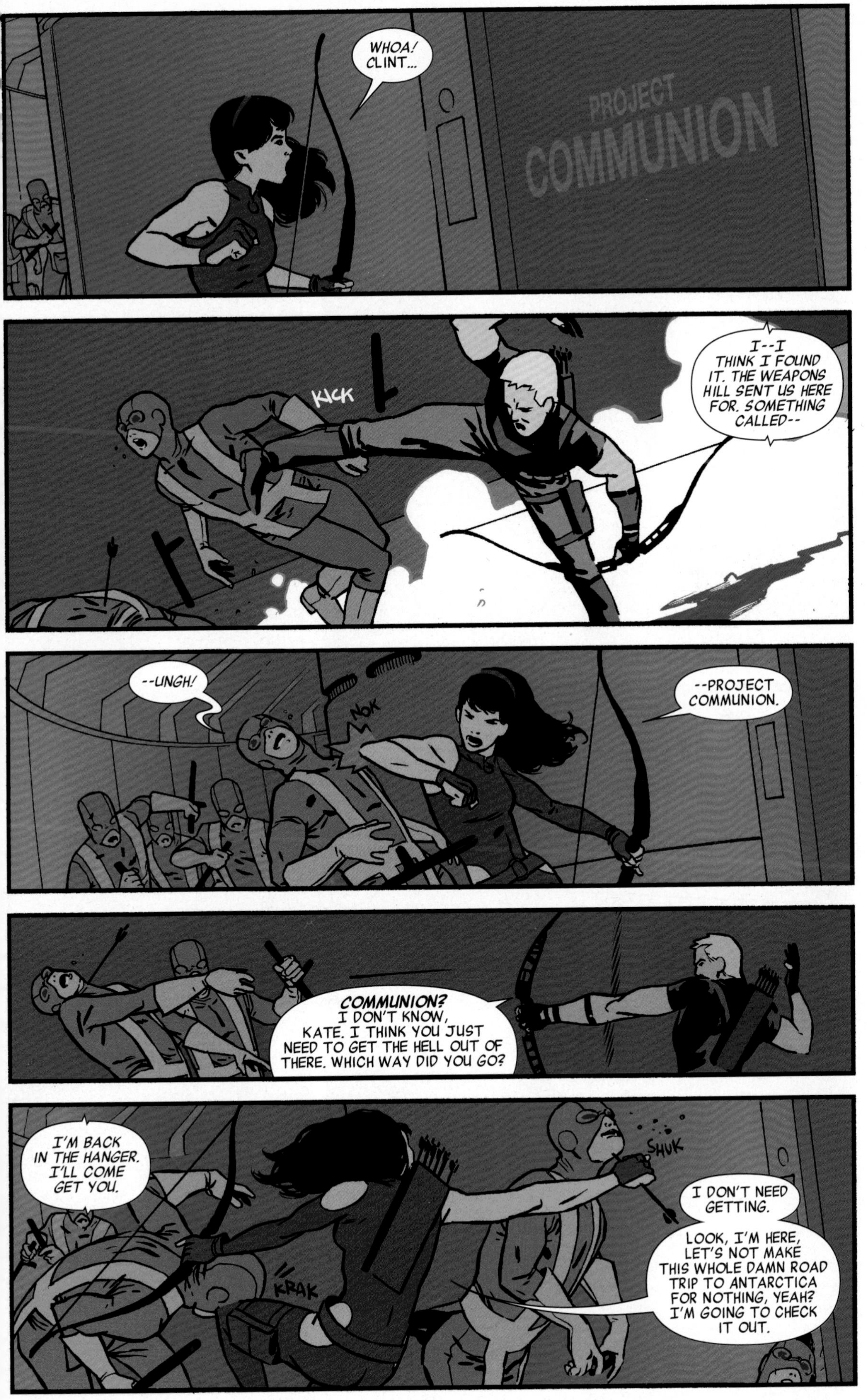

WHOA! CLINT...
PROJECT COMMUNION
KICK
I--I THINK I FOUND IT. THE WEAPONS HILL SENT US HERE FOR. SOMETHING CALLED--
--UNGH!
NOK
--PROJECT COMMUNION.
COMMUNION? I DON'T KNOW, KATE. I THINK YOU JUST NEED TO GET THE HELL OUT OF THERE. WHICH WAY DID YOU GO?
I'M BACK IN THE HANGER. I'LL COME GET YOU.
SHUK
I DON'T NEED GETTING.
LOOK, I'M HERE, LET'S NOT MAKE THIS WHOLE DAMN ROAD TRIP TO ANTARCTICA FOR NOTHING, YEAH? I'M GOING TO CHECK IT OUT.
KRAK

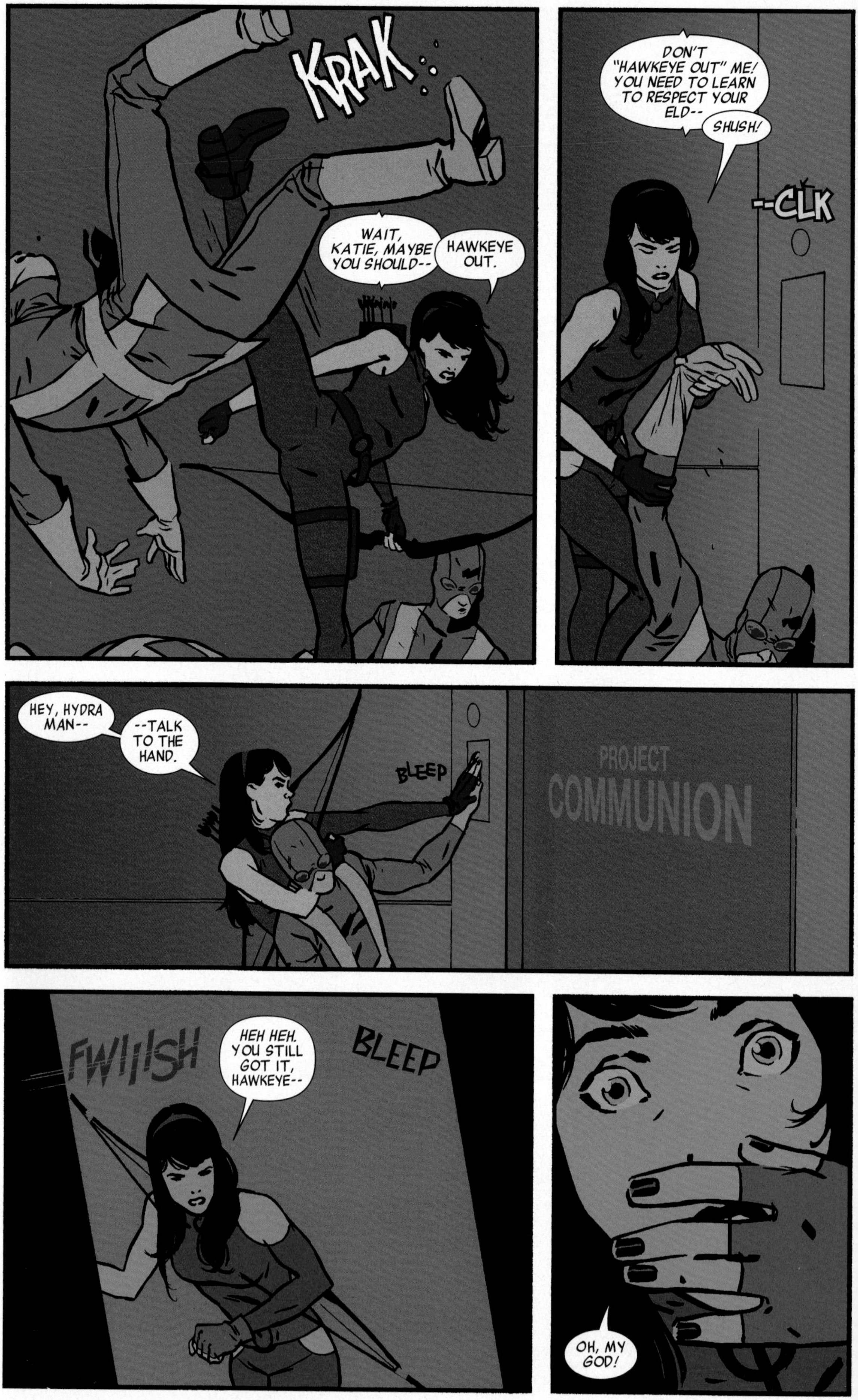
KRAK
WAIT, KATIE, MAYBE YOU SHOULD--
HAWKEYE OUT.
DON'T "HAWKEYE OUT" ME! YOU NEED TO LEARN TO RESPECT YOUR ELD--
SHUSH!
--CLK
HEY, HYDRA MAN--
--TALK TO THE HAND.
BLEEP
PROJECT COMMUNION
FWIIISH
HEH HEH. YOU STILL GOT IT, HAWKEYE--
BLEEP
OH, MY GOD!

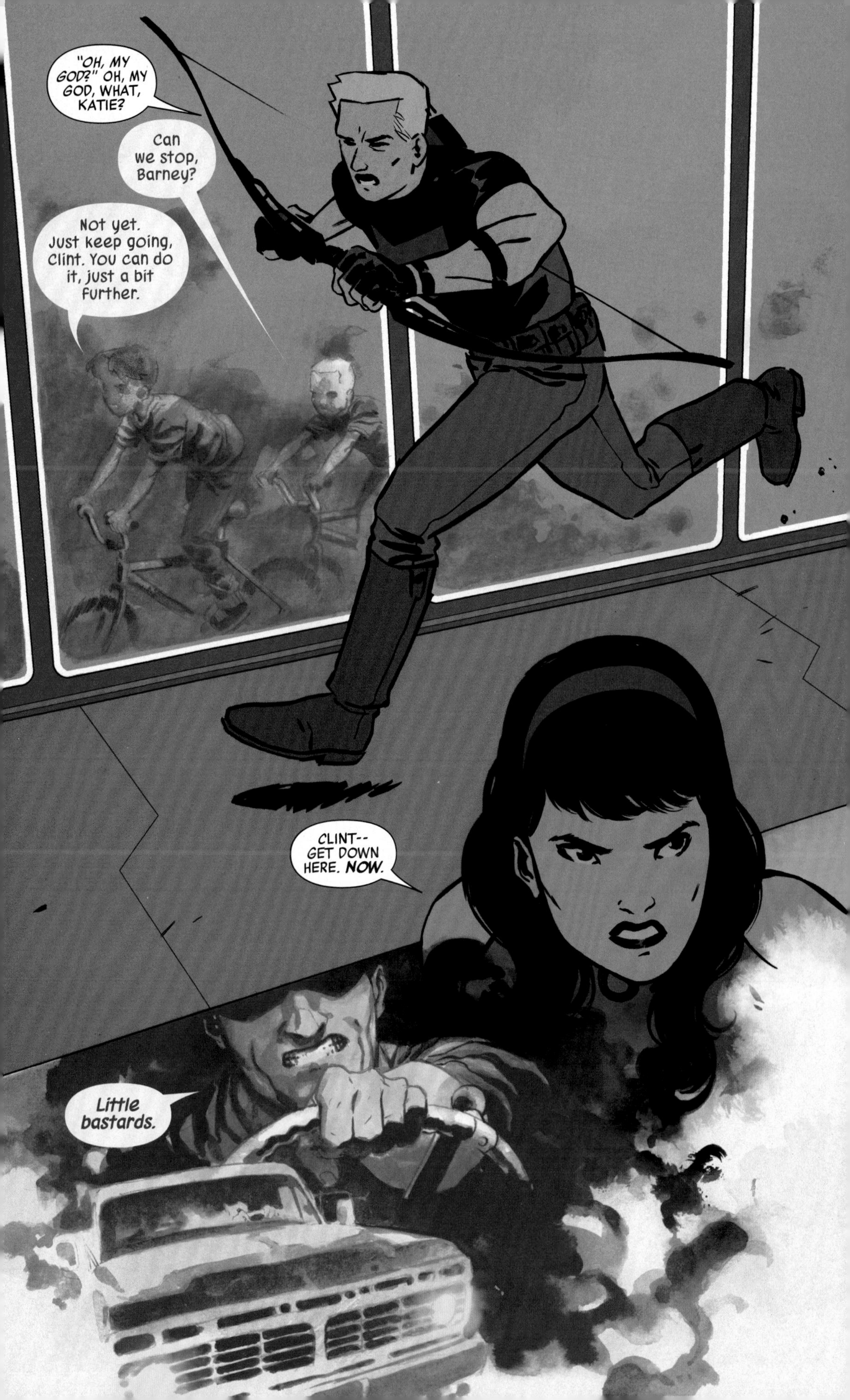
"OH, MY GOD?" OH, MY GOD, WHAT, KATIE?
Can we stop, Barney?
Not yet. Just keep going, Clint. You can do it, just a bit further.
CLINT-- GET DOWN HERE. NOW.
Little bastards.

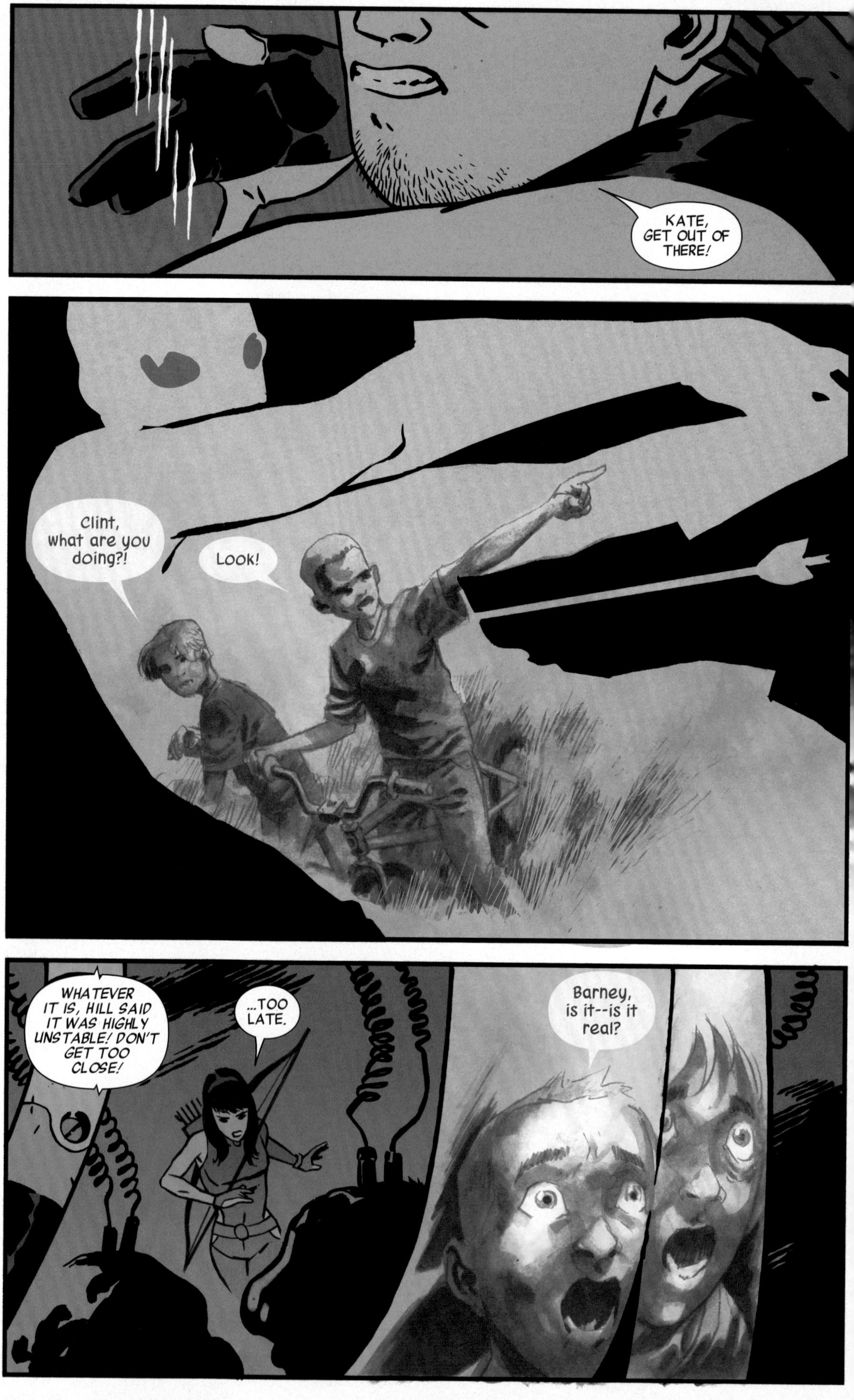
KATE, GET OUT OF THERE!
Clint, what are you doing?!
LOOK!
WHATEVER IT IS, HILL SAID IT WAS HIGHLY UNSTABLE! DON'T GET TOO CLOSE!
...TOO LATE.
Barney, is it--is it real?

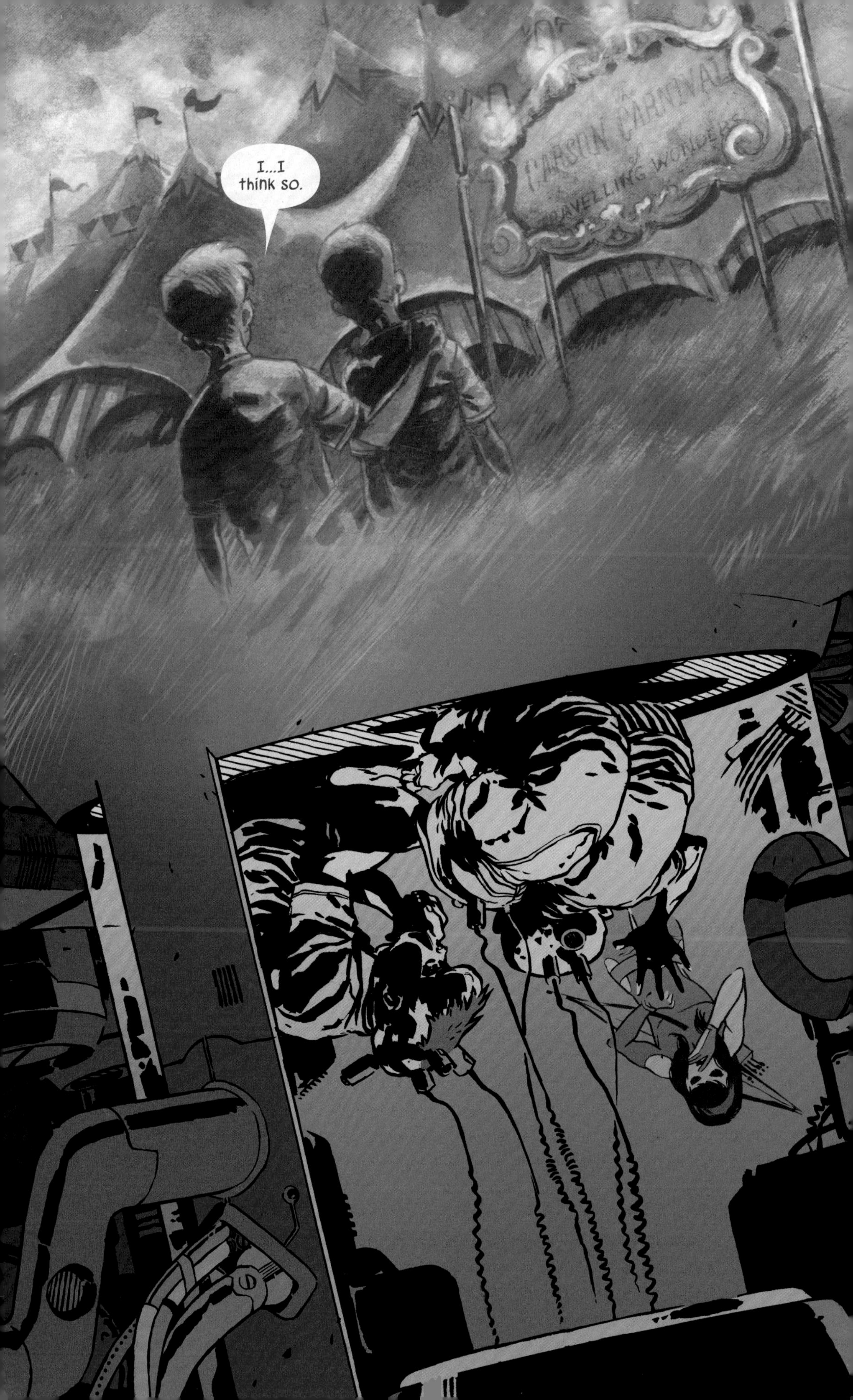
I...I think so.

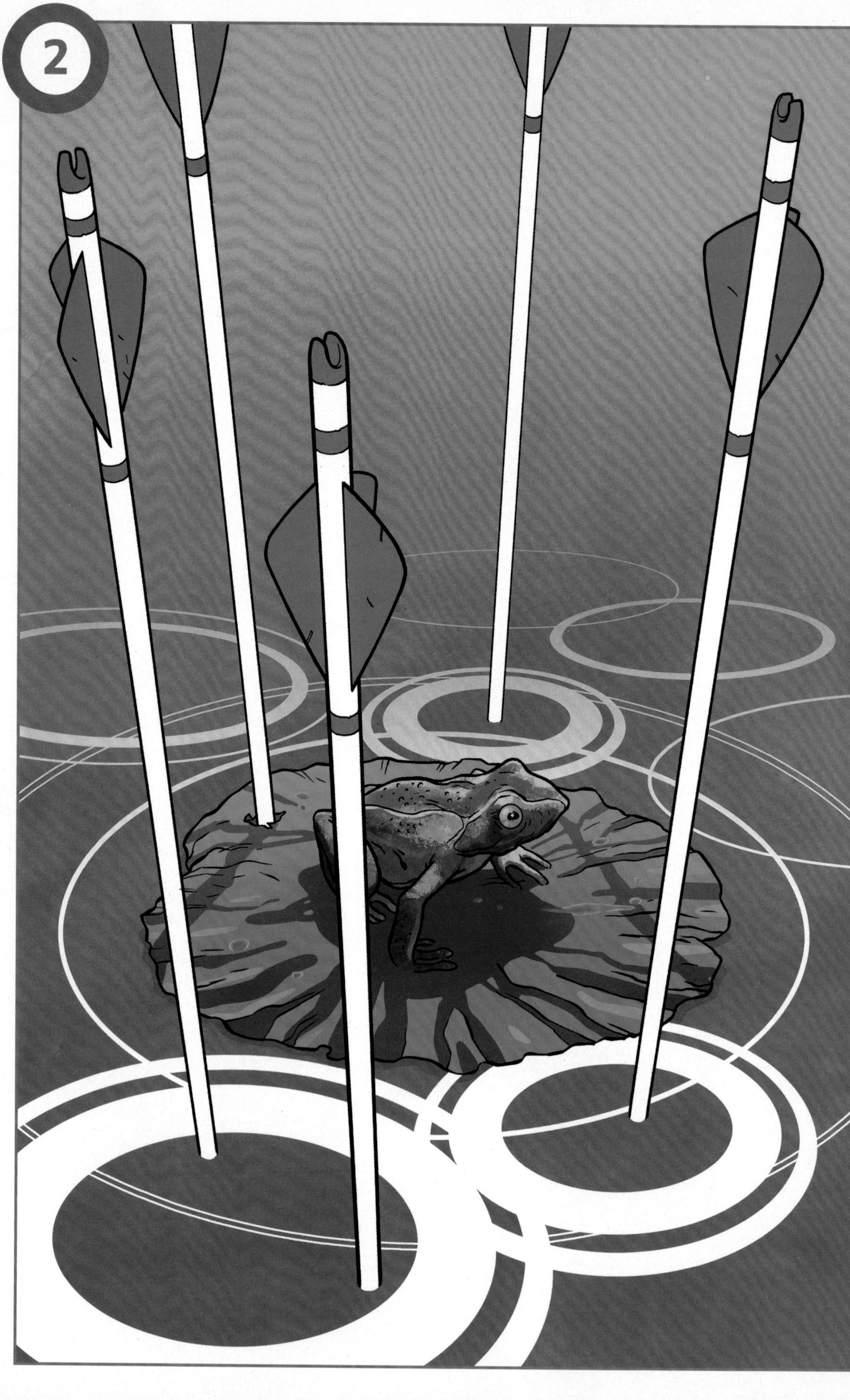
2

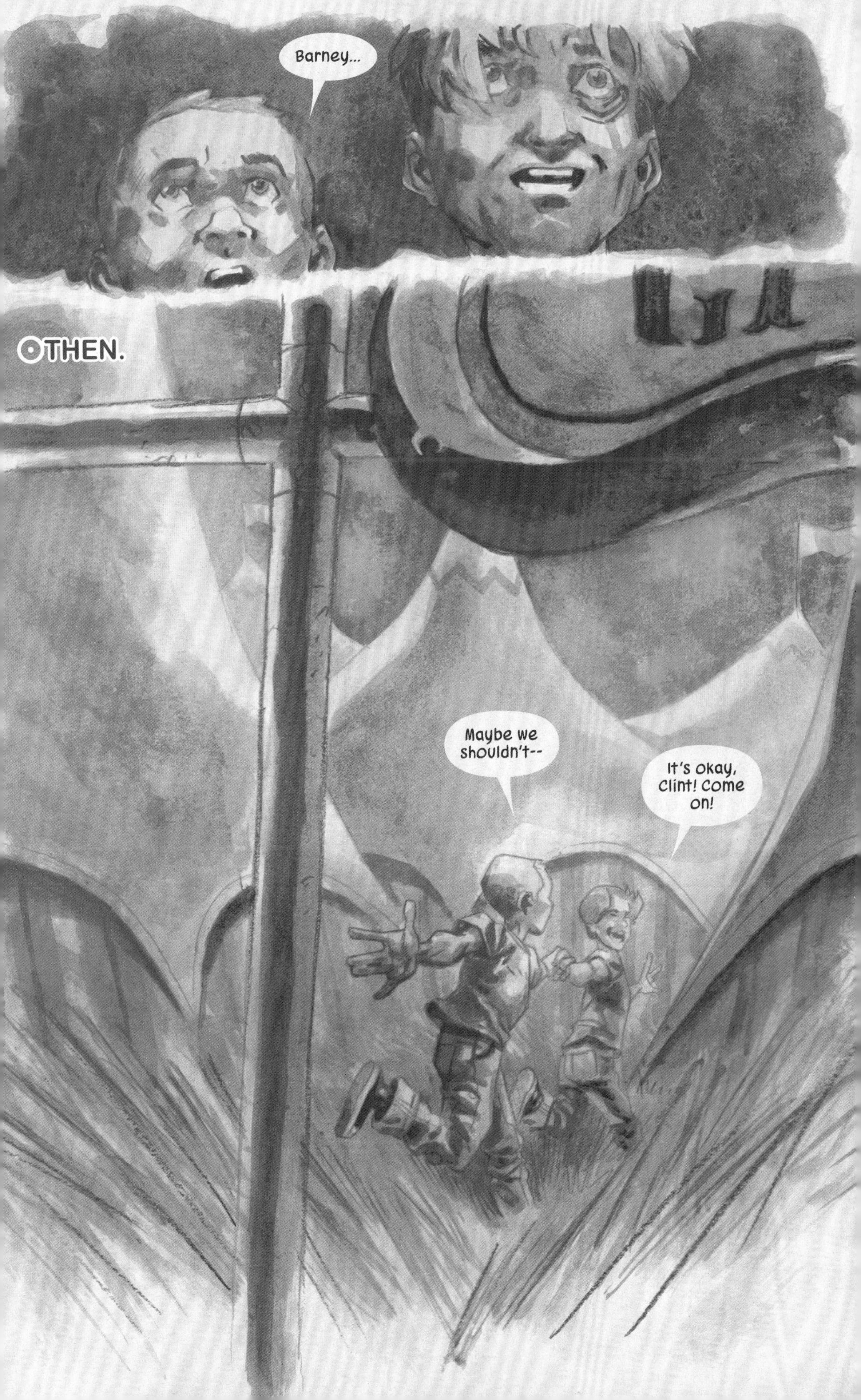
Barney...
THEN.
Maybe we shouldn't--
It's okay, Clint! Come on!

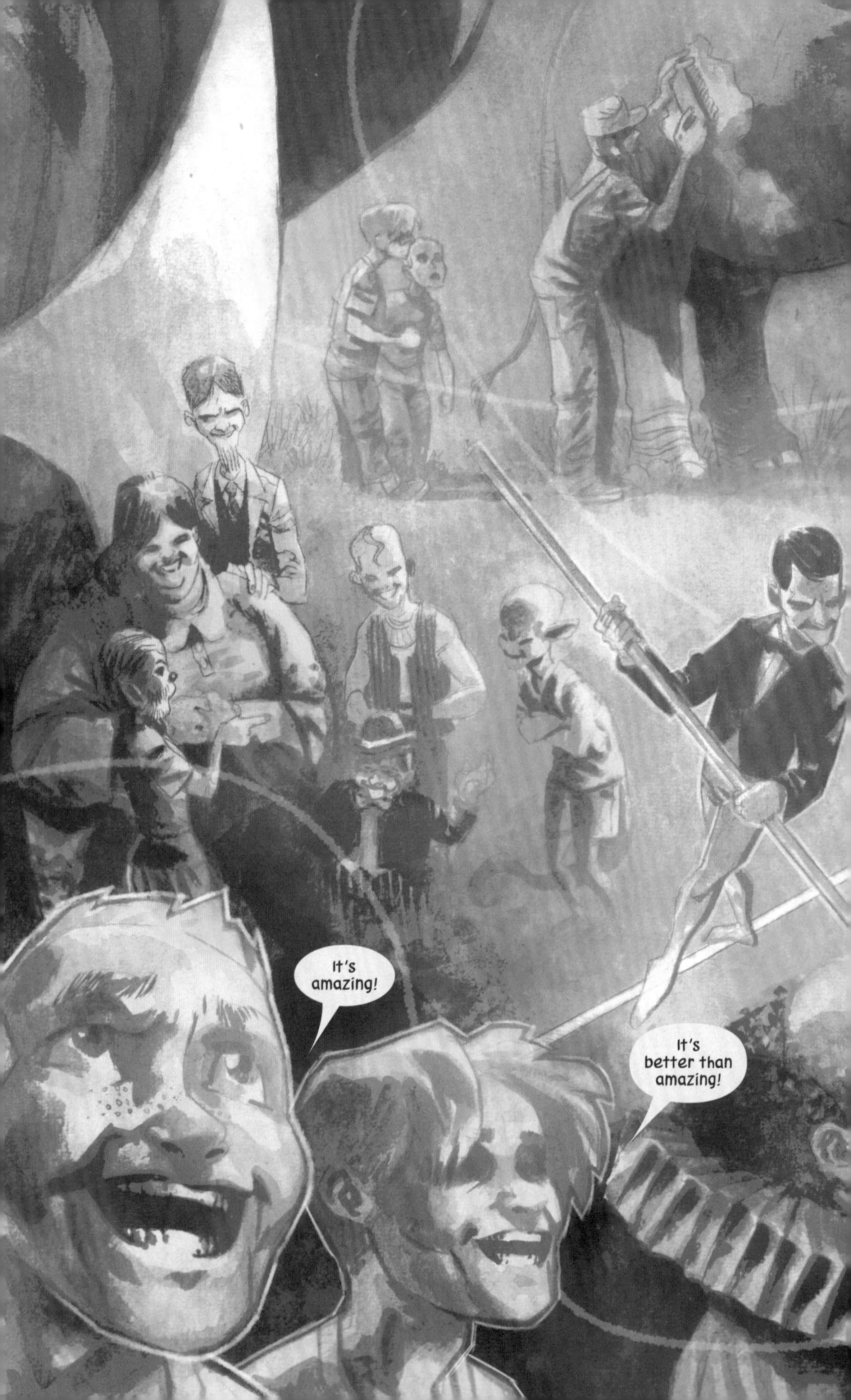
It's amazing!
It's better than amazing!

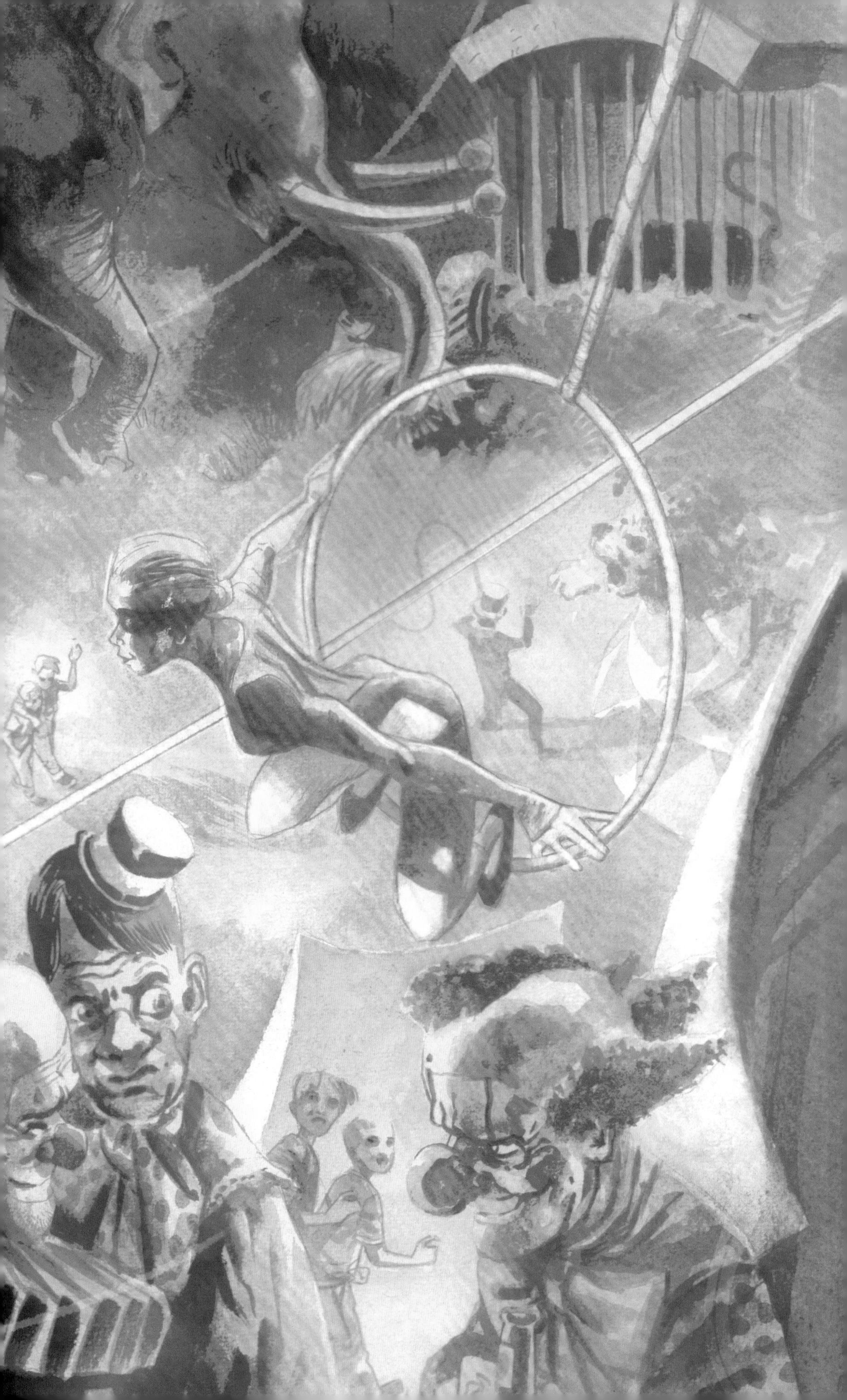

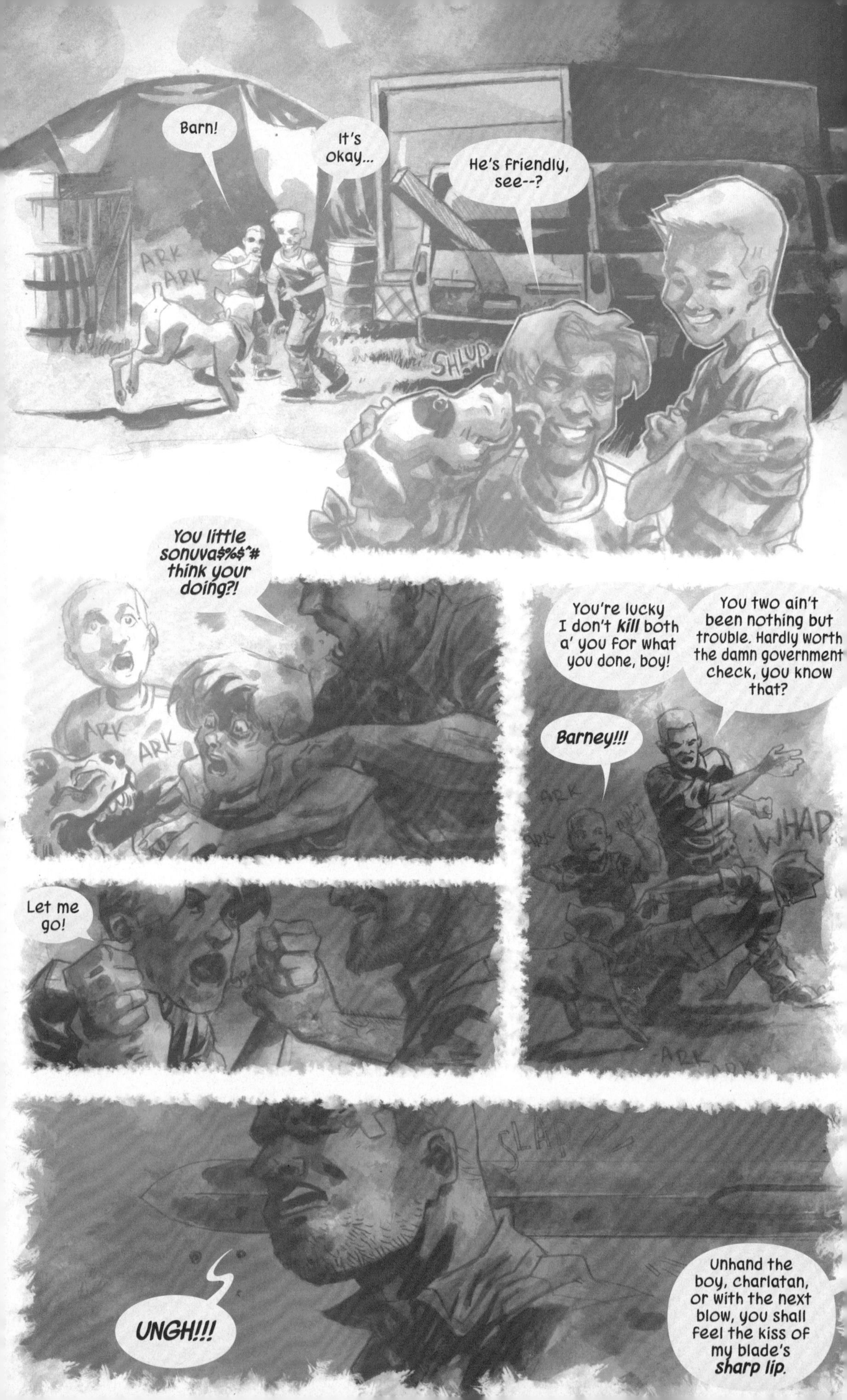
Barn!
It's okay...
He's friendly, see--?
ARK ARK
SHLUP
You little sonuva$%$^# think your doing?!
ARK ARK
Let me go!
You're lucky I don't *kill* both a' you for what you done, boy!
You two ain't been nothing but trouble. Hardly worth the damn government check, you know that?
Barney!!!
WHAP
SLAP
UNGH!!!
Unhand the boy, charlatan, or with the next blow, you shall feel the kiss of my blade's *sharp lip*.

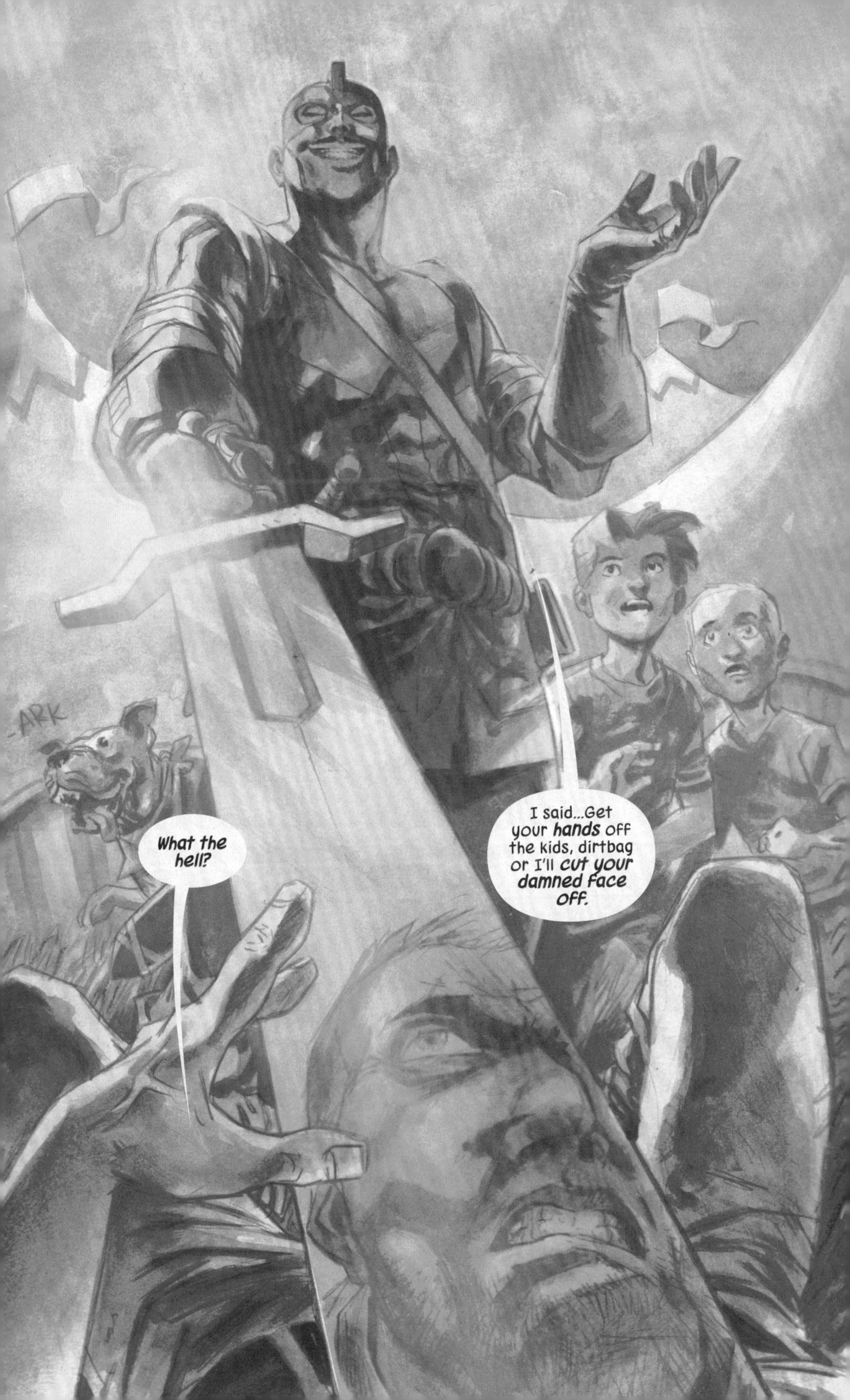
-ARK
What the hell?
I said...Get your hands off the kids, dirtbag or I'll cut your damned face off.

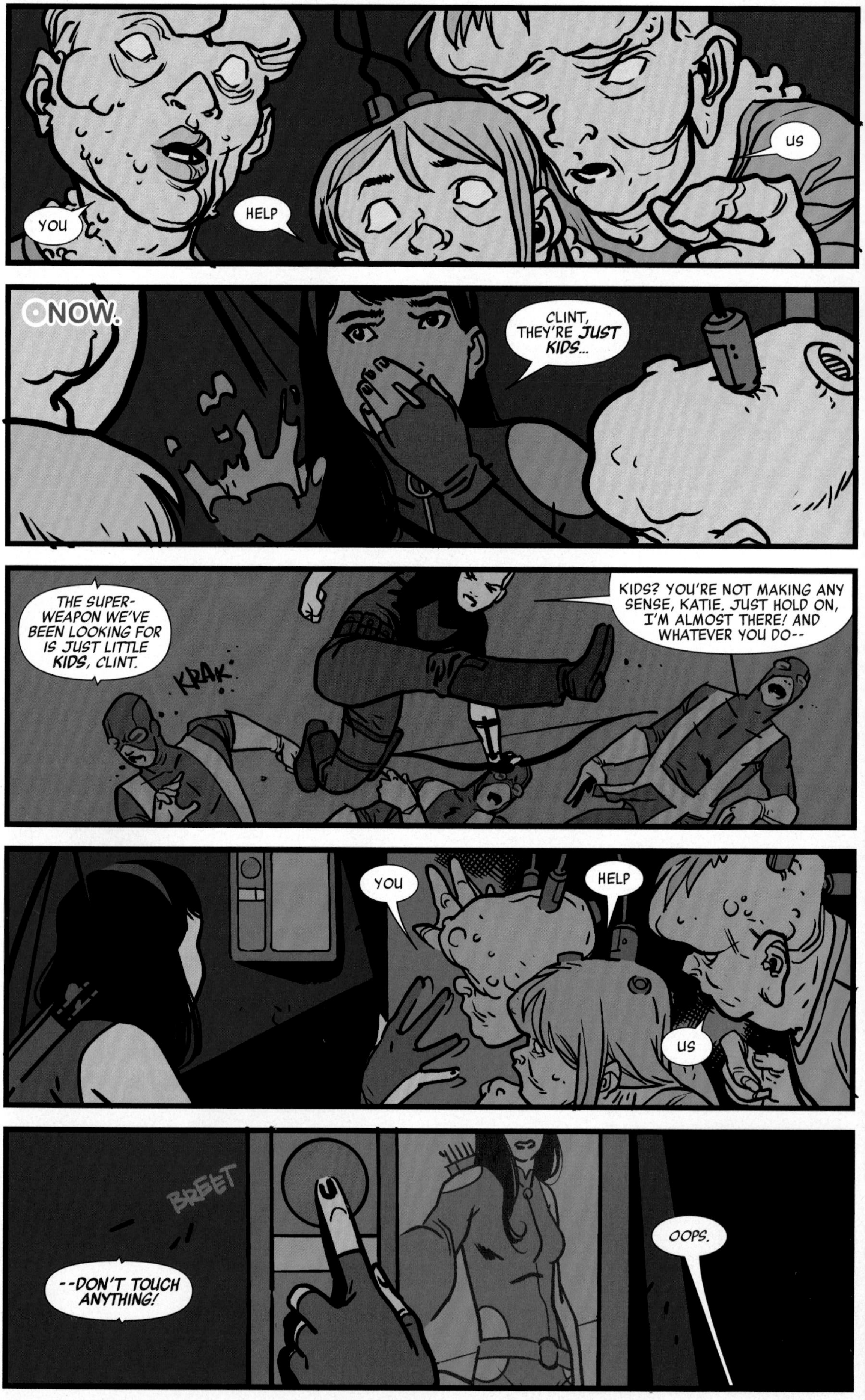
YOU
HELP
US
NOW.
CLINT, THEY'RE JUST KIDS...
THE SUPER-WEAPON WE'VE BEEN LOOKING FOR IS JUST LITTLE KIDS, CLINT.
KIDS? YOU'RE NOT MAKING ANY SENSE, KATIE. JUST HOLD ON, I'M ALMOST THERE! AND WHATEVER YOU DO--
KRAK
YOU
HELP
US
BREET
--DON'T TOUCH ANYTHING!
OOPS.

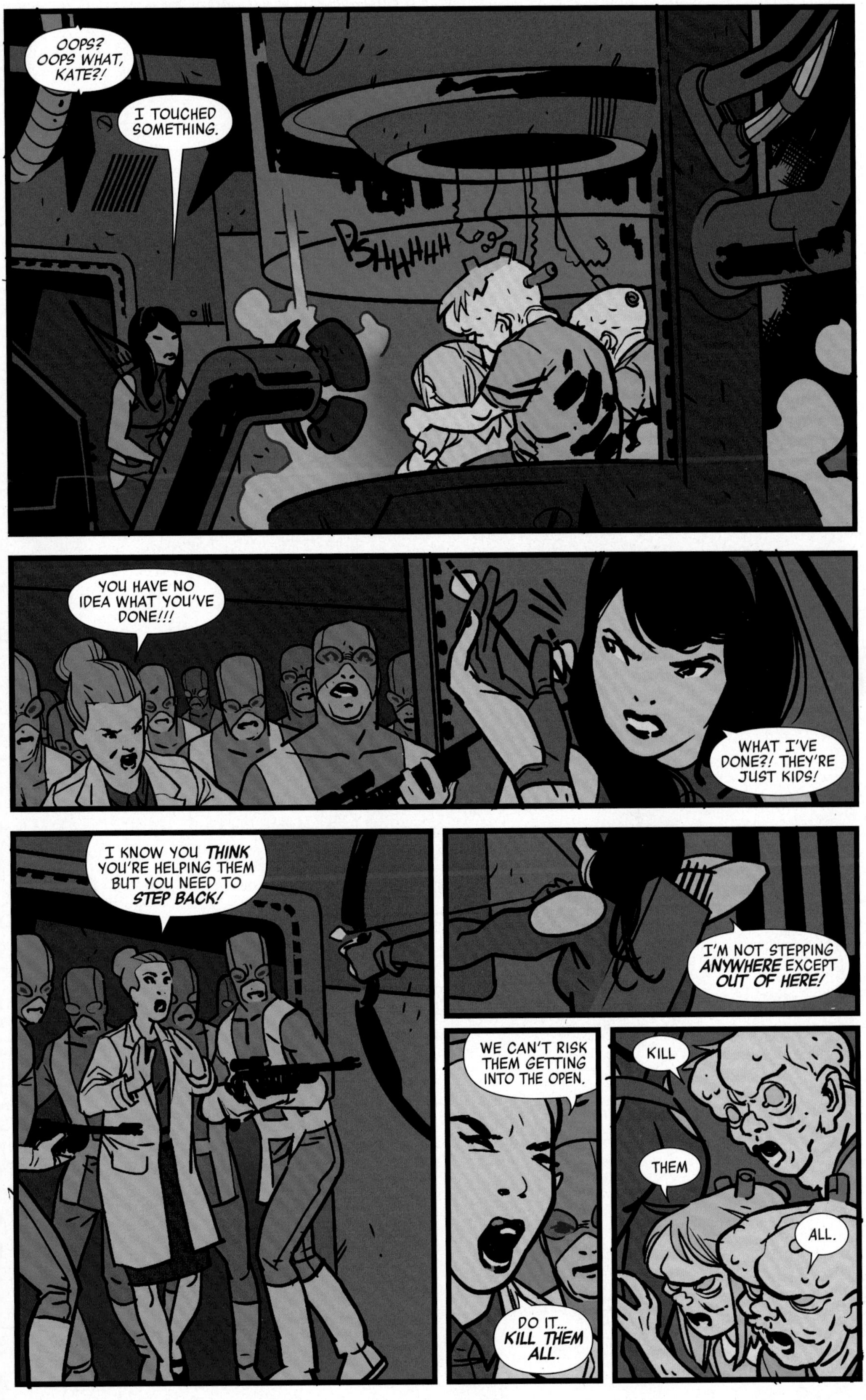
OOPS? OOPS WHAT, KATE?!
I TOUCHED SOMETHING.
PSHHHHH
YOU HAVE NO IDEA WHAT YOU'VE DONE!!!
WHAT I'VE DONE?! THEY'RE JUST KIDS!
I KNOW YOU THINK YOU'RE HELPING THEM BUT YOU NEED TO STEP BACK!
I'M NOT STEPPING ANYWHERE EXCEPT OUT OF HERE!
WE CAN'T RISK THEM GETTING INTO THE OPEN.
DO IT... KILL THEM ALL.
KILL
THEM
ALL.

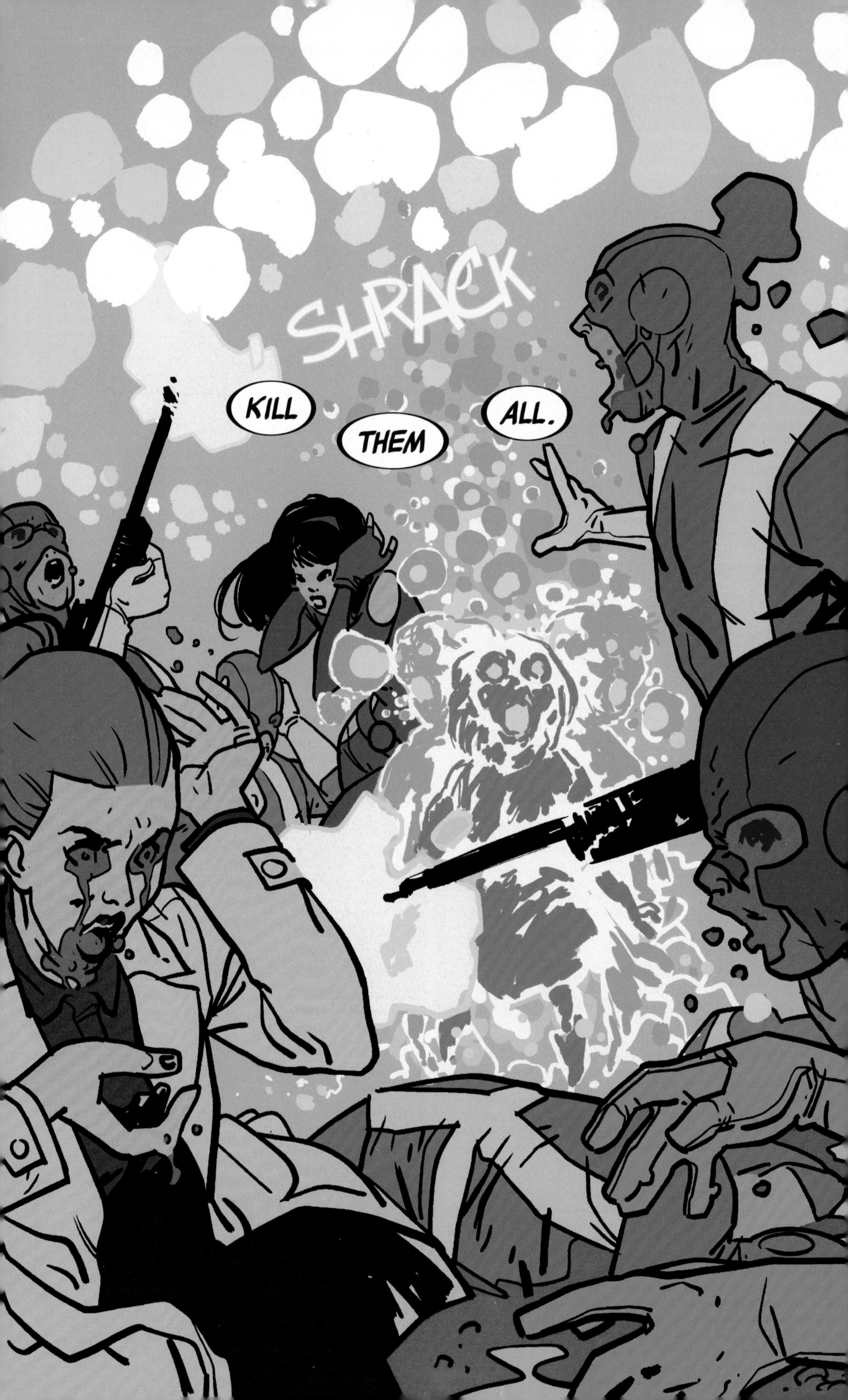
SHRACK
KILL
THEM
ALL.

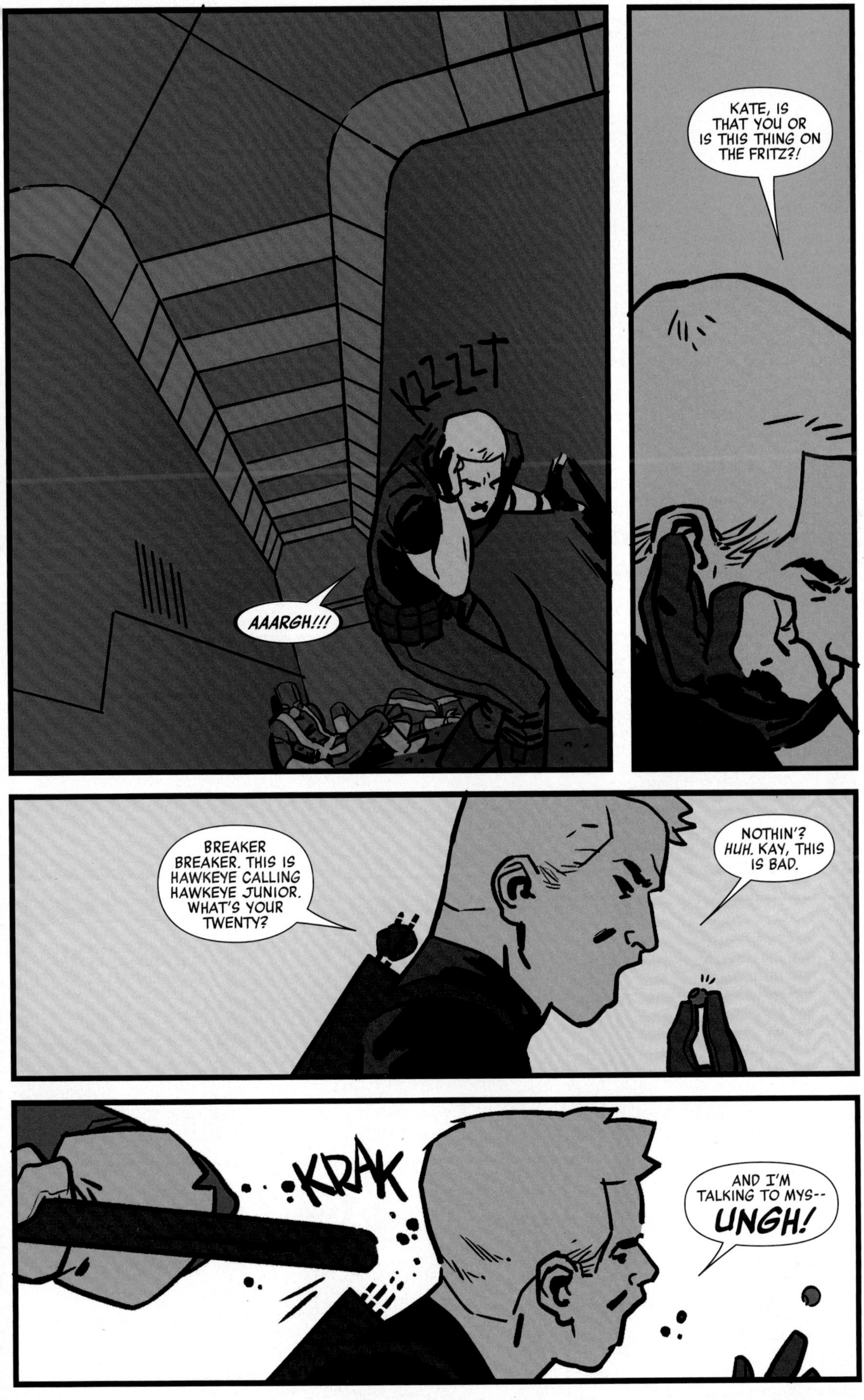
KZZZZT
AAARGH!!!
KATE, IS THAT YOU OR IS THIS THING ON THE FRITZ?!
BREAKER BREAKER. THIS IS HAWKEYE CALLING HAWKEYE JUNIOR. WHAT'S YOUR TWENTY?
NOTHIN'? HUH. KAY, THIS IS BAD.
KRAK
AND I'M TALKING TO MYS-- UNGH!

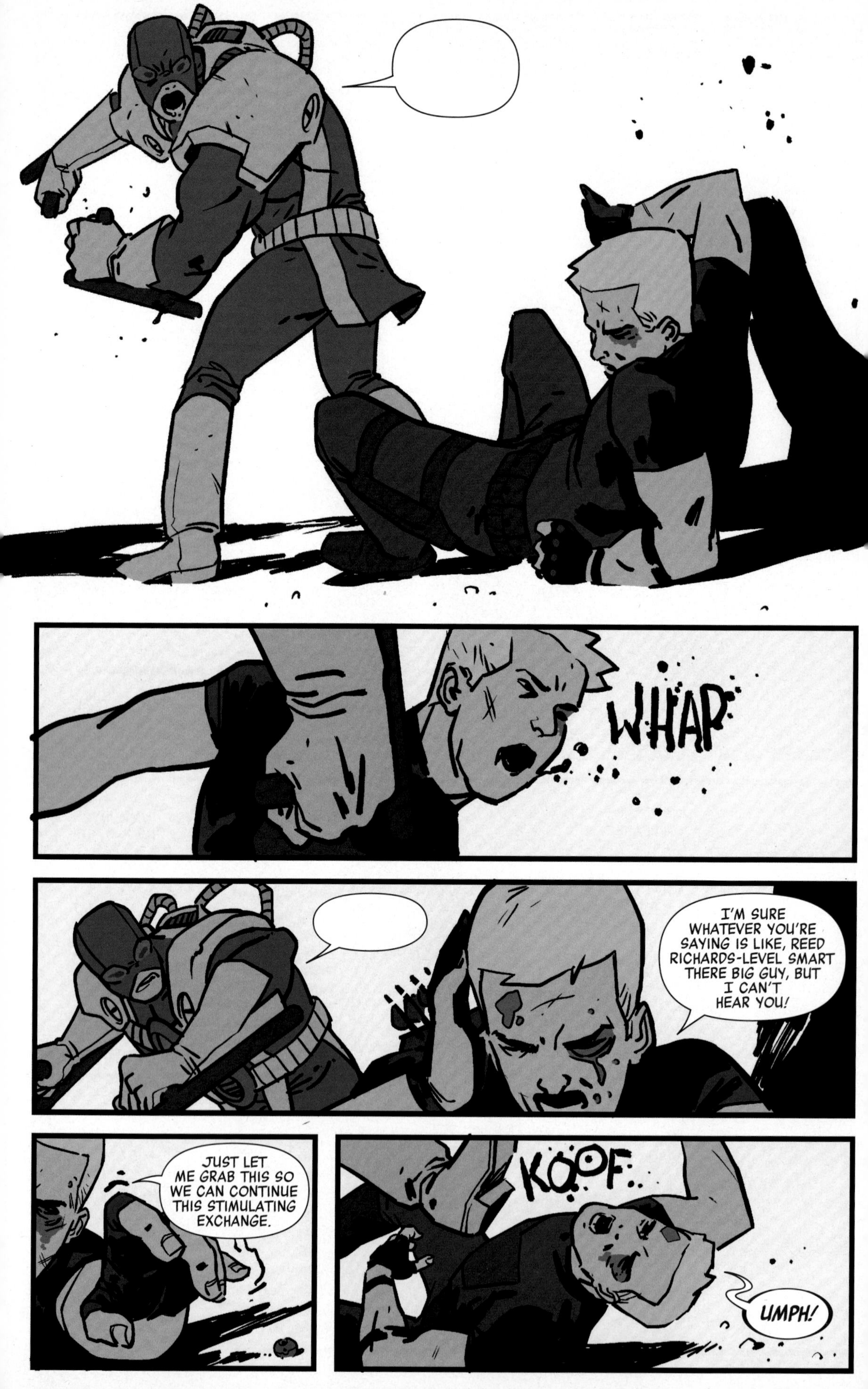
WHAP
I'M SURE WHATEVER YOU'RE SAYING IS LIKE, REED RICHARDS-LEVEL SMART THERE BIG GUY, BUT I CAN'T HEAR YOU!
JUST LET ME GRAB THIS SO WE CAN CONTINUE THIS STIMULATING EXCHANGE.
KOOF
UMPH!

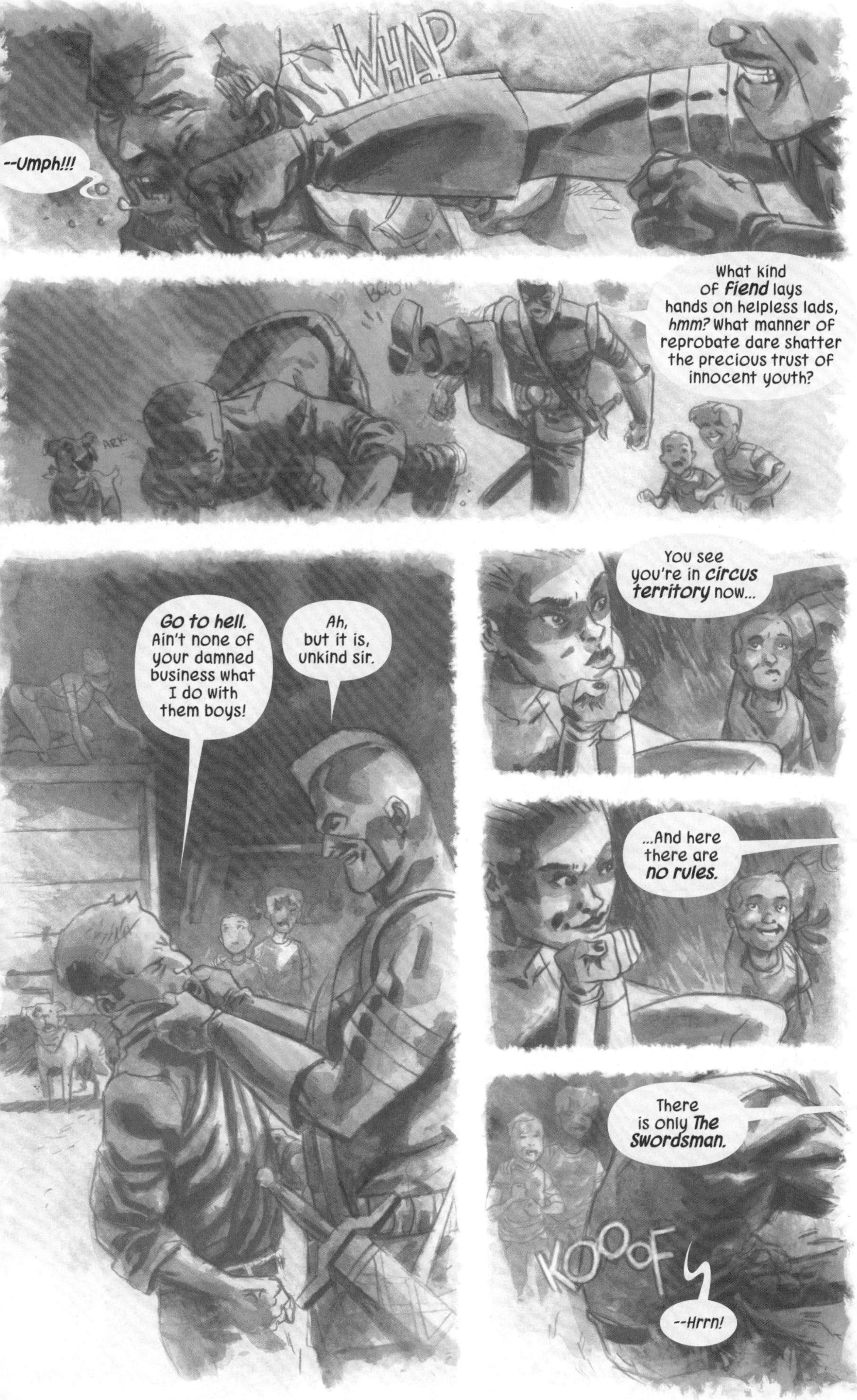
WHAP
--Umph!!!
What kind of fiend lays hands on helpless lads, hmm? What manner of reprobate dare shatter the precious trust of innocent youth?
Go to hell. Ain't none of your damned business what I do with them boys!
Ah, but it is, unkind sir.
You see you're in circus territory now...
...And here there are no rules.
There is only The Swordsman.
KOOOF
--Hrrn!

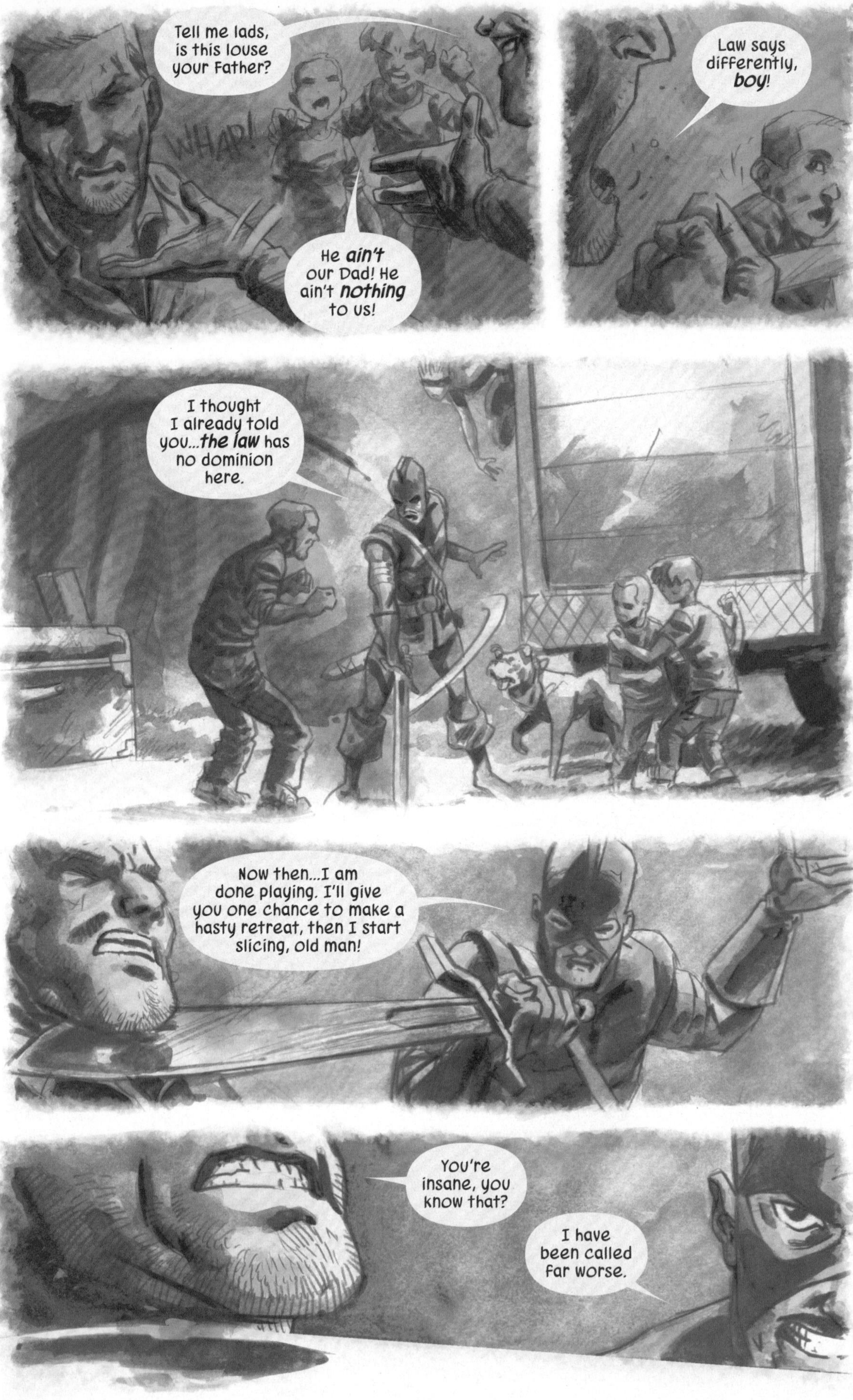
Tell me lads, is this louse your Father?
WHAP!
He ain't our Dad! He ain't nothing to us!
Law says differently, boy!
I thought I already told you...the law has no dominion here.
Now then...I am done playing. I'll give you one chance to make a hasty retreat, then I start slicing, old man!
You're insane, you know that?
I have been called far worse.

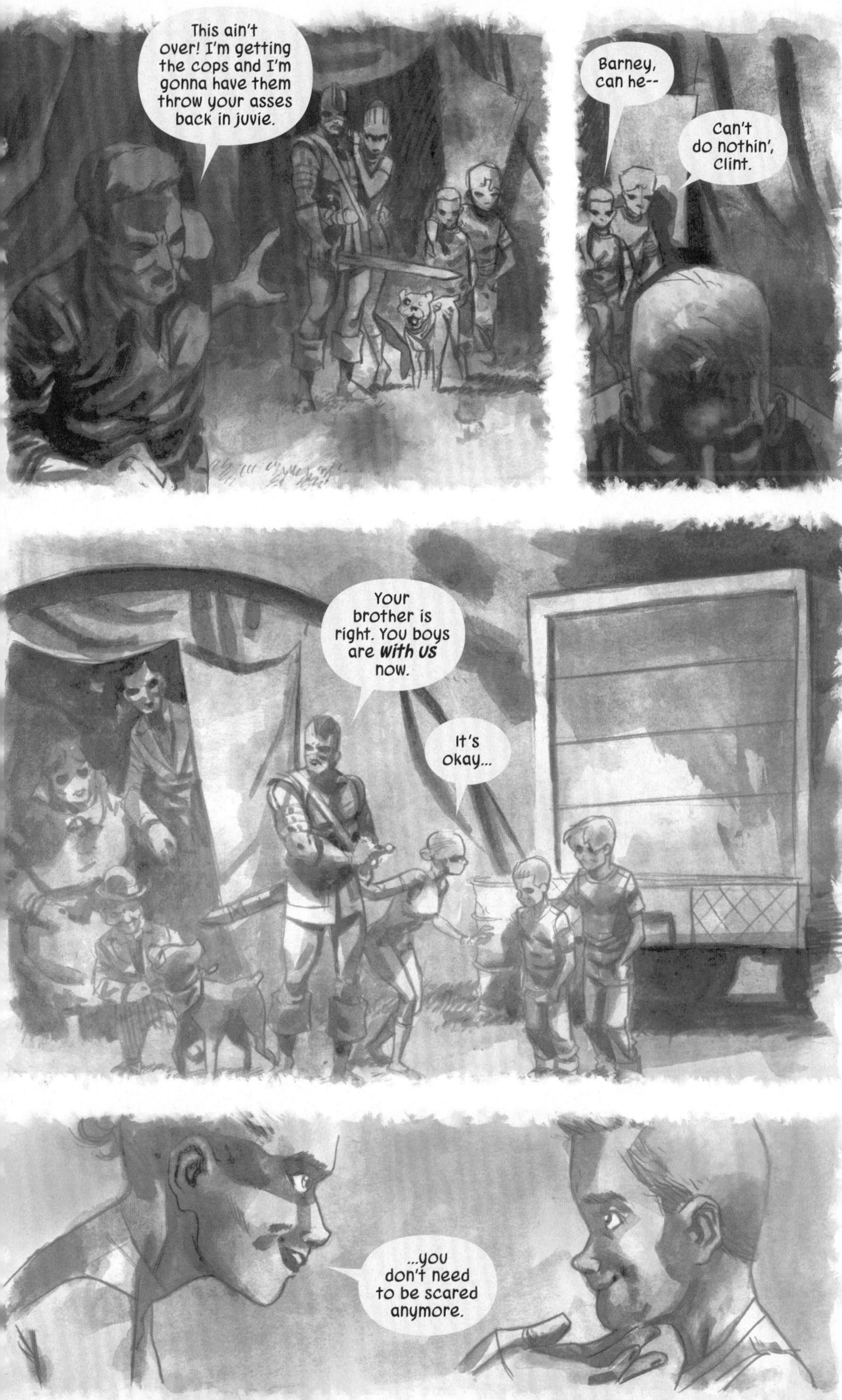
This ain't over! I'm getting the cops and I'm gonna have them throw your asses back in juvie.
Barney, can he--
Can't do nothin', Clint.
Your brother is right. You boys are **With Us** now.
It's okay...
...you don't need to be scared anymore.

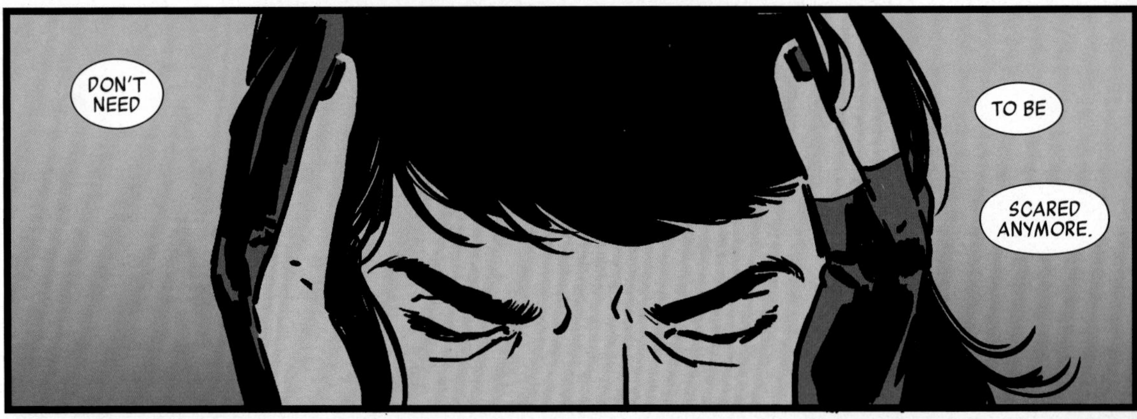
DON'T NEED
TO BE
SCARED ANYMORE.

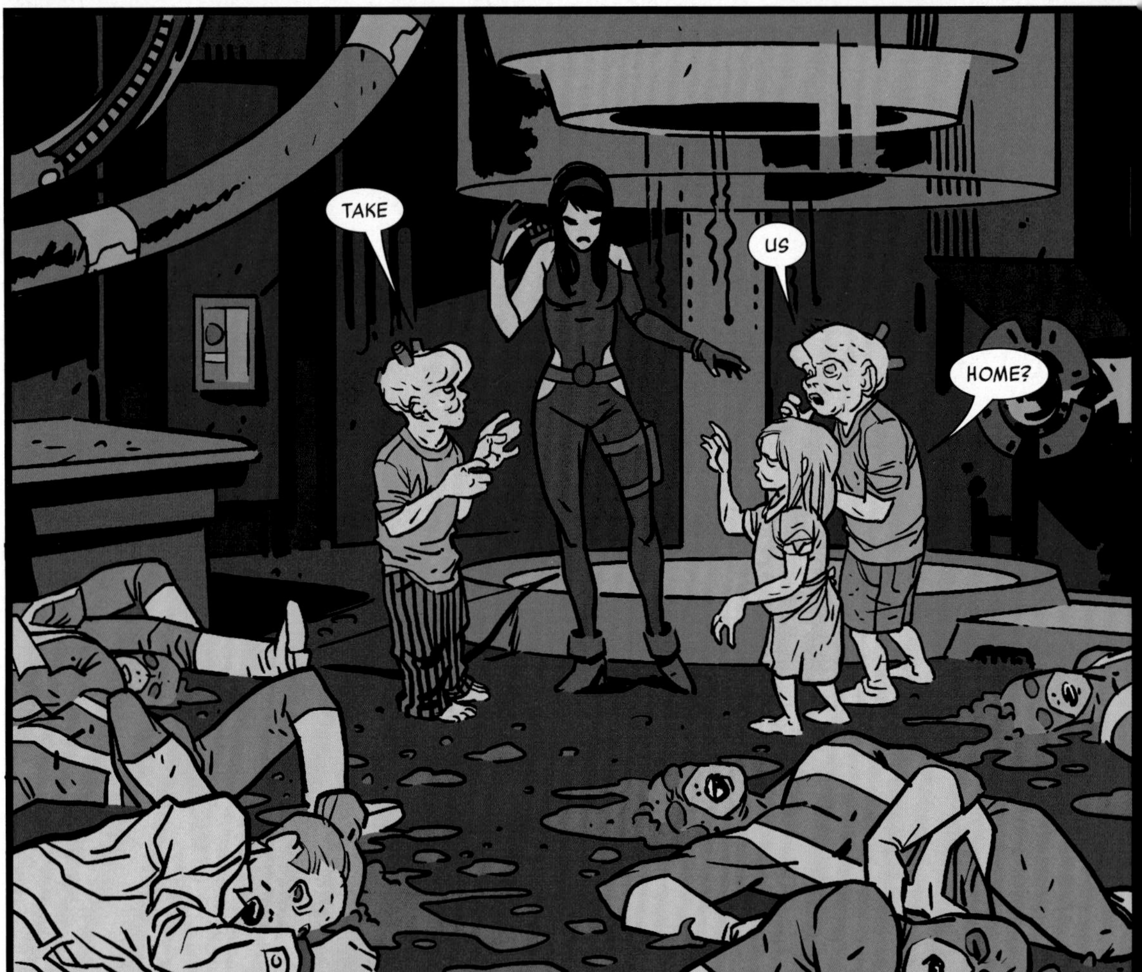
TAKE
US
HOME?

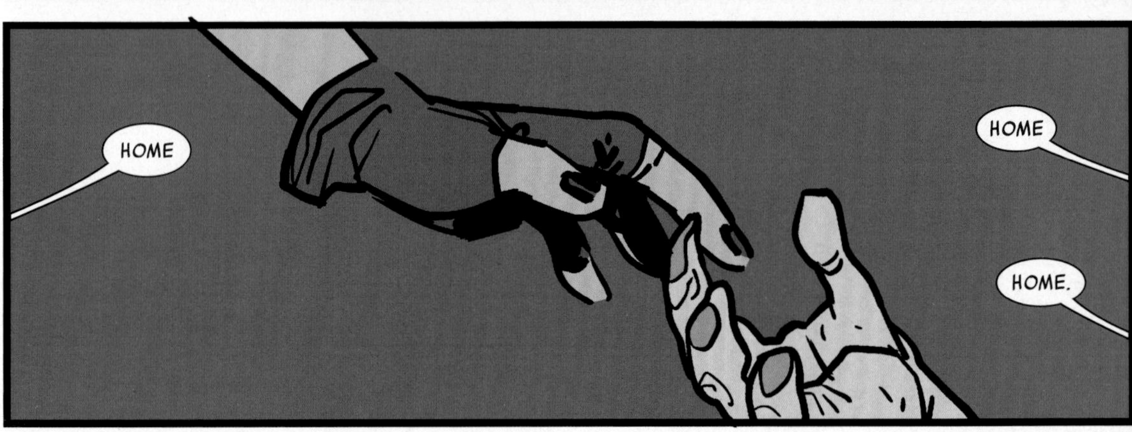
HOME
HOME
HOME.

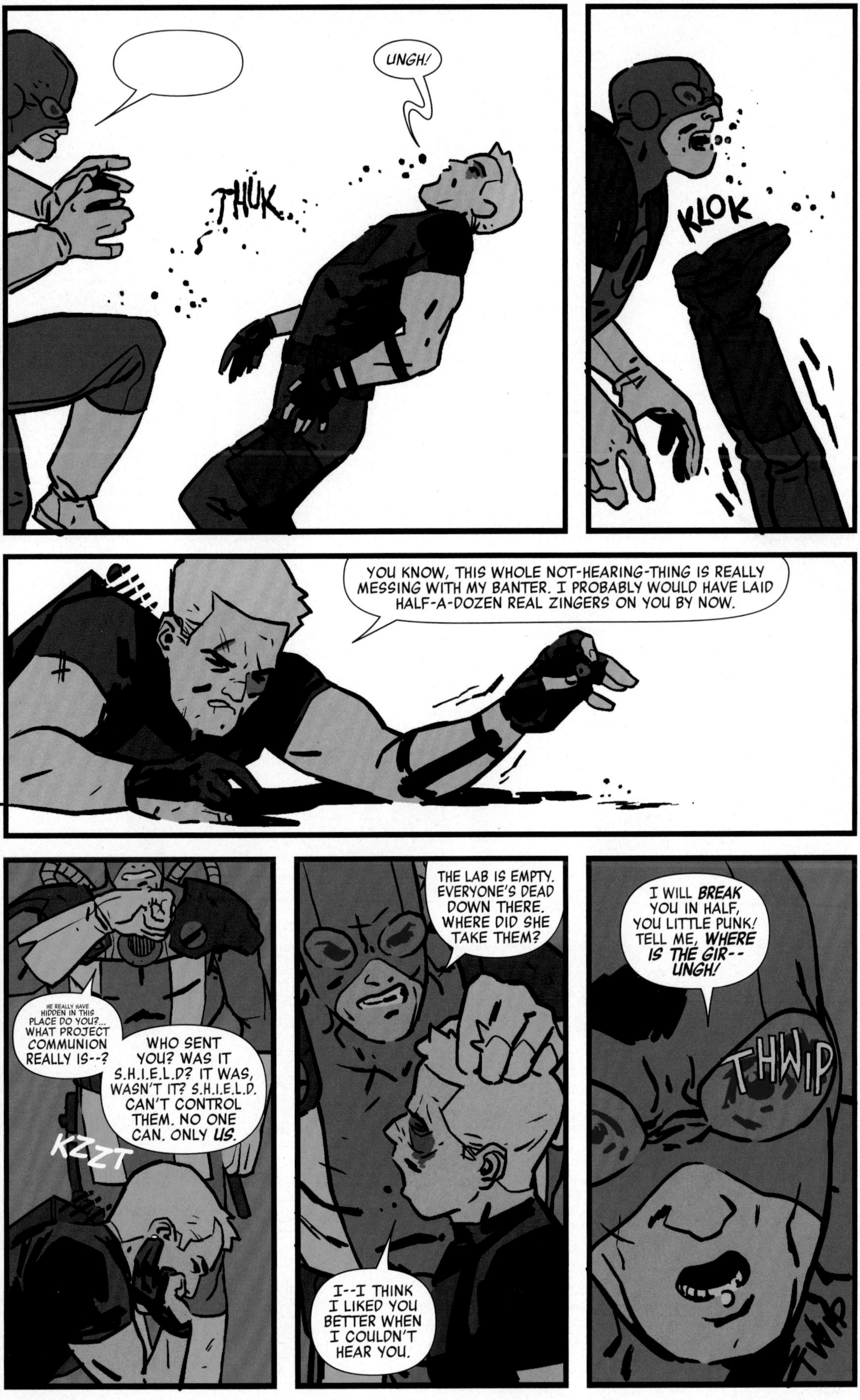
UNGH!
THUK
KLOK
YOU KNOW, THIS WHOLE NOT-HEARING-THING IS REALLY MESSING WITH MY BANTER. I PROBABLY WOULD HAVE LAID HALF-A-DOZEN REAL ZINGERS ON YOU BY NOW.
HE REALLY HAVE HIDDEN IN THIS PLACE DO YOU?... WHAT PROJECT COMMUNION REALLY IS--?
WHO SENT YOU? WAS IT S.H.I.E.L.D? IT WAS, WASN'T IT? S.H.I.E.L.D. CAN'T CONTROL THEM. NO ONE CAN. ONLY US.
KZZT
THE LAB IS EMPTY. EVERYONE'S DEAD DOWN THERE. WHERE DID SHE TAKE THEM?
I--I THINK I LIKED YOU BETTER WHEN I COULDN'T HEAR YOU.
I WILL BREAK YOU IN HALF, YOU LITTLE PUNK! TELL ME, WHERE IS THE GIR-- UNGH!
THWIP

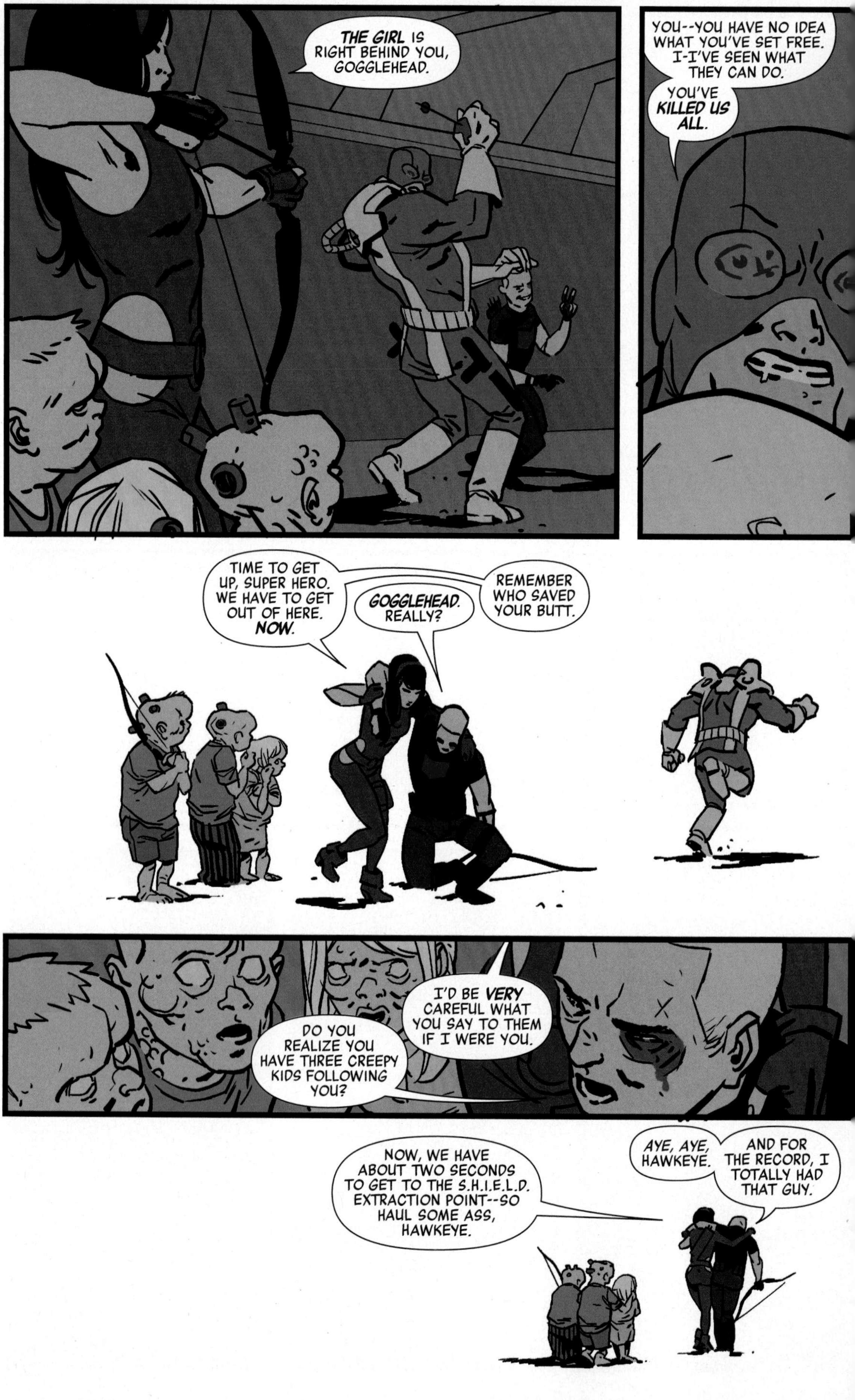
THE GIRL IS RIGHT BEHIND YOU, GOGGLEHEAD.
YOU--YOU HAVE NO IDEA WHAT YOU'VE SET FREE. I-I'VE SEEN WHAT THEY CAN DO.
YOU'VE KILLED US ALL.
TIME TO GET UP, SUPER HERO. WE HAVE TO GET OUT OF HERE. NOW.
GOGGLEHEAD. REALLY?
REMEMBER WHO SAVED YOUR BUTT.
DO YOU REALIZE YOU HAVE THREE CREEPY KIDS FOLLOWING YOU?
I'D BE VERY CAREFUL WHAT YOU SAY TO THEM IF I WERE YOU.
NOW, WE HAVE ABOUT TWO SECONDS TO GET TO THE S.H.I.E.L.D. EXTRACTION POINT--SO HAUL SOME ASS, HAWKEYE.
AYE, AYE, HAWKEYE.
AND FOR THE RECORD, I TOTALLY HAD THAT GUY.

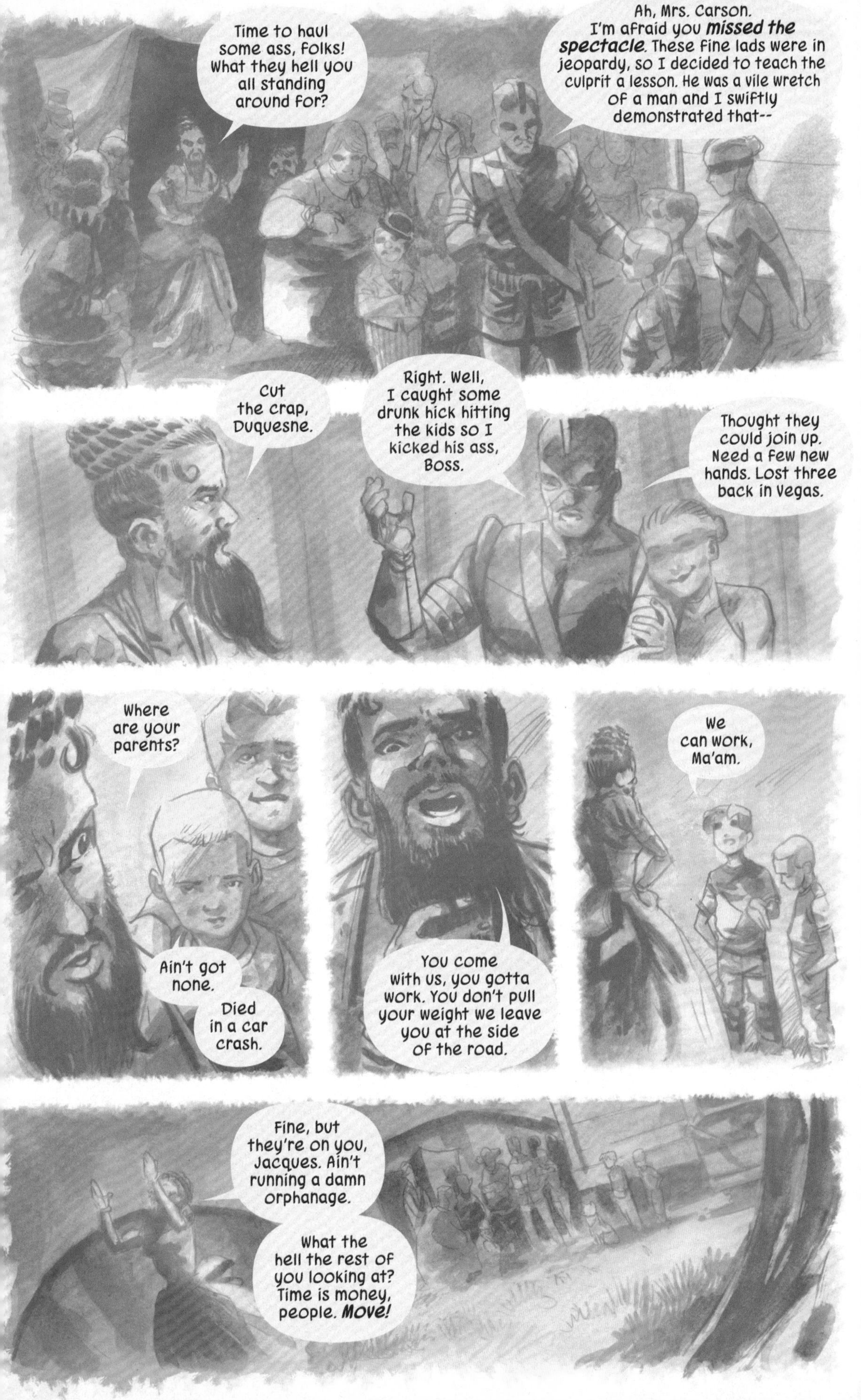
Time to haul some ass, folks! What they hell you all standing around for?
Ah, Mrs. Carson. I'm afraid you **missed the spectacle**. These fine lads were in jeopardy, so I decided to teach the culprit a lesson. He was a vile wretch of a man and I swiftly demonstrated that--
Cut the crap, Duquesne.
Right. Well, I caught some drunk hick hitting the kids so I kicked his ass, Boss.
Thought they could join up. Need a few new hands. Lost three back in Vegas.
Where are your parents?
Ain't got none.
Died in a car crash.
You come with us, you gotta work. You don't pull your weight we leave you at the side of the road.
We can work, Ma'am.
Fine, but they're on you, Jacques. Ain't running a damn orphanage.
What the hell the rest of you looking at? Time is money, people. **Move!**

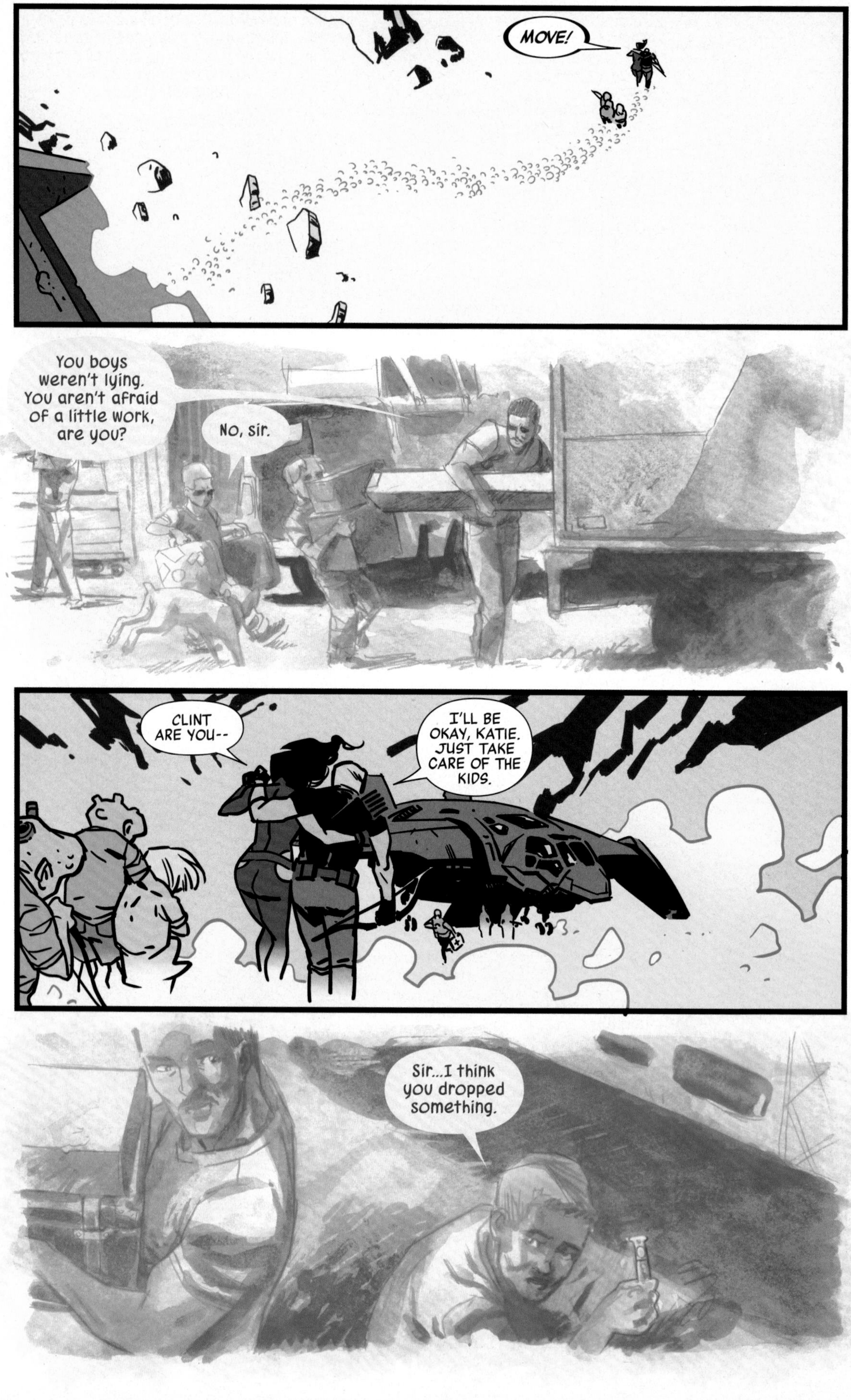
MOVE!
You boys weren't lying. You aren't afraid of a little work, are you?
No, sir.
CLINT ARE YOU--
I'LL BE OKAY, KATIE. JUST TAKE CARE OF THE KIDS.
Sir...I think you dropped something.

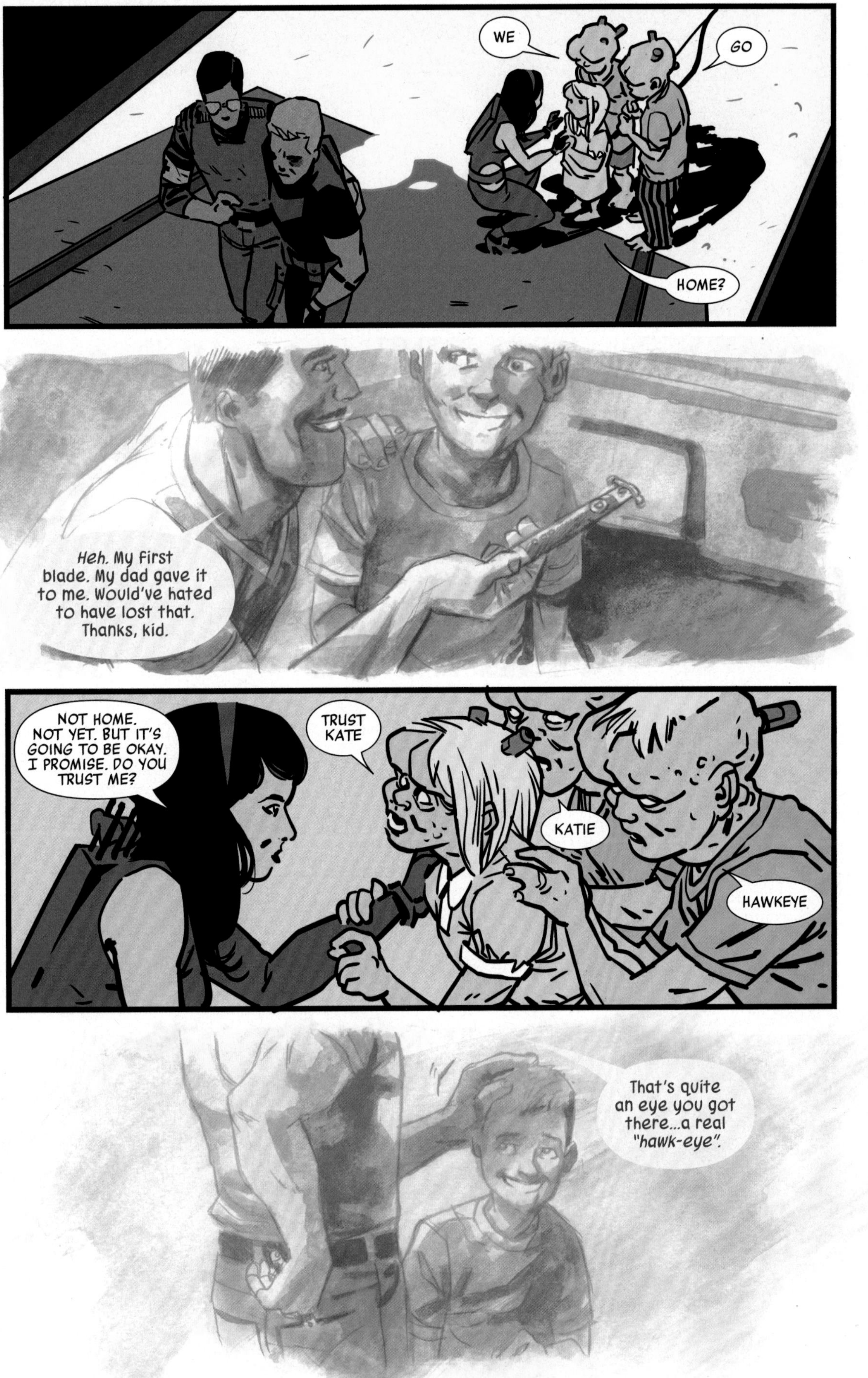
WE
GO
HOME?
Heh. My first blade. My dad gave it to me. Would've hated to have lost that. Thanks, kid.
NOT HOME. NOT YET. BUT IT'S GOING TO BE OKAY. I PROMISE. DO YOU TRUST ME?
TRUST KATE
KATIE
HAWKEYE
That's quite an eye you got there...a real "hawk-eye".

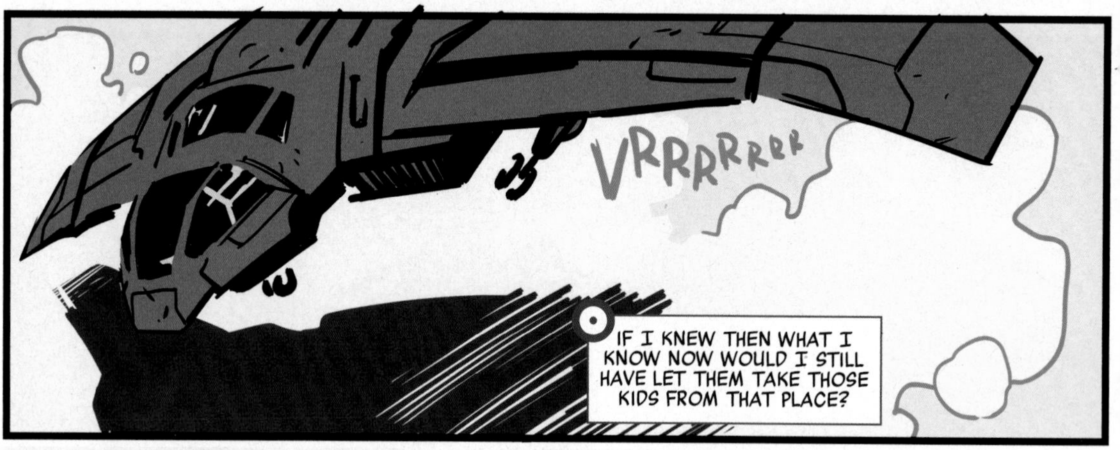
VRRRRrrr
IF I KNEW THEN WHAT I KNOW NOW WOULD I STILL HAVE LET THEM TAKE THOSE KIDS FROM THAT PLACE?

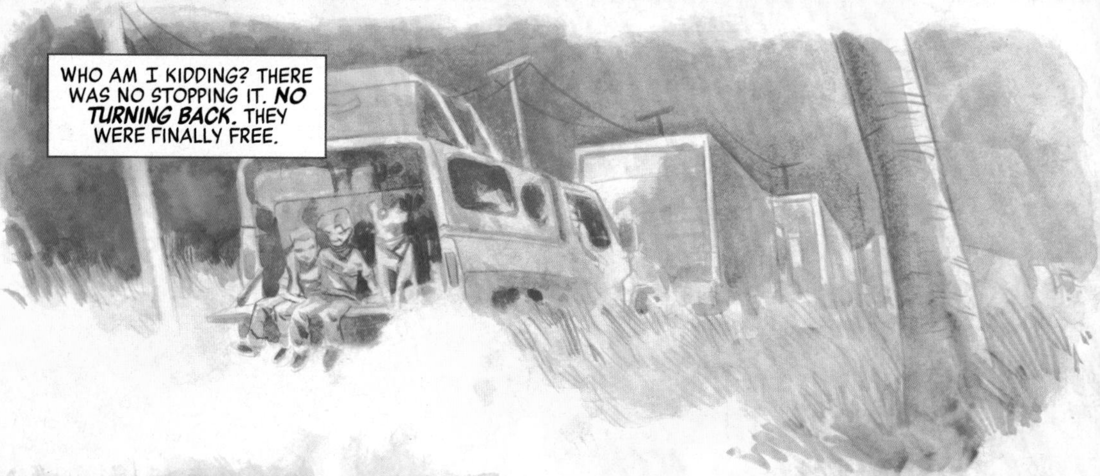
WHO AM I KIDDING? THERE WAS NO STOPPING IT. NO TURNING BACK. THEY WERE FINALLY FREE.

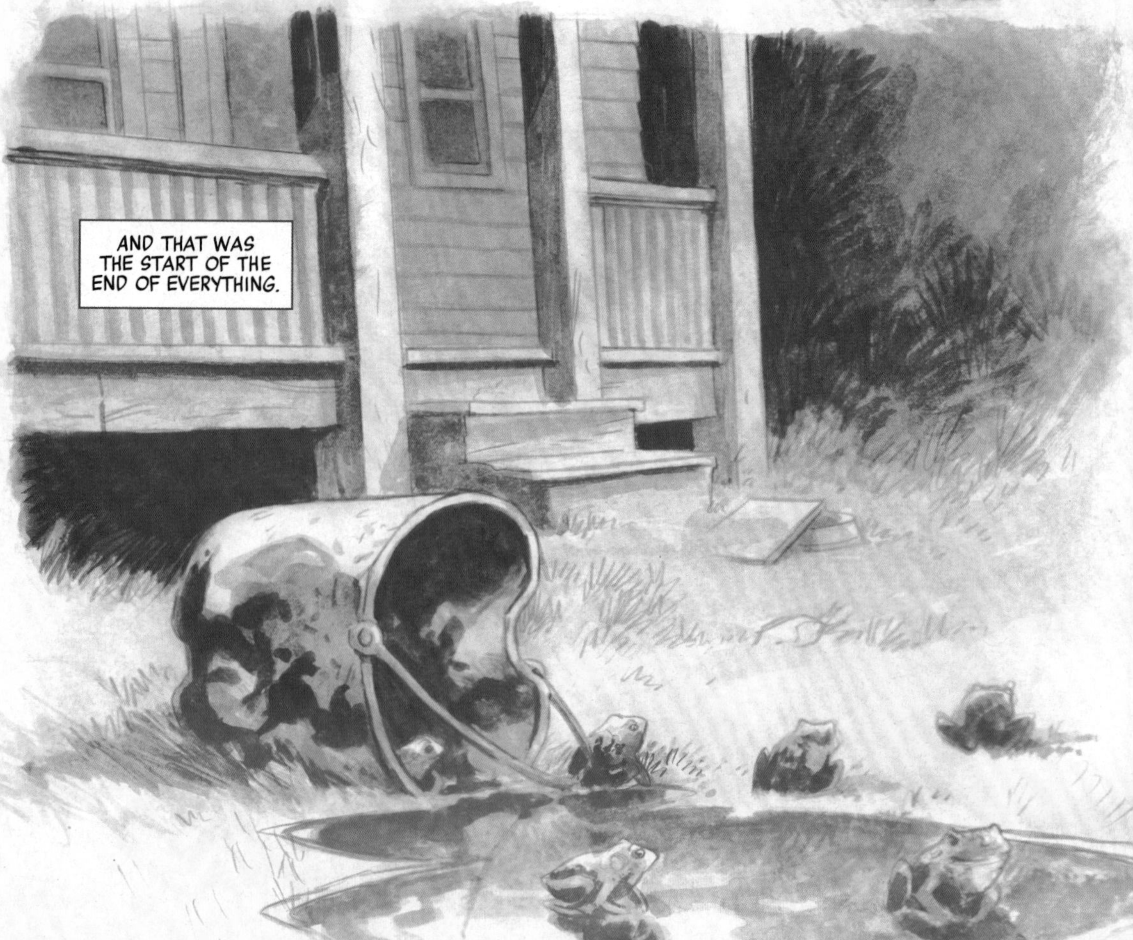
AND THAT WAS THE START OF THE END OF EVERYTHING.

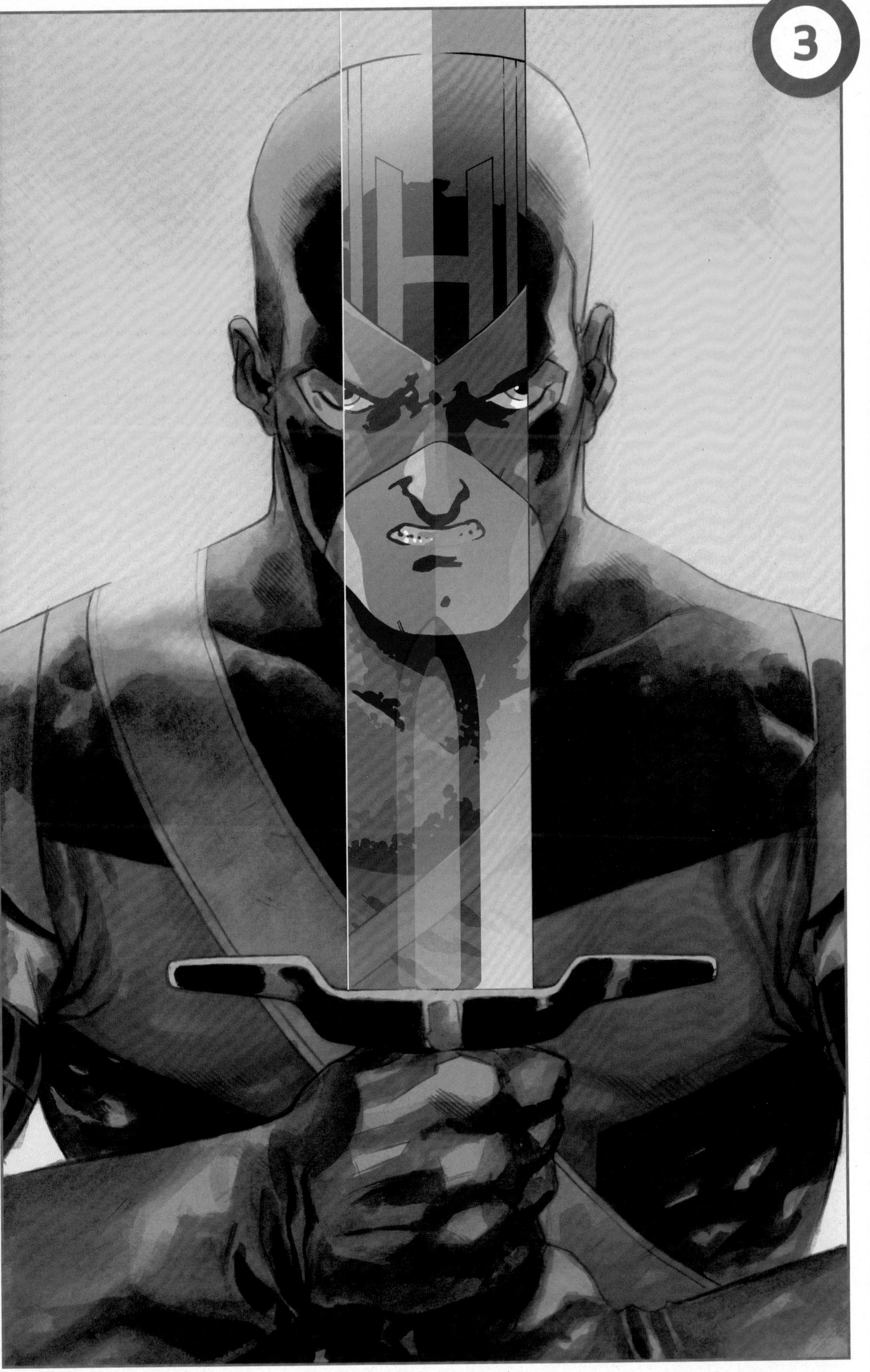
3

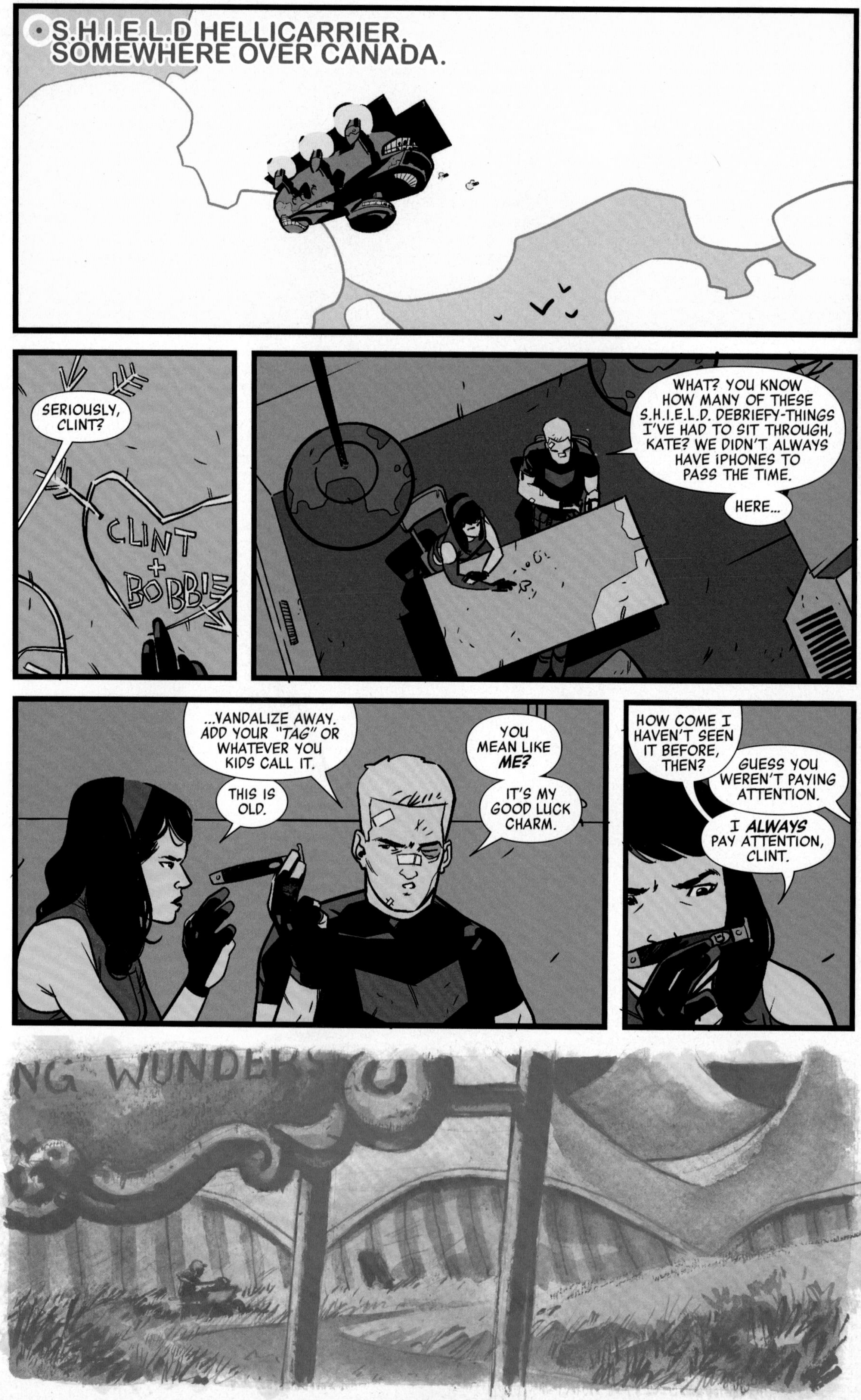
S.H.I.E.L.D HELLICARRIER. SOMEWHERE OVER CANADA.
SERIOUSLY, CLINT?
CLINT + BOBBIE
WHAT? YOU KNOW HOW MANY OF THESE S.H.I.E.L.D. DEBRIEFY-THINGS I'VE HAD TO SIT THROUGH, KATE? WE DIDN'T ALWAYS HAVE iPHONES TO PASS THE TIME.
HERE...
...VANDALIZE AWAY. ADD YOUR "TAG" OR WHATEVER YOU KIDS CALL IT.
THIS IS OLD.
YOU MEAN LIKE ME?
IT'S MY GOOD LUCK CHARM.
HOW COME I HAVEN'T SEEN IT BEFORE, THEN?
GUESS YOU WEREN'T PAYING ATTENTION.
I ALWAYS PAY ATTENTION, CLINT.
NG WUNDERS

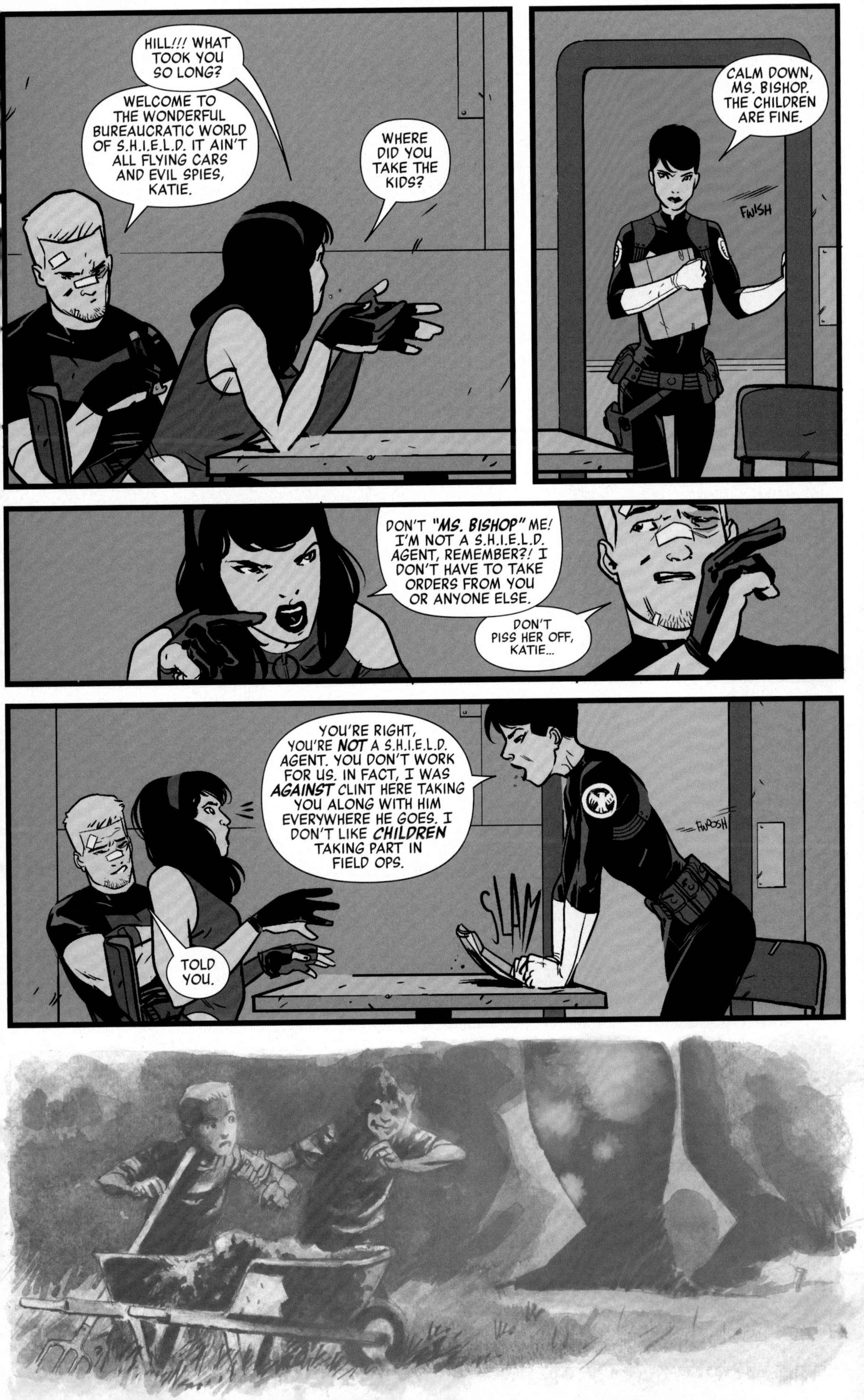
HILL!!! WHAT TOOK YOU SO LONG?
WELCOME TO THE WONDERFUL BUREAUCRATIC WORLD OF S.H.I.E.L.D. IT AIN'T ALL FLYING CARS AND EVIL SPIES, KATIE.
WHERE DID YOU TAKE THE KIDS?
CALM DOWN, MS. BISHOP. THE CHILDREN ARE FINE.
FWISH
DON'T "MS. BISHOP" ME! I'M NOT A S.H.I.E.L.D. AGENT, REMEMBER?! I DON'T HAVE TO TAKE ORDERS FROM YOU OR ANYONE ELSE.
DON'T PISS HER OFF, KATIE...
YOU'RE RIGHT, YOU'RE NOT A S.H.I.E.L.D. AGENT. YOU DON'T WORK FOR US. IN FACT, I WAS AGAINST CLINT HERE TAKING YOU ALONG WITH HIM EVERYWHERE HE GOES. I DON'T LIKE CHILDREN TAKING PART IN FIELD OPS.
FWOOSH
SLAM
TOLD YOU.

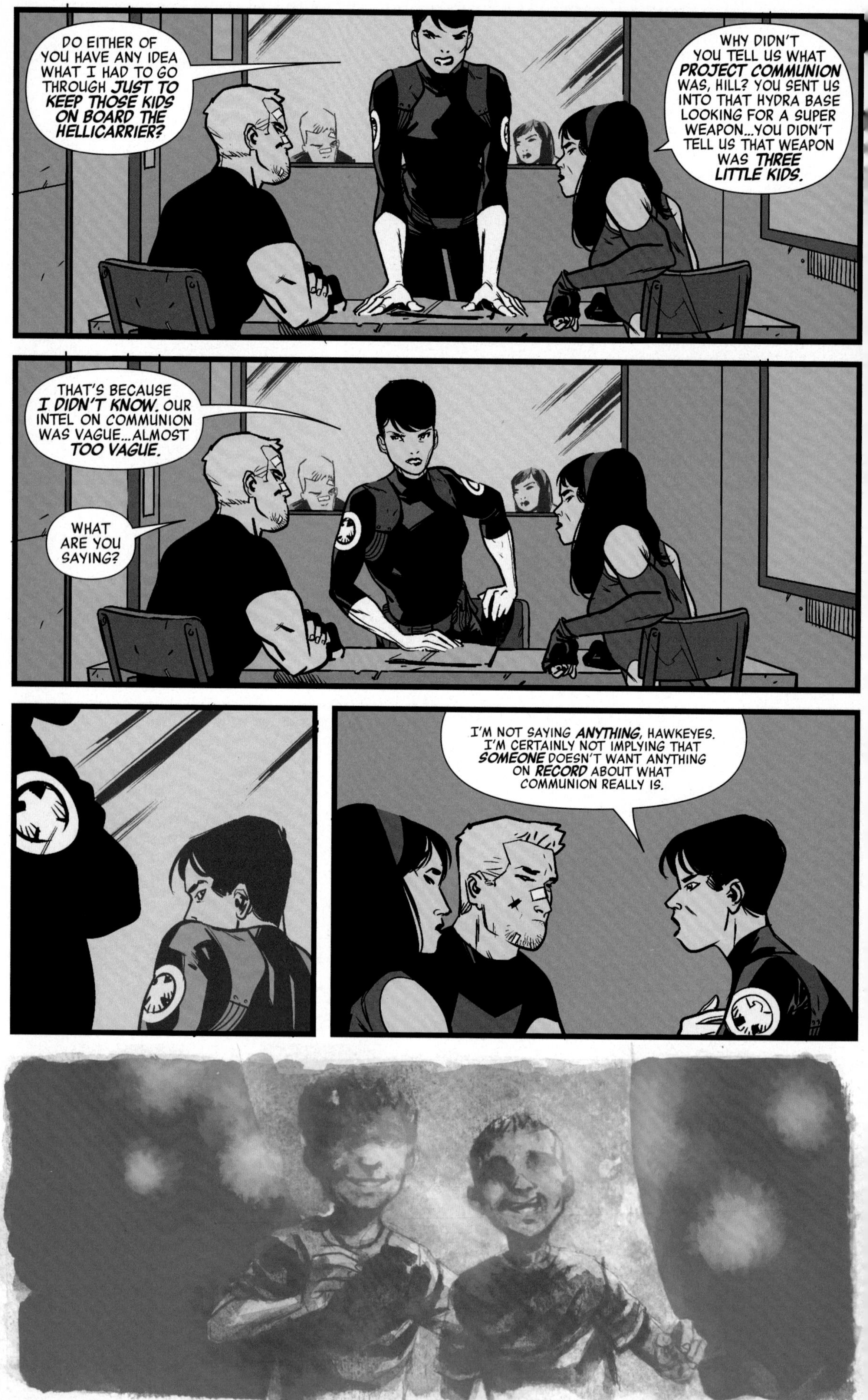
DO EITHER OF YOU HAVE ANY IDEA WHAT I HAD TO GO THROUGH JUST TO KEEP THOSE KIDS ON BOARD THE HELLICARRIER?
WHY DIDN'T YOU TELL US WHAT PROJECT COMMUNION WAS, HILL? YOU SENT US INTO THAT HYDRA BASE LOOKING FOR A SUPER WEAPON...YOU DIDN'T TELL US THAT WEAPON WAS THREE LITTLE KIDS.
THAT'S BECAUSE I DIDN'T KNOW. OUR INTEL ON COMMUNION WAS VAGUE...ALMOST TOO VAGUE.
WHAT ARE YOU SAYING?
I'M NOT SAYING ANYTHING, HAWKEYES. I'M CERTAINLY NOT IMPLYING THAT SOMEONE DOESN'T WANT ANYTHING ON RECORD ABOUT WHAT COMMUNION REALLY IS.

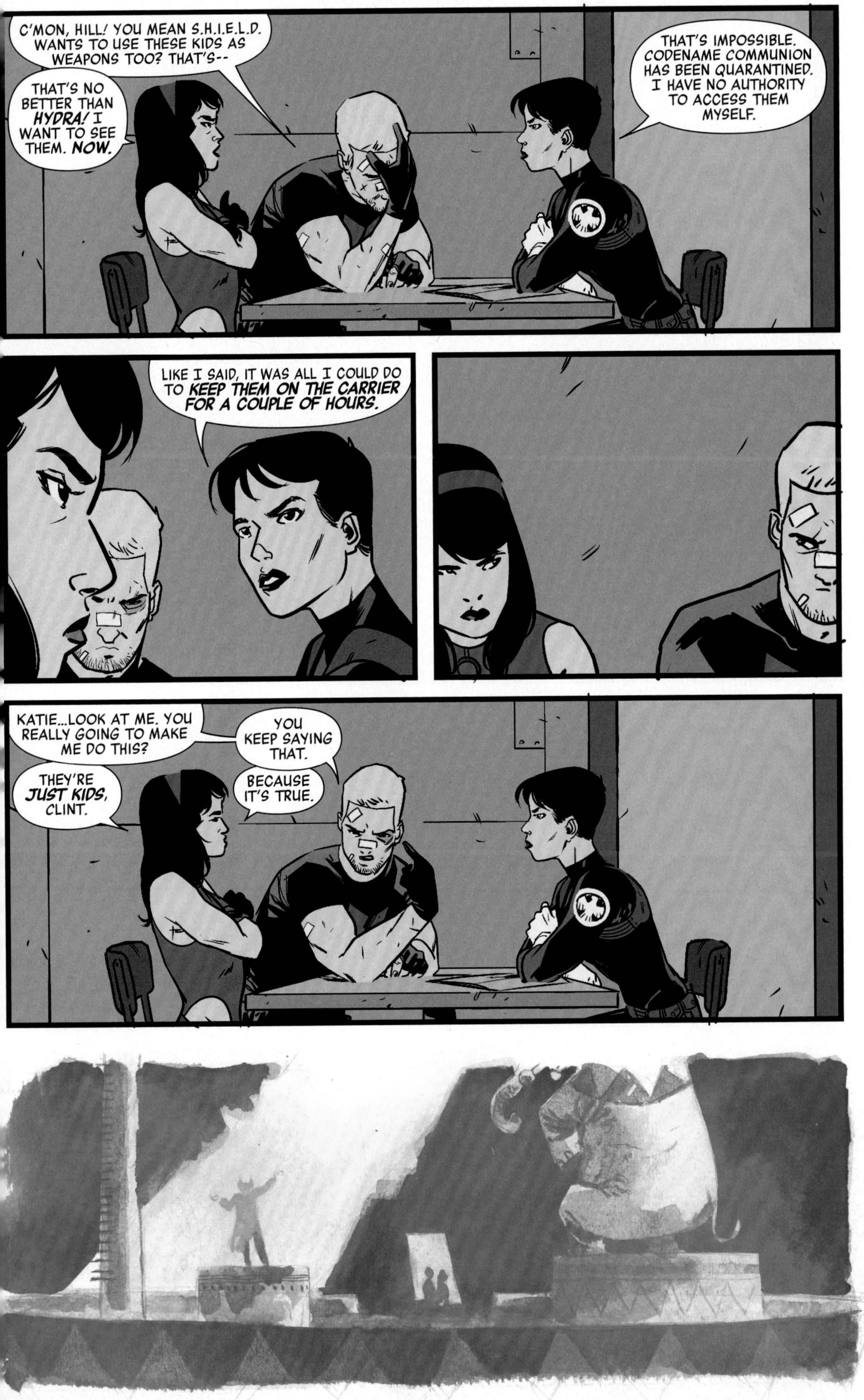
C'MON, HILL! YOU MEAN S.H.I.E.L.D. WANTS TO USE THESE KIDS AS WEAPONS TOO? THAT'S--
THAT'S NO BETTER THAN HYDRA! I WANT TO SEE THEM. NOW.
THAT'S IMPOSSIBLE. CODENAME COMMUNION HAS BEEN QUARANTINED. I HAVE NO AUTHORITY TO ACCESS THEM MYSELF.
LIKE I SAID, IT WAS ALL I COULD DO TO KEEP THEM ON THE CARRIER FOR A COUPLE OF HOURS.
KATIE...LOOK AT ME. YOU REALLY GOING TO MAKE ME DO THIS?
THEY'RE JUST KIDS, CLINT.
YOU KEEP SAYING THAT.
BECAUSE IT'S TRUE.

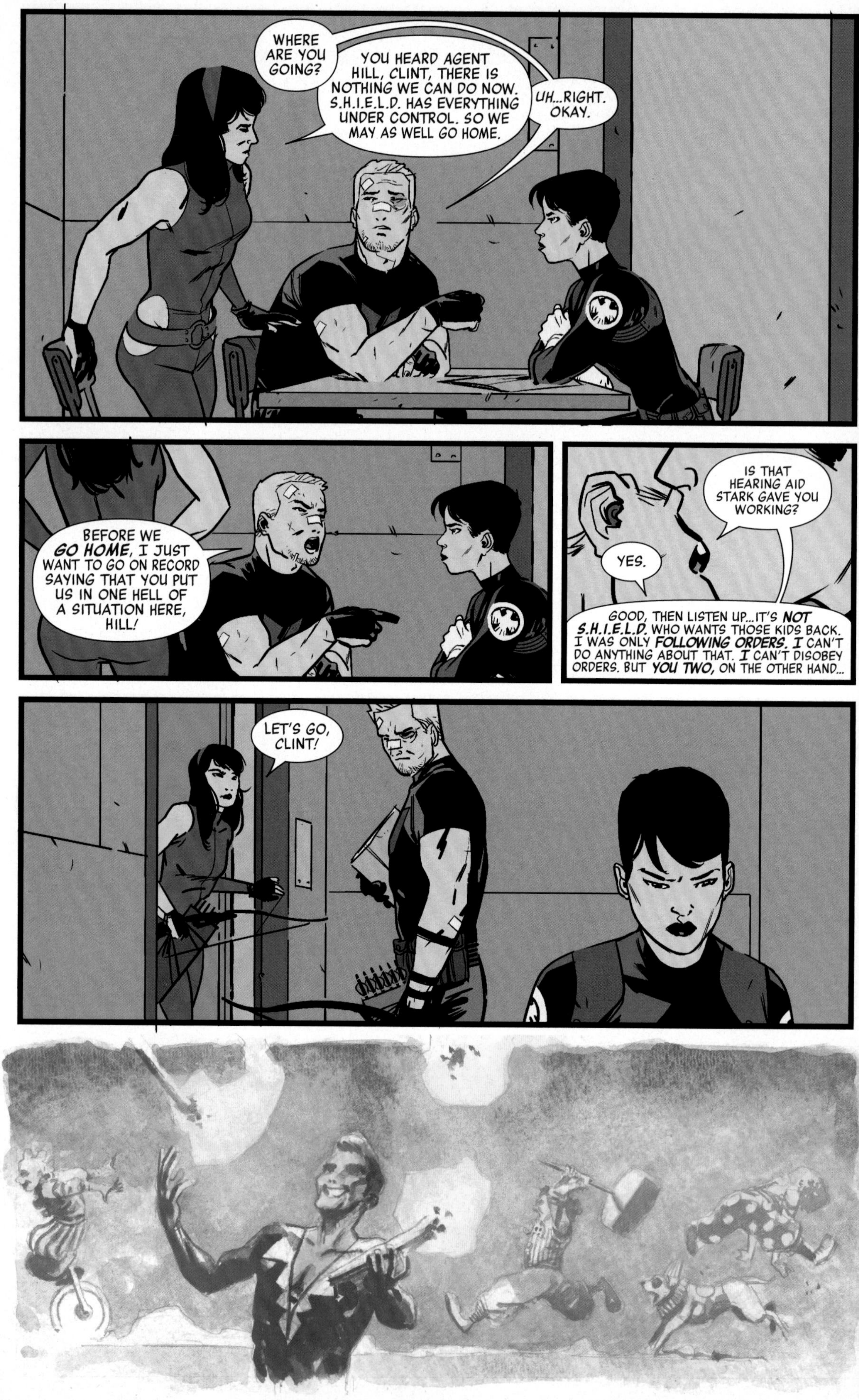
WHERE ARE YOU GOING?
YOU HEARD AGENT HILL, CLINT, THERE IS NOTHING WE CAN DO NOW. S.H.I.E.L.D. HAS EVERYTHING UNDER CONTROL. SO WE MAY AS WELL GO HOME.
UH...RIGHT. OKAY.
BEFORE WE GO HOME, I JUST WANT TO GO ON RECORD SAYING THAT YOU PUT US IN ONE HELL OF A SITUATION HERE, HILL!
IS THAT HEARING AID STARK GAVE YOU WORKING?
YES.
GOOD, THEN LISTEN UP...IT'S NOT S.H.I.E.L.D. WHO WANTS THOSE KIDS BACK. I WAS ONLY FOLLOWING ORDERS. I CAN'T DO ANYTHING ABOUT THAT. I CAN'T DISOBEY ORDERS. BUT YOU TWO, ON THE OTHER HAND...
LET'S GO, CLINT!

KATE, WE NEED TO THINK ABOUT THIS. IF WE DO THIS-- I MEAN, WHERE DO WE GO?

WE GO TO THE AVENGERS. MAYBE THEY CAN HELP.

HELP WITH WHAT? OPENING A DAY CARE? WHAT ARE WE EVEN DOING HERE?! I MEAN, WHO KNOWS WHAT THOSE KIDS ARE CAPABLE OF?!

I DO. I WAS THERE, REMEMBER? AND THEY DIDN'T HURT *ME*, CLINT. I WAS RIGHT THERE AND THEY DIDN'T *HURT ME*. THEY CAN CONTROL IT. WE CAN HELP THEM.

IT'S JUST THAT--

WHAT?

I JUST DON'T WANT YOU TO *BECOME ATTACHED*.

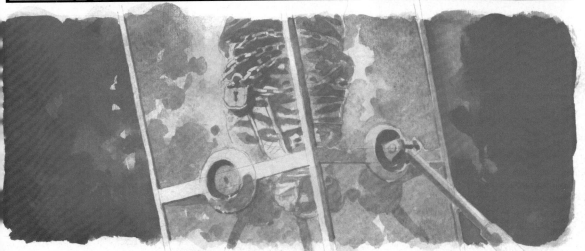

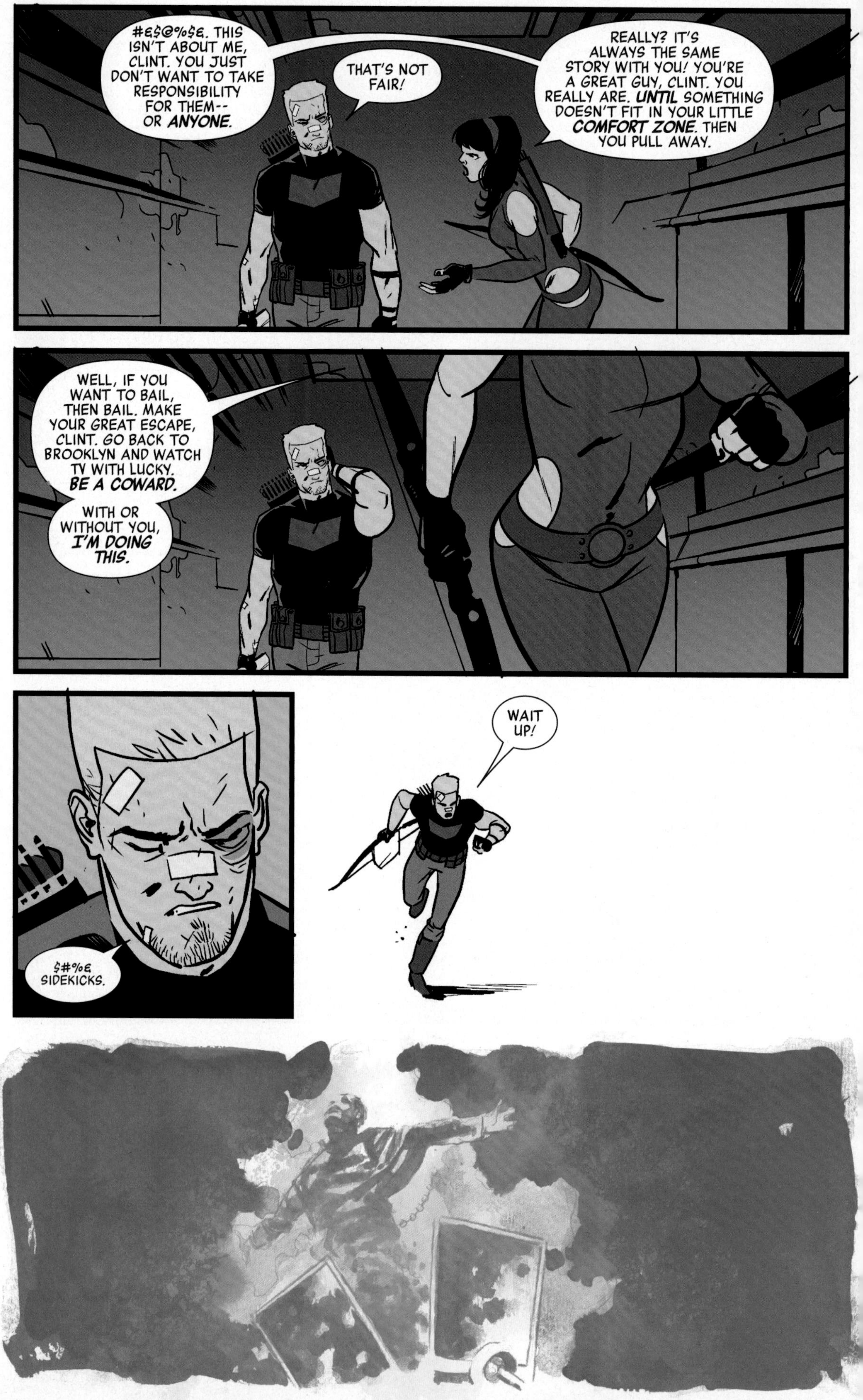

#€$@%$€. THIS ISN'T ABOUT ME, CLINT. YOU JUST DON'T WANT TO TAKE RESPONSIBILITY FOR THEM-- OR ANYONE.
THAT'S NOT FAIR!
REALLY? IT'S ALWAYS THE SAME STORY WITH YOU! YOU'RE A GREAT GUY, CLINT. YOU REALLY ARE. UNTIL SOMETHING DOESN'T FIT IN YOUR LITTLE COMFORT ZONE. THEN YOU PULL AWAY.
WELL, IF YOU WANT TO BAIL, THEN BAIL. MAKE YOUR GREAT ESCAPE, CLINT. GO BACK TO BROOKLYN AND WATCH TV WITH LUCKY. BE A COWARD.
WITH OR WITHOUT YOU, I'M DOING THIS.
$#%€ SIDEKICKS.
WAIT UP!

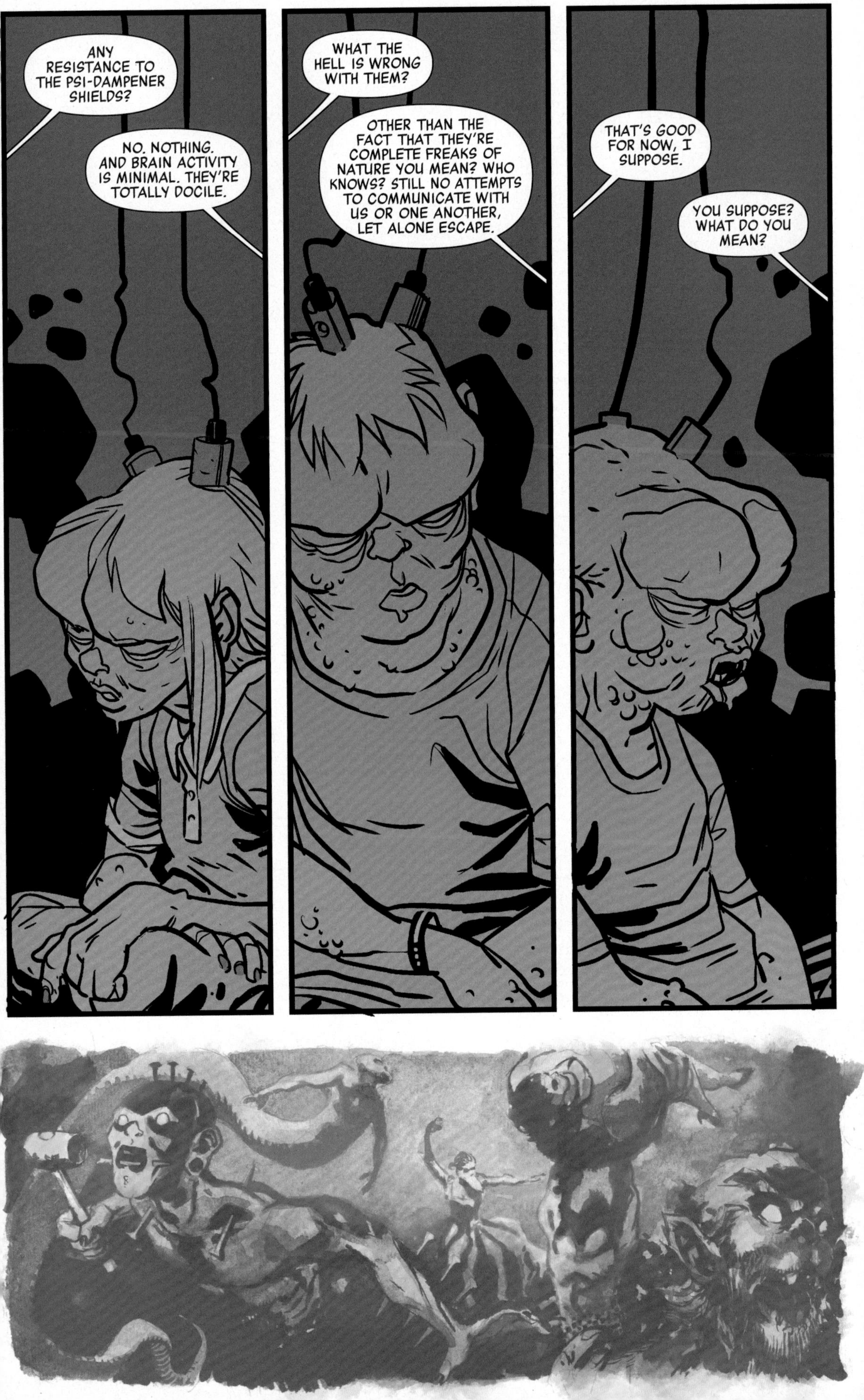
ANY RESISTANCE TO THE PSI-DAMPENER SHIELDS?
NO. NOTHING. AND BRAIN ACTIVITY IS MINIMAL. THEY'RE TOTALLY DOCILE.
WHAT THE HELL IS WRONG WITH THEM?
OTHER THAN THE FACT THAT THEY'RE COMPLETE FREAKS OF NATURE YOU MEAN? WHO KNOWS? STILL NO ATTEMPTS TO COMMUNICATE WITH US OR ONE ANOTHER, LET ALONE ESCAPE.
THAT'S GOOD FOR NOW, I SUPPOSE.
YOU SUPPOSE? WHAT DO YOU MEAN?

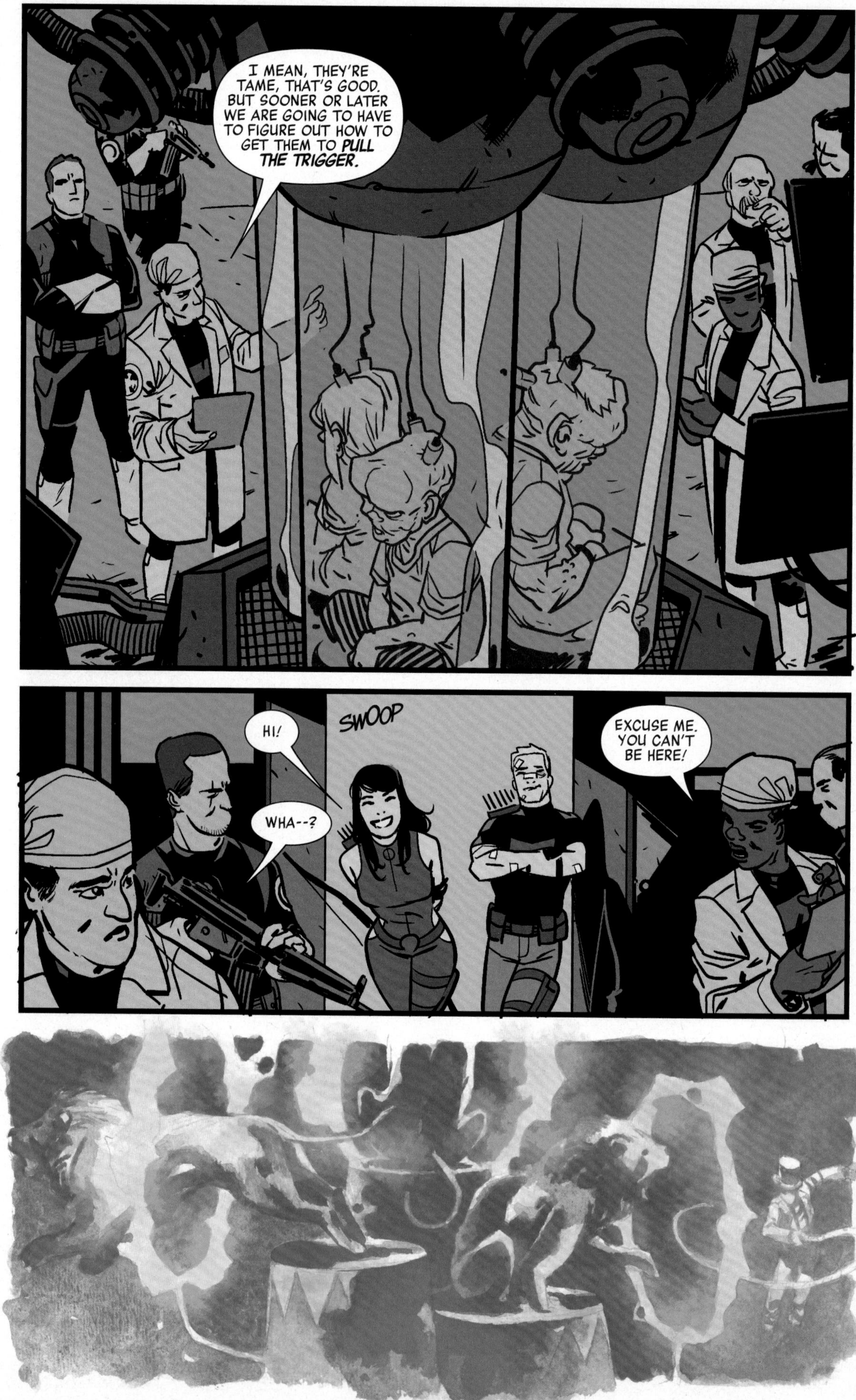
I MEAN, THEY'RE TAME, THAT'S GOOD. BUT SOONER OR LATER WE ARE GOING TO HAVE TO FIGURE OUT HOW TO GET THEM TO PULL THE TRIGGER.
SWOOP
HI!
WHA--?
EXCUSE ME. YOU CAN'T BE HERE!

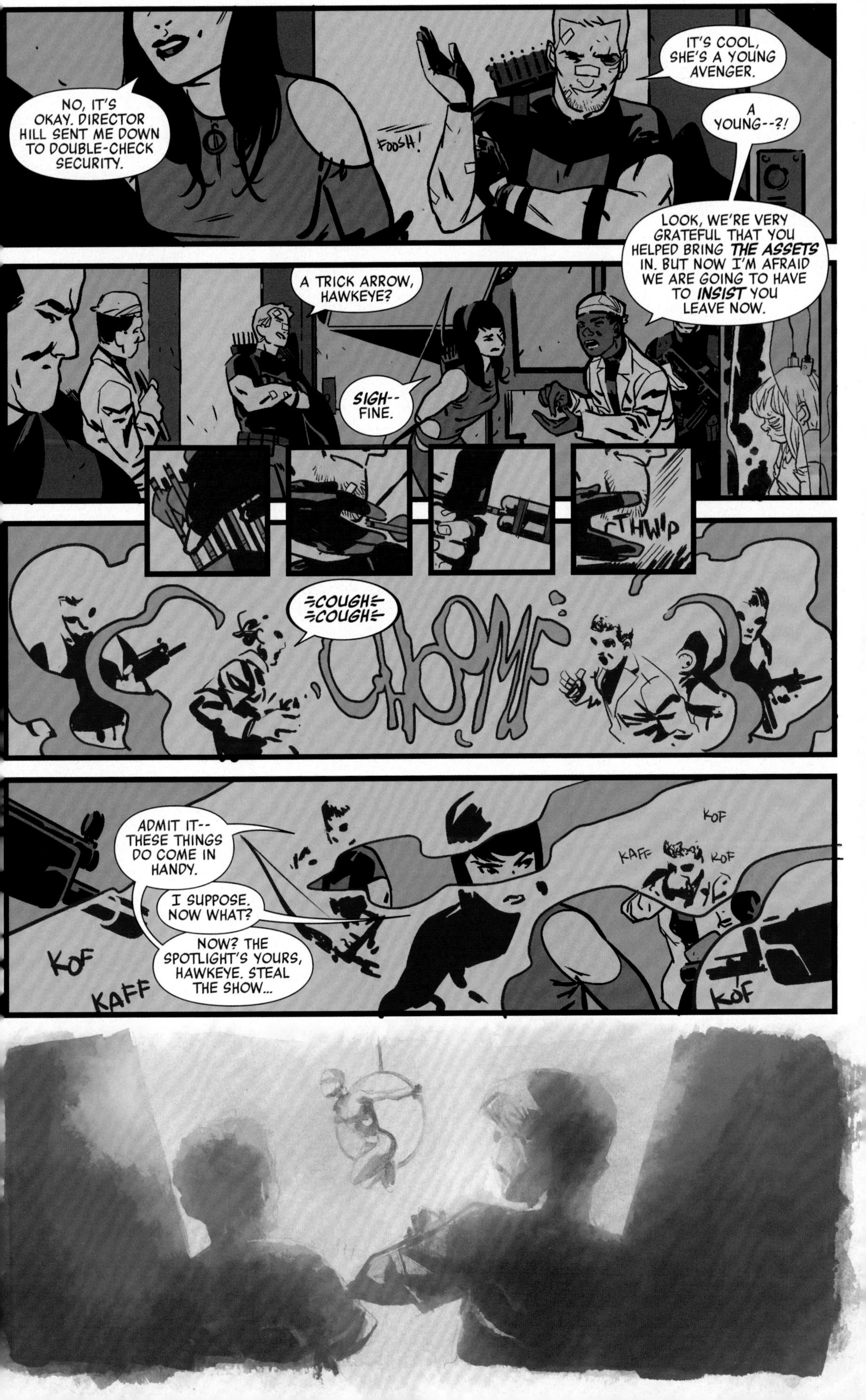
NO, IT'S OKAY. DIRECTOR HILL SENT ME DOWN TO DOUBLE-CHECK SECURITY.
FOOSH!
IT'S COOL, SHE'S A YOUNG AVENGER.
A YOUNG--?!
LOOK, WE'RE VERY GRATEFUL THAT YOU HELPED BRING THE ASSETS IN. BUT NOW I'M AFRAID WE ARE GOING TO HAVE TO INSIST YOU LEAVE NOW.
A TRICK ARROW, HAWKEYE?
SIGH-- FINE.
THWIP
COUGH COUGH
CHOOMF
ADMIT IT-- THESE THINGS DO COME IN HANDY.
I SUPPOSE. NOW WHAT?
NOW? THE SPOTLIGHT'S YOURS, HAWKEYE. STEAL THE SHOW...
KOF
KAFF
KOF
KAFF
KOF
KOF

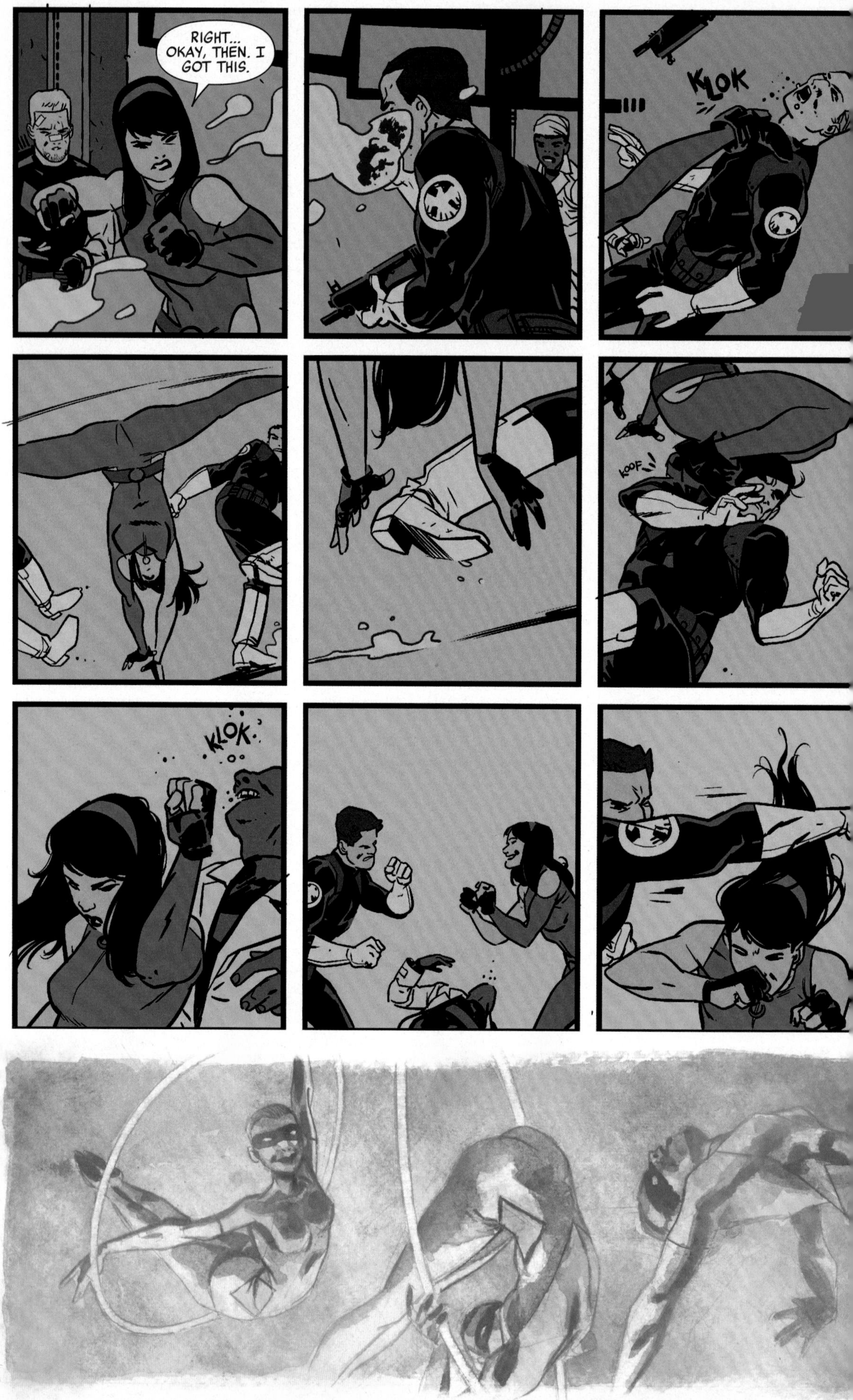
RIGHT... OKAY, THEN. I GOT THIS.
KLOK
KOOF
KLOK

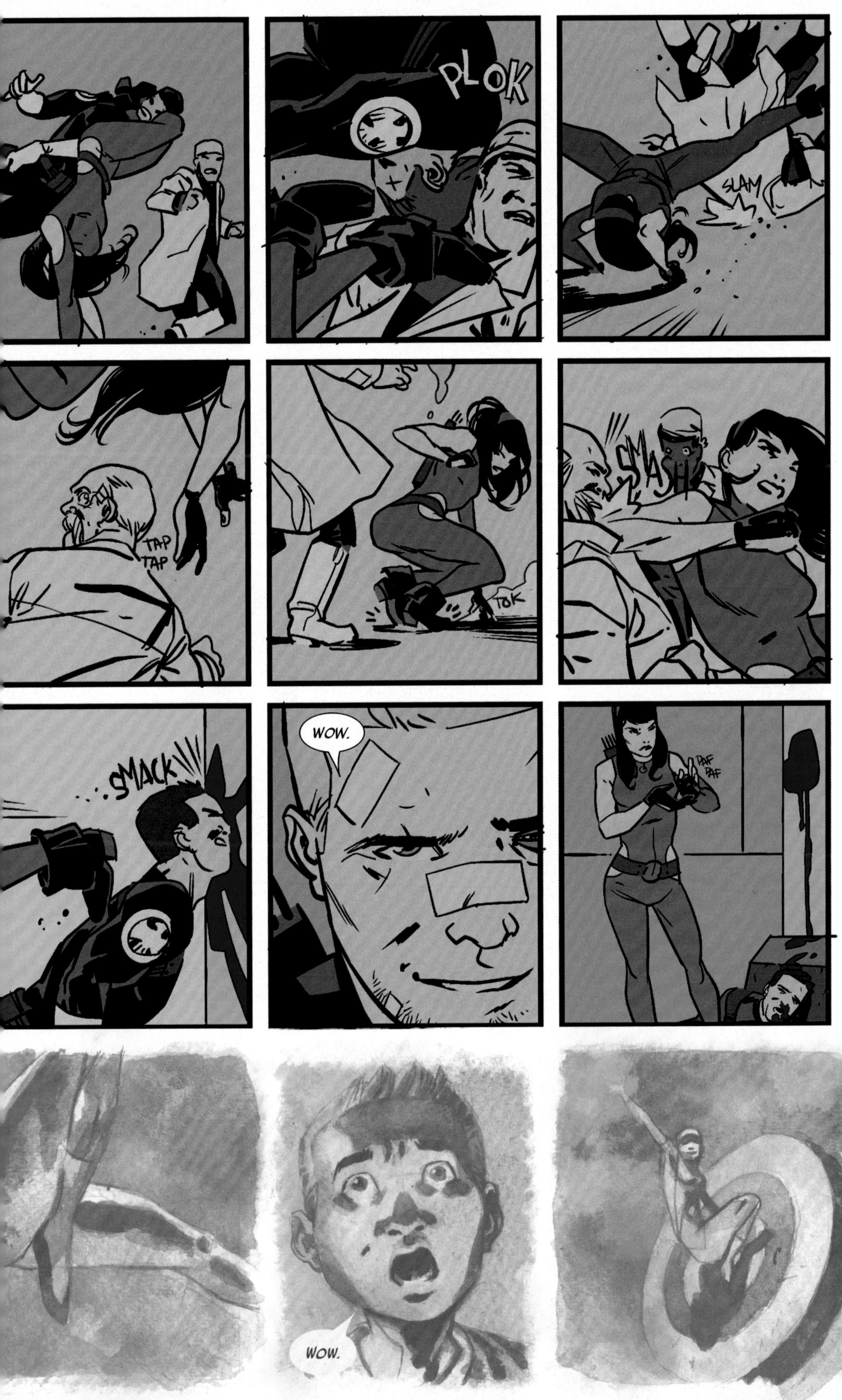
PLOK
SLAM
TAP
TAP
TOK
SMASH
SMACK
WOW.
PAF
PAF
WOW.

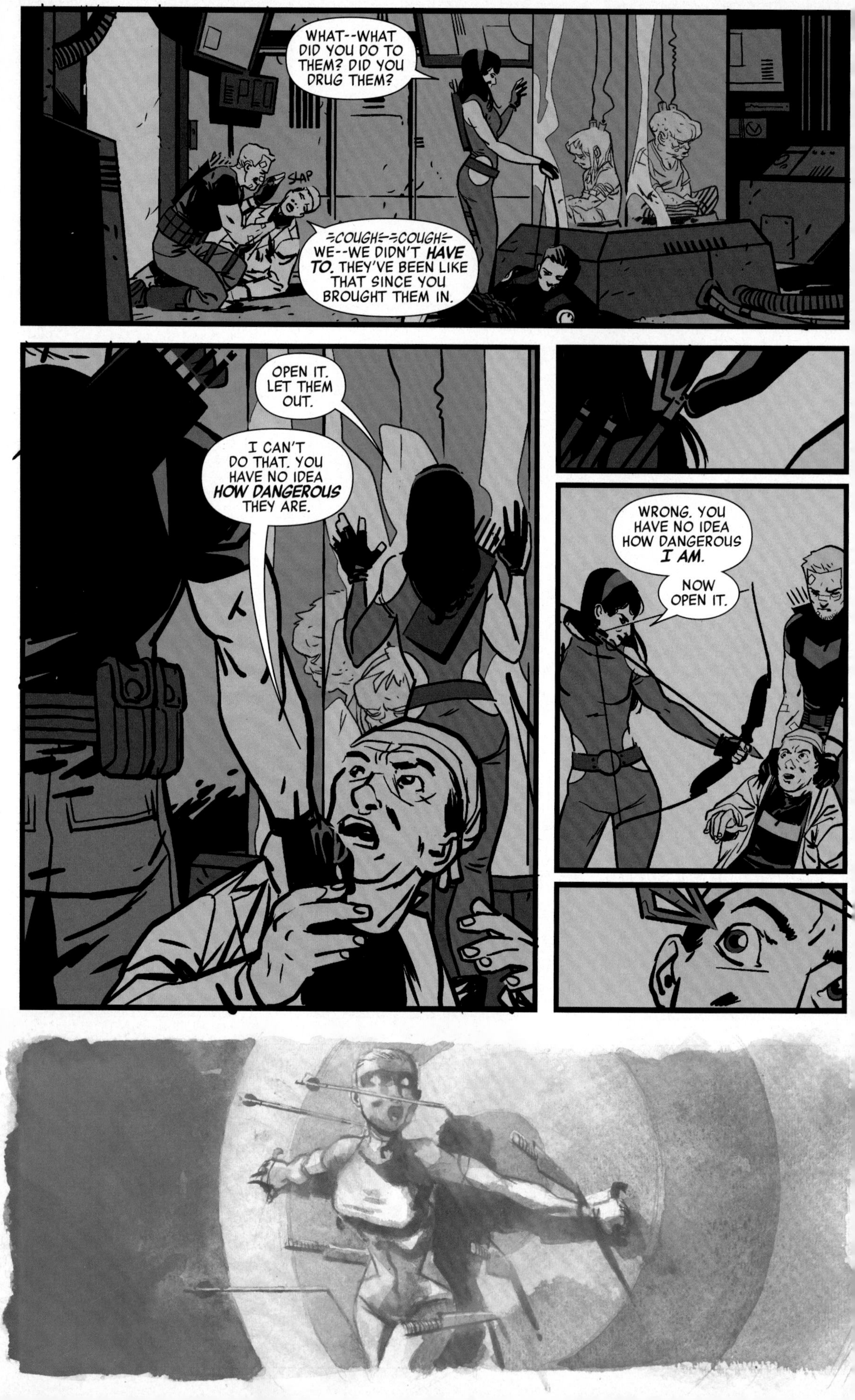
WHAT--WHAT DID YOU DO TO THEM? DID YOU DRUG THEM?
SLAP
=COUGH= =COUGH= WE--WE DIDN'T **HAVE TO.** THEY'VE BEEN LIKE THAT SINCE YOU BROUGHT THEM IN.
OPEN IT. LET THEM OUT.
I CAN'T DO THAT. YOU HAVE NO IDEA ***HOW DANGEROUS*** THEY ARE.
WRONG. YOU HAVE NO IDEA HOW DANGEROUS ***I AM.***
NOW OPEN IT.

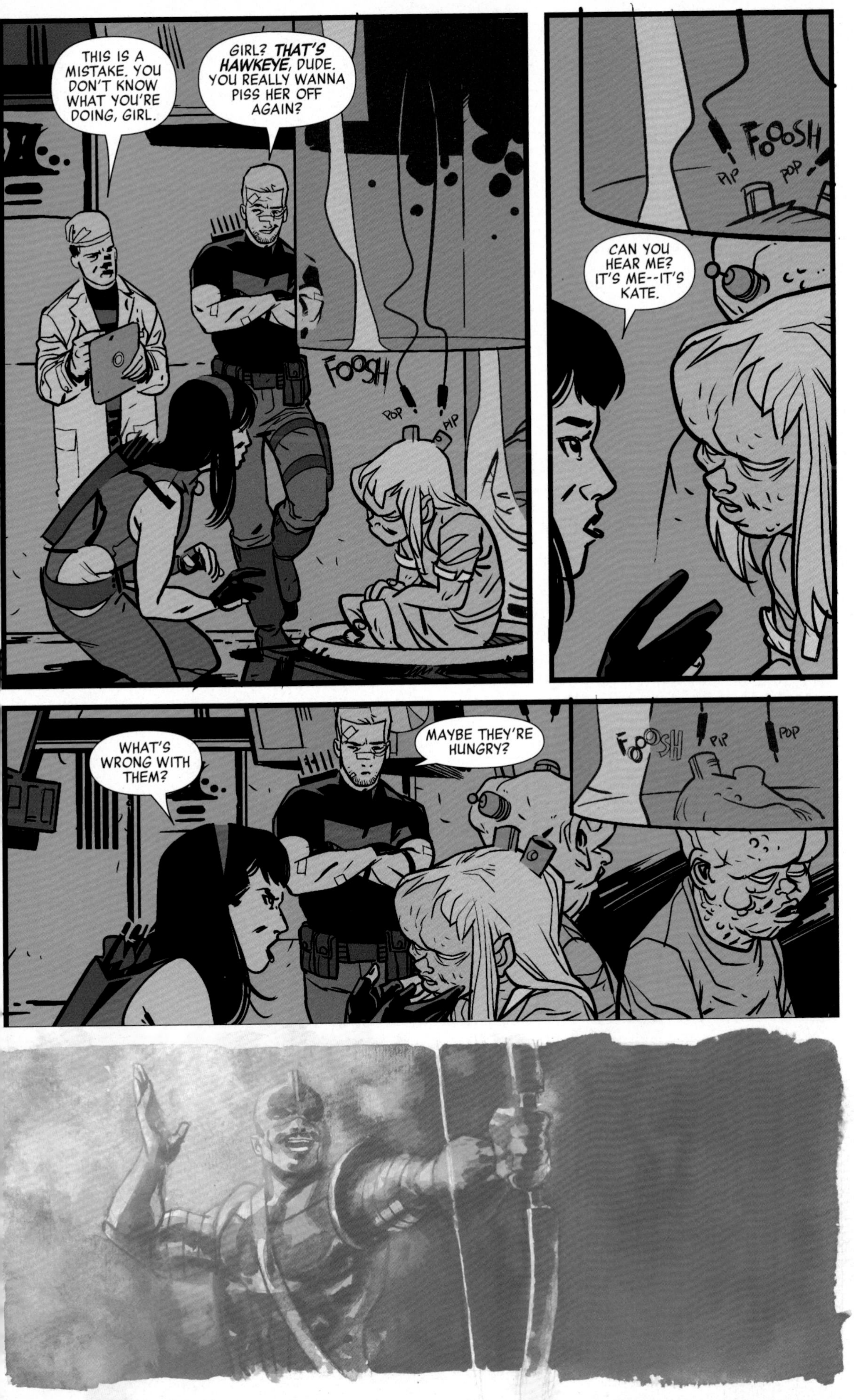

THIS IS A MISTAKE. YOU DON'T KNOW WHAT YOU'RE DOING, GIRL.
GIRL? THAT'S HAWKEYE, DUDE. YOU REALLY WANNA PISS HER OFF AGAIN?
FOOSH
POP
PIP
FOOOSH
PIP
POP
CAN YOU HEAR ME? IT'S ME--IT'S KATE.
WHAT'S WRONG WITH THEM?
MAYBE THEY'RE HUNGRY?
FOOOSH
PIP
POP

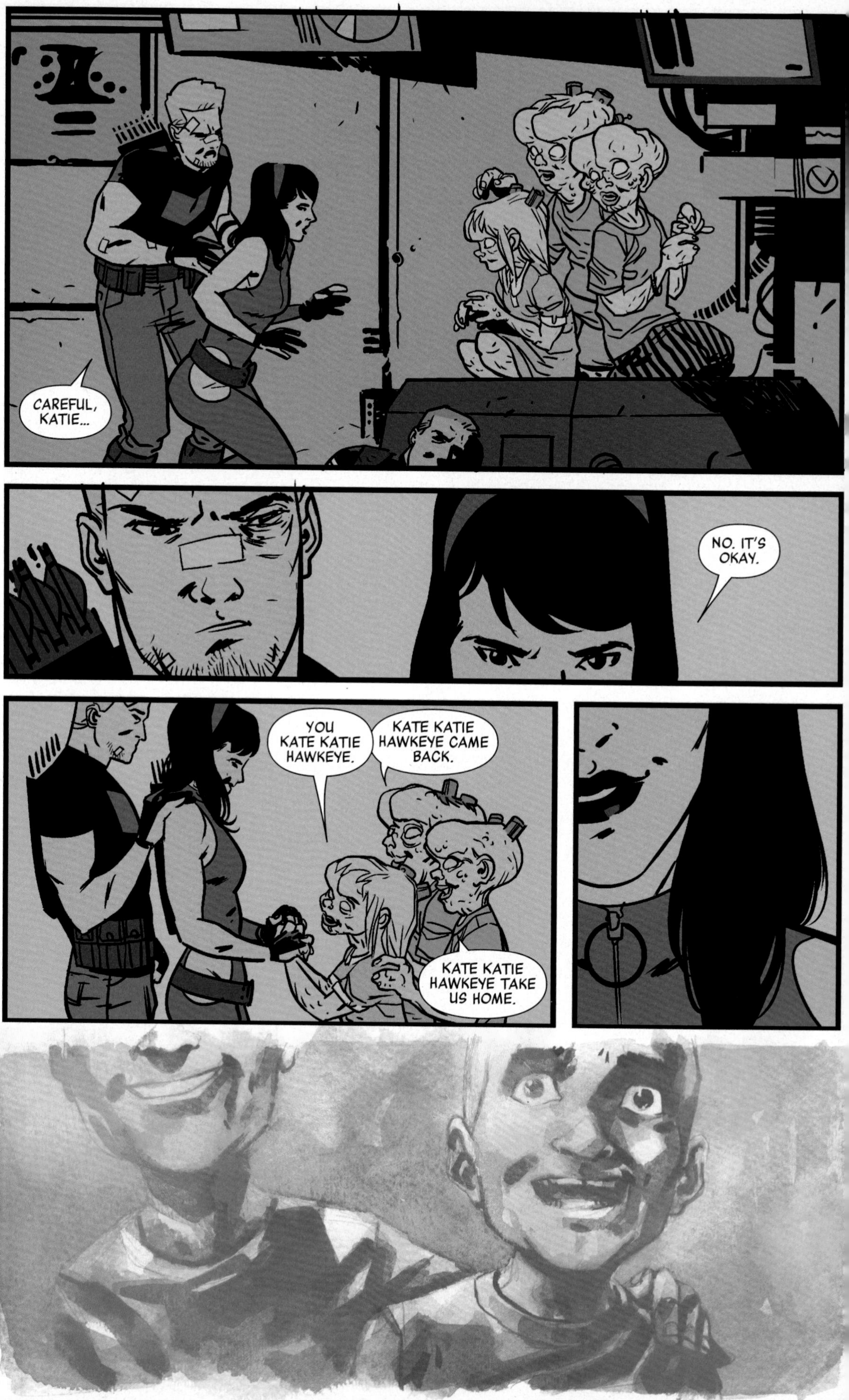
CAREFUL, KATIE...
NO. IT'S OKAY.
YOU KATE KATIE HAWKEYE.
KATE KATIE HAWKEYE CAME BACK.
KATE KATIE HAWKEYE TAKE US HOME.

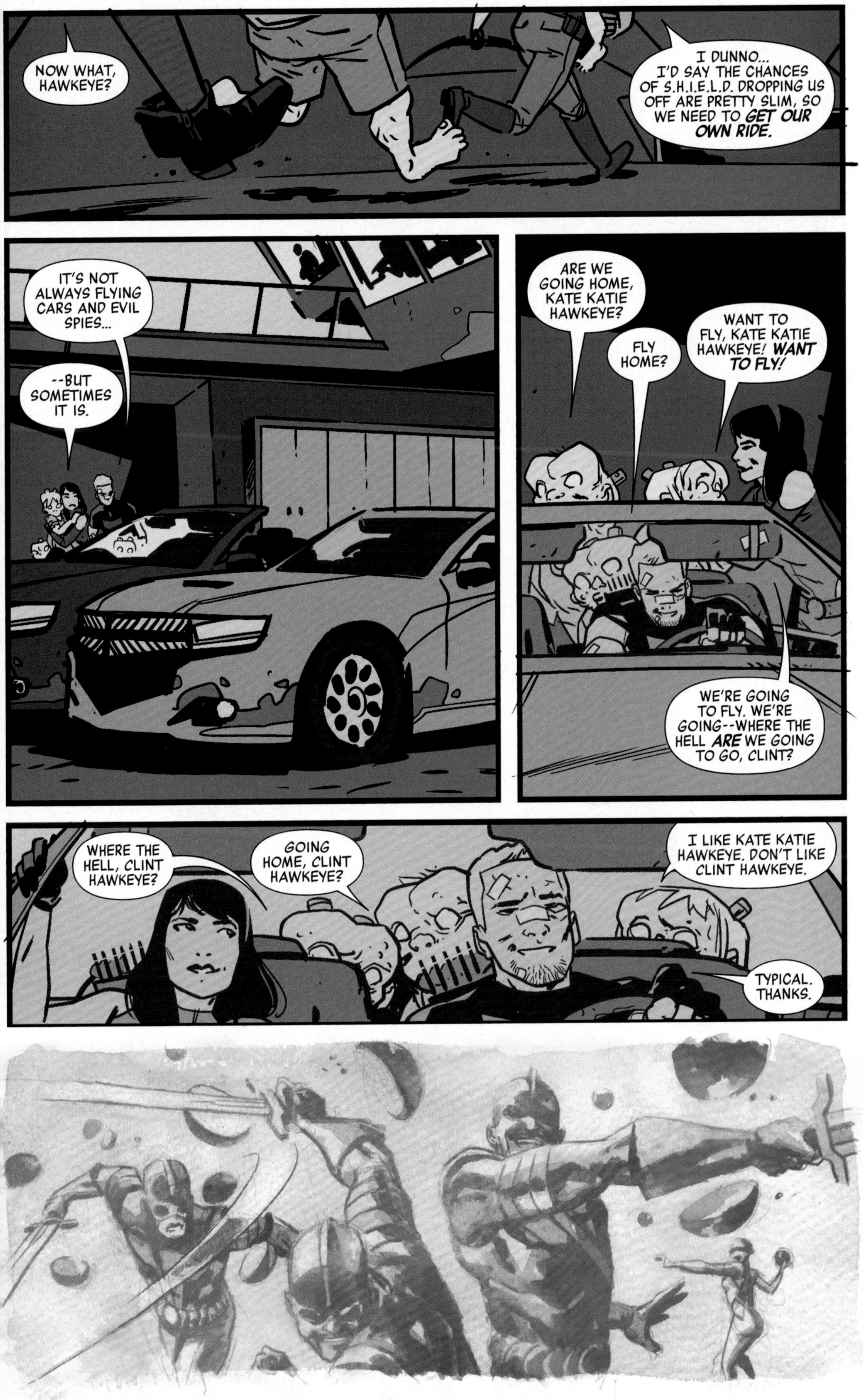
NOW WHAT, HAWKEYE?
I DUNNO... I'D SAY THE CHANCES OF S.H.I.E.L.D. DROPPING US OFF ARE PRETTY SLIM, SO WE NEED TO GET OUR OWN RIDE.
IT'S NOT ALWAYS FLYING CARS AND EVIL SPIES...
--BUT SOMETIMES IT IS.
ARE WE GOING HOME, KATE KATIE HAWKEYE?
FLY HOME?
WANT TO FLY, KATE KATIE HAWKEYE! WANT TO FLY!
WE'RE GOING TO FLY. WE'RE GOING--WHERE THE HELL ARE WE GOING TO GO, CLINT?
WHERE THE HELL, CLINT HAWKEYE?
GOING HOME, CLINT HAWKEYE?
I LIKE KATE KATIE HAWKEYE. DON'T LIKE CLINT HAWKEYE.
TYPICAL. THANKS.

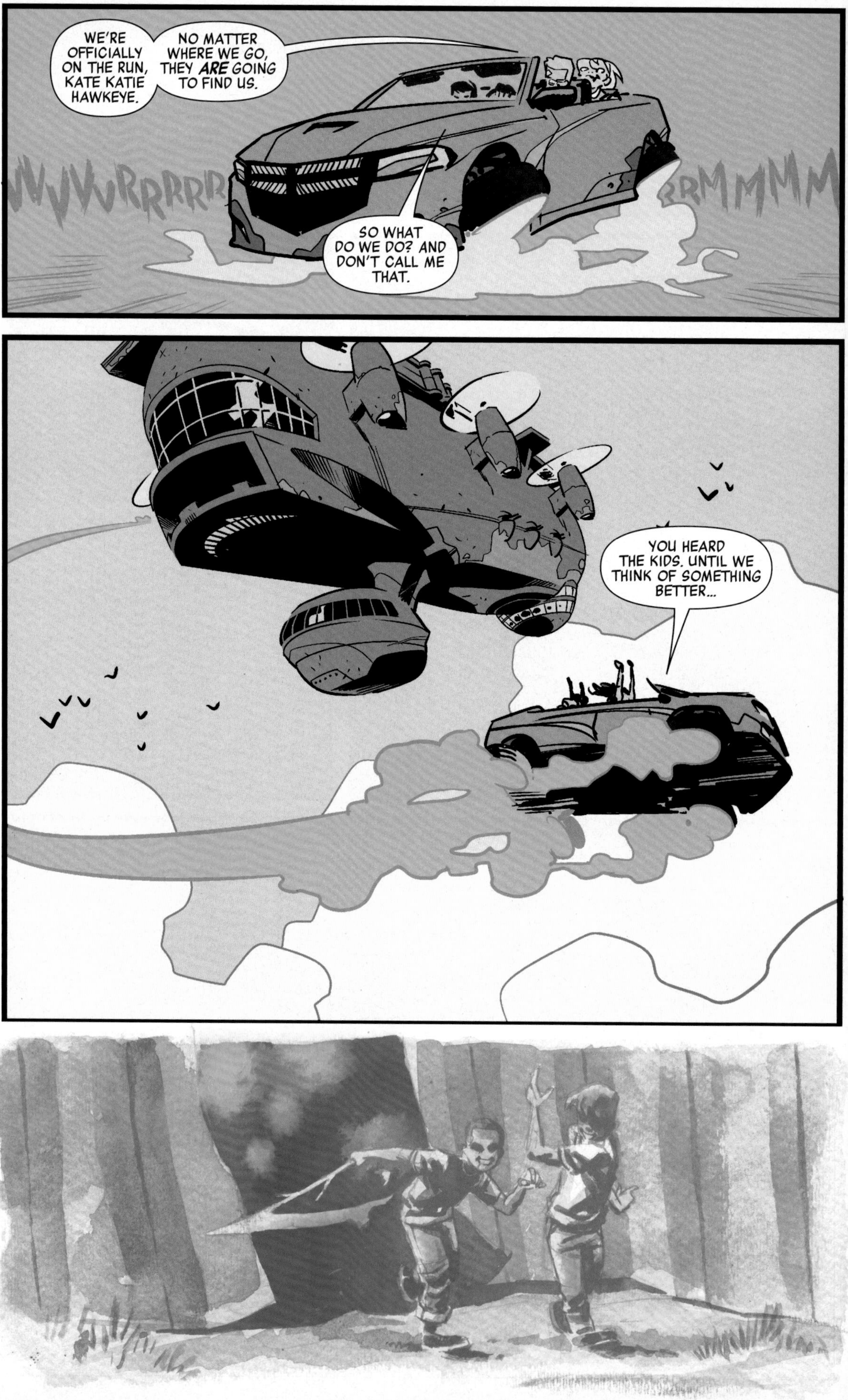
WE'RE OFFICIALLY ON THE RUN, KATE KATIE HAWKEYE.
NO MATTER WHERE WE GO, THEY ARE GOING TO FIND US.
VVVVVRRRRR
RMMMMM
SO WHAT DO WE DO? AND DON'T CALL ME THAT.
YOU HEARD THE KIDS. UNTIL WE THINK OF SOMETHING BETTER...

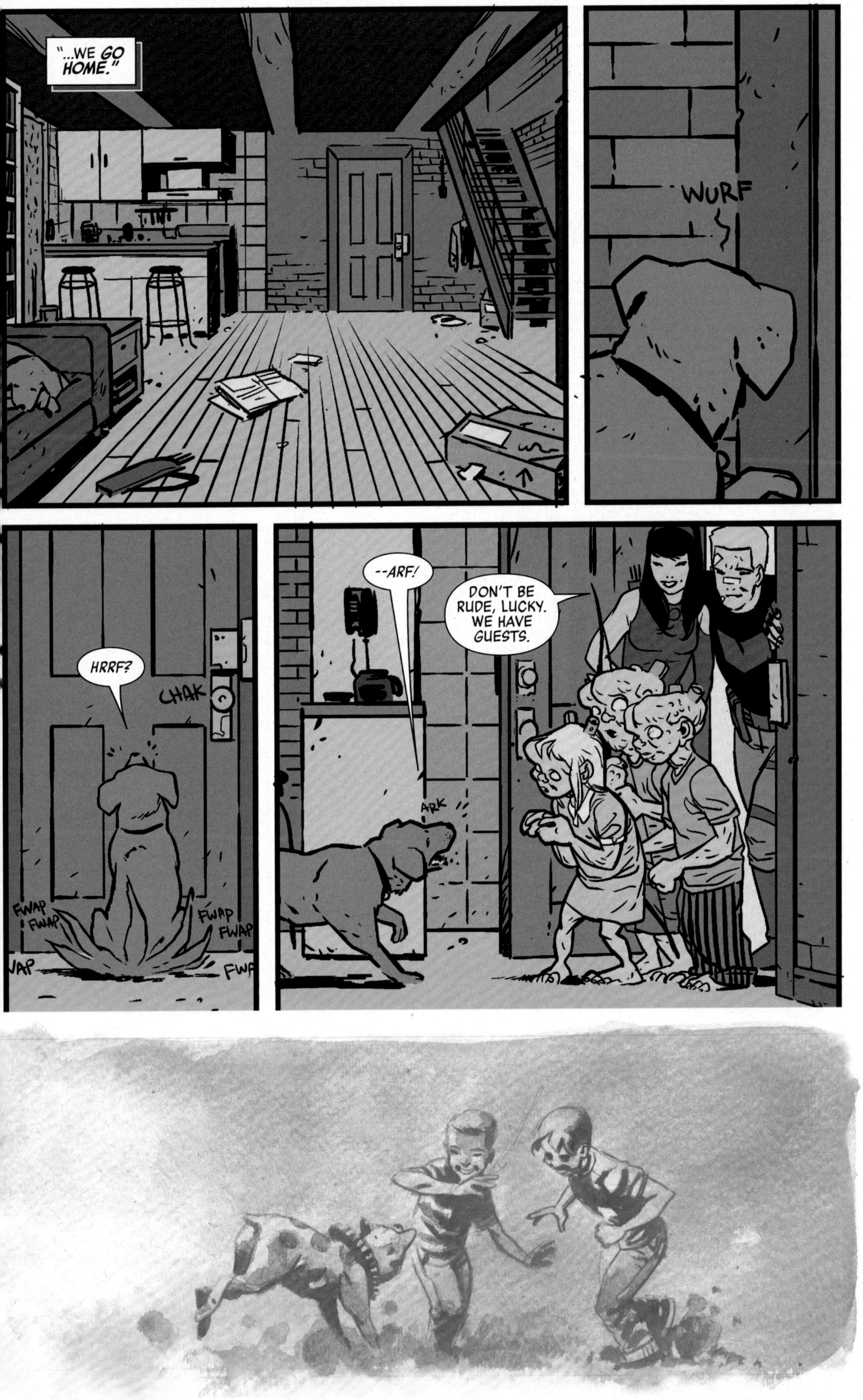
"...WE GO HOME."
WURF
HRRF?
CHAK
FWAP
FWAP
FWAP
FWAP
FWAP
--ARF!
DON'T BE RUDE, LUCKY. WE HAVE GUESTS.
ARK

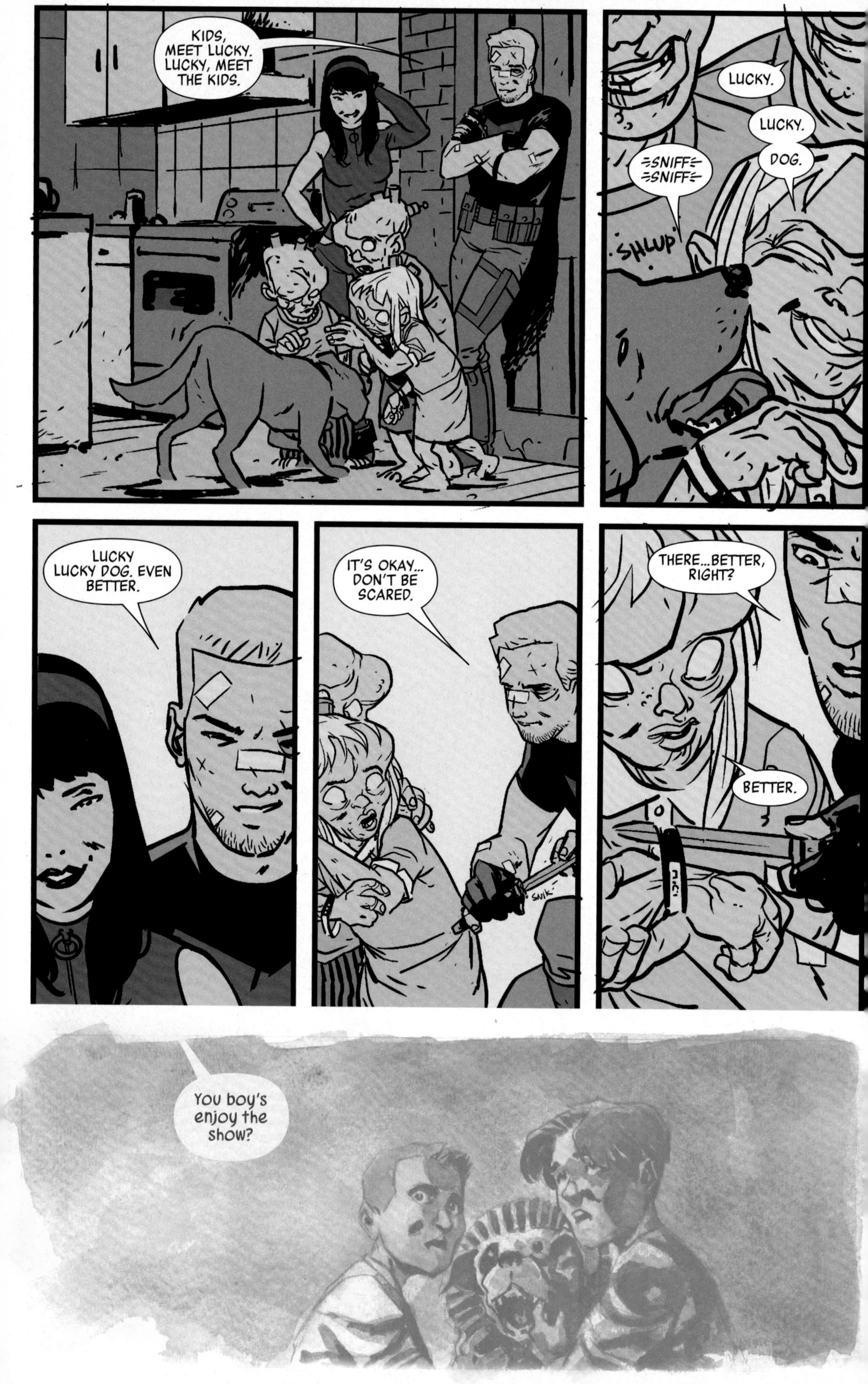
KIDS, MEET LUCKY. LUCKY, MEET THE KIDS.
LUCKY.
LUCKY.
DOG.
=SNIFF= =SNIFF=
SHLUP
LUCKY LUCKY DOG. EVEN BETTER.
IT'S OKAY... DON'T BE SCARED.
SNIK
THERE...BETTER, RIGHT?
BETTER.
You boy's enjoy the show?

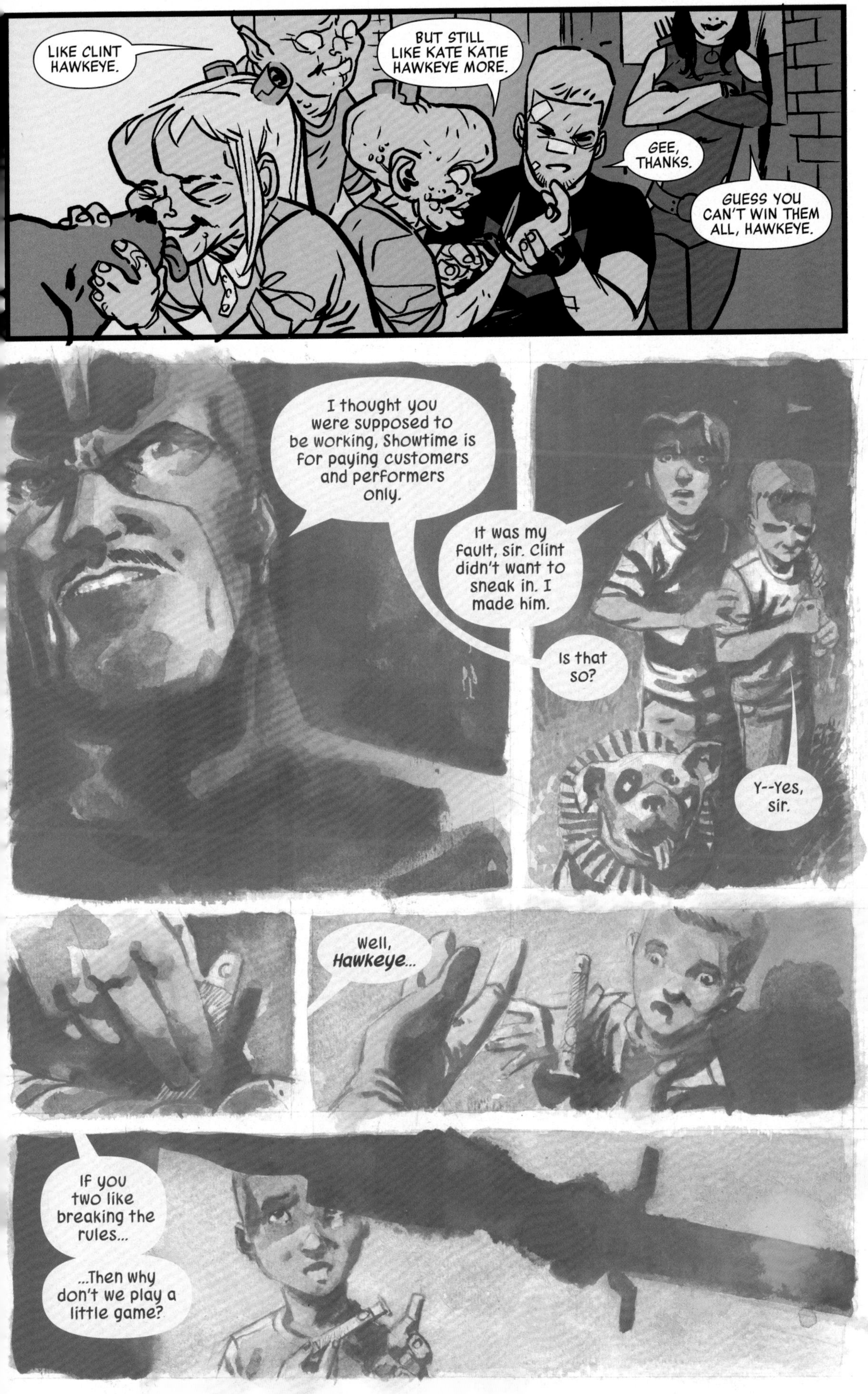
LIKE CLINT HAWKEYE.
BUT STILL LIKE KATE KATIE HAWKEYE MORE.
GEE, THANKS.
GUESS YOU CAN'T WIN THEM ALL, HAWKEYE.
I thought you were supposed to be working, Showtime is for paying customers and performers only.
It was my fault, sir. Clint didn't want to sneak in. I made him.
Is that so?
Y--Yes, sir.
Well, Hawkeye...
If you two like breaking the rules...
...Then why don't we play a little game?

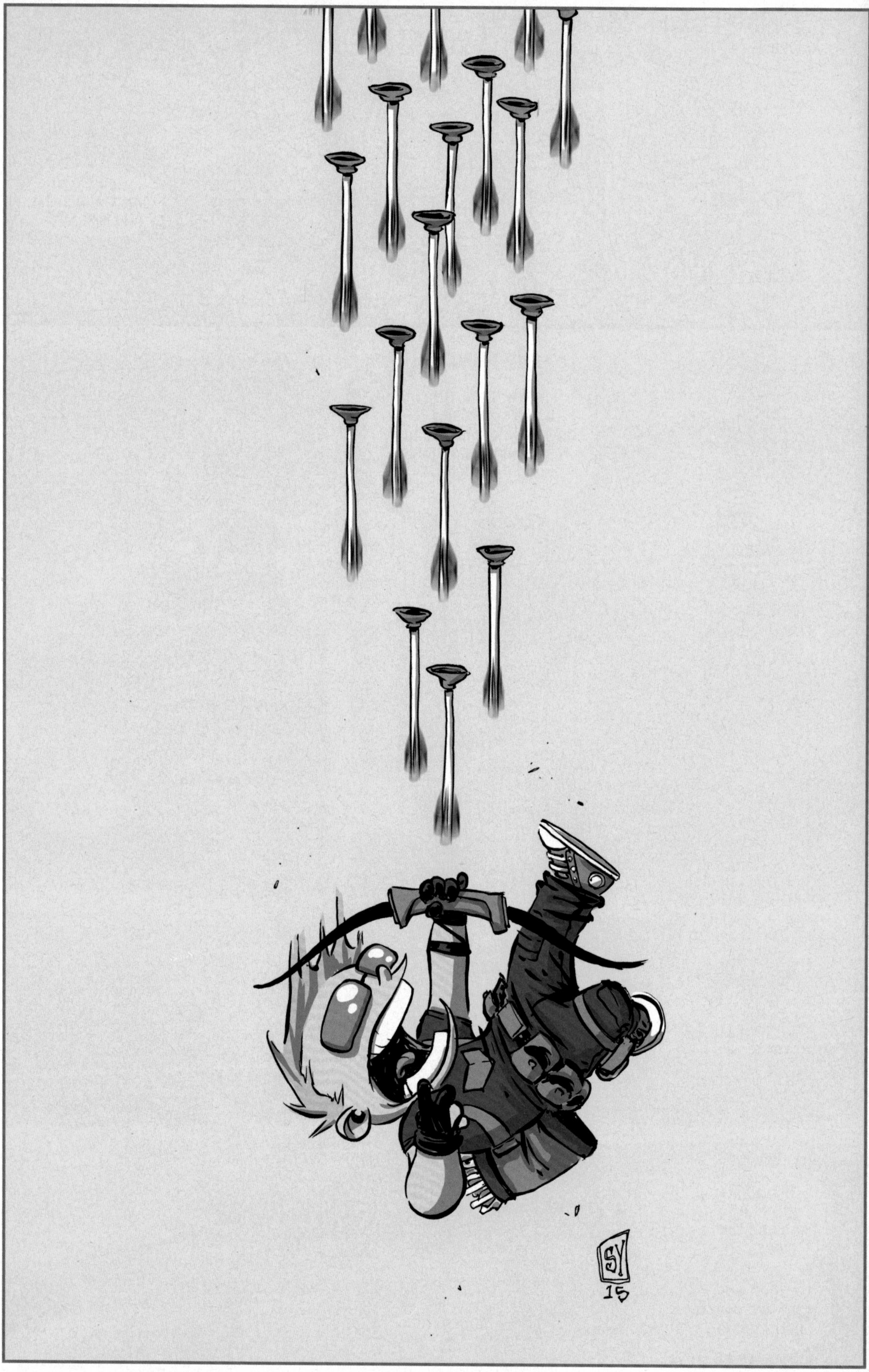
SY
15

ALL-NEW HAWKEYE #1 VARIANT BY **SKOTTIE YOUNG**

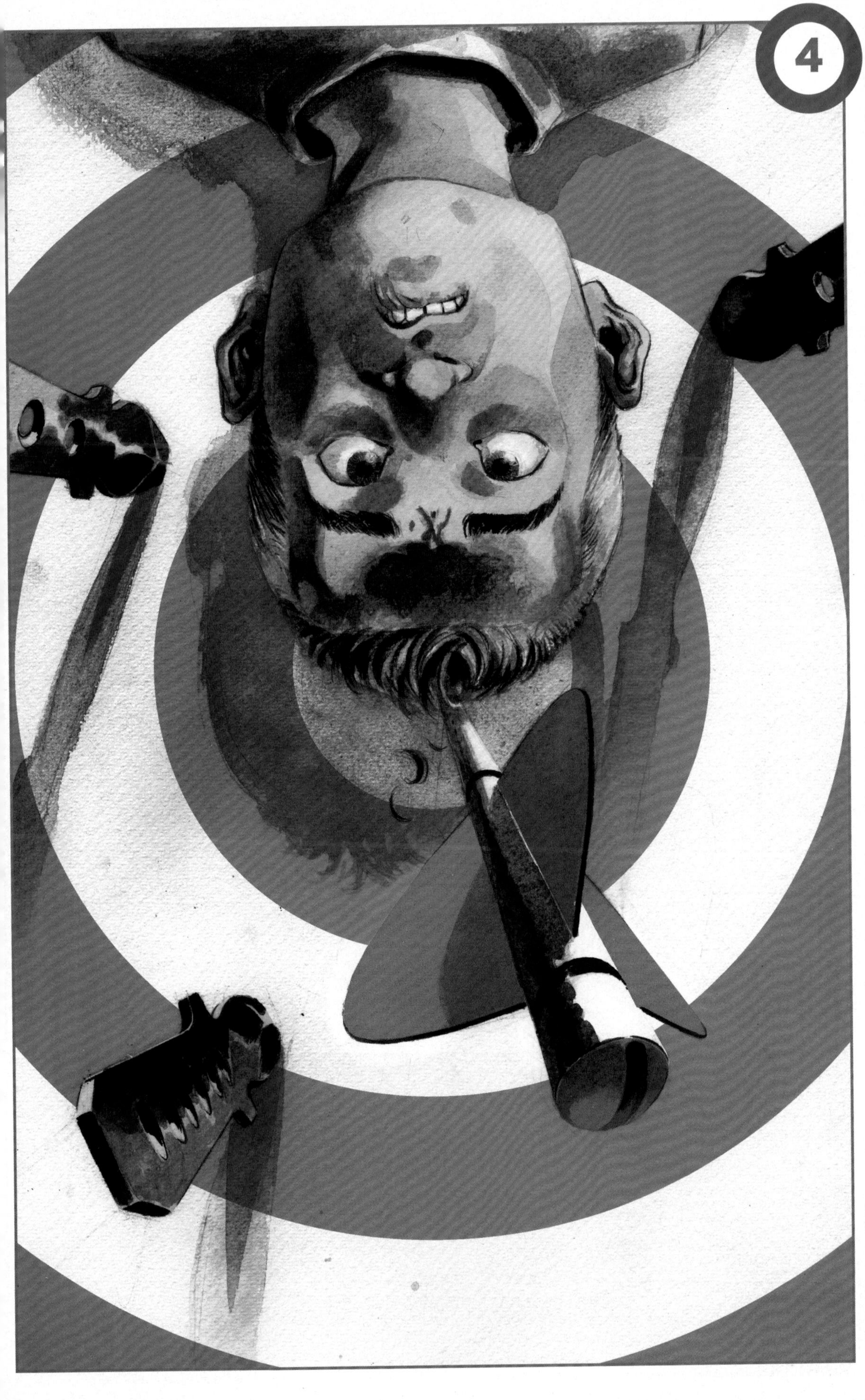
4

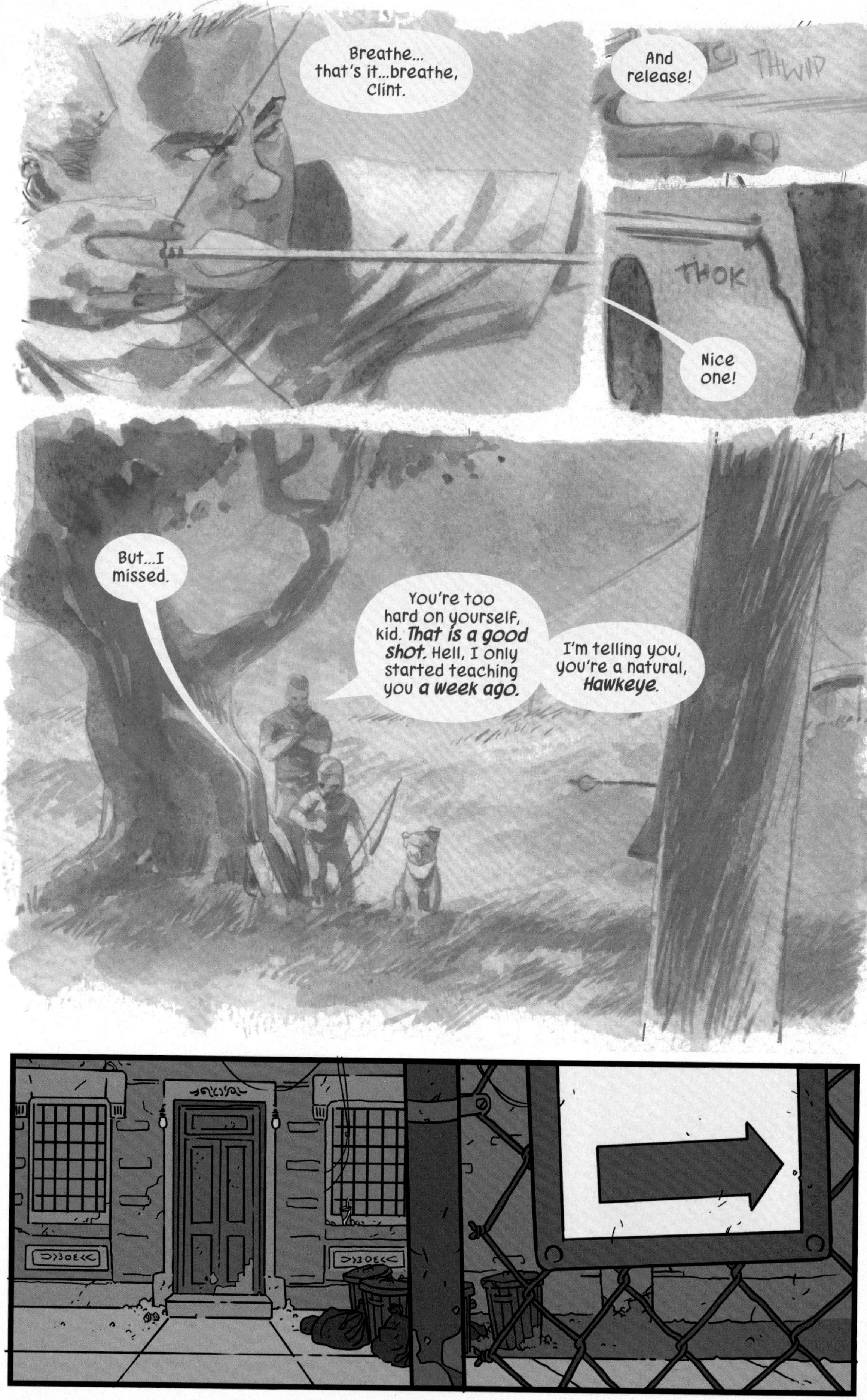
Breathe... that's it...breathe, Clint.
And release!
THWIP
THOK
Nice one!
But...I missed.
You're too hard on yourself, kid. That is a good shot. Hell, I only started teaching you a week ago.
I'm telling you, you're a natural, Hawkeye.

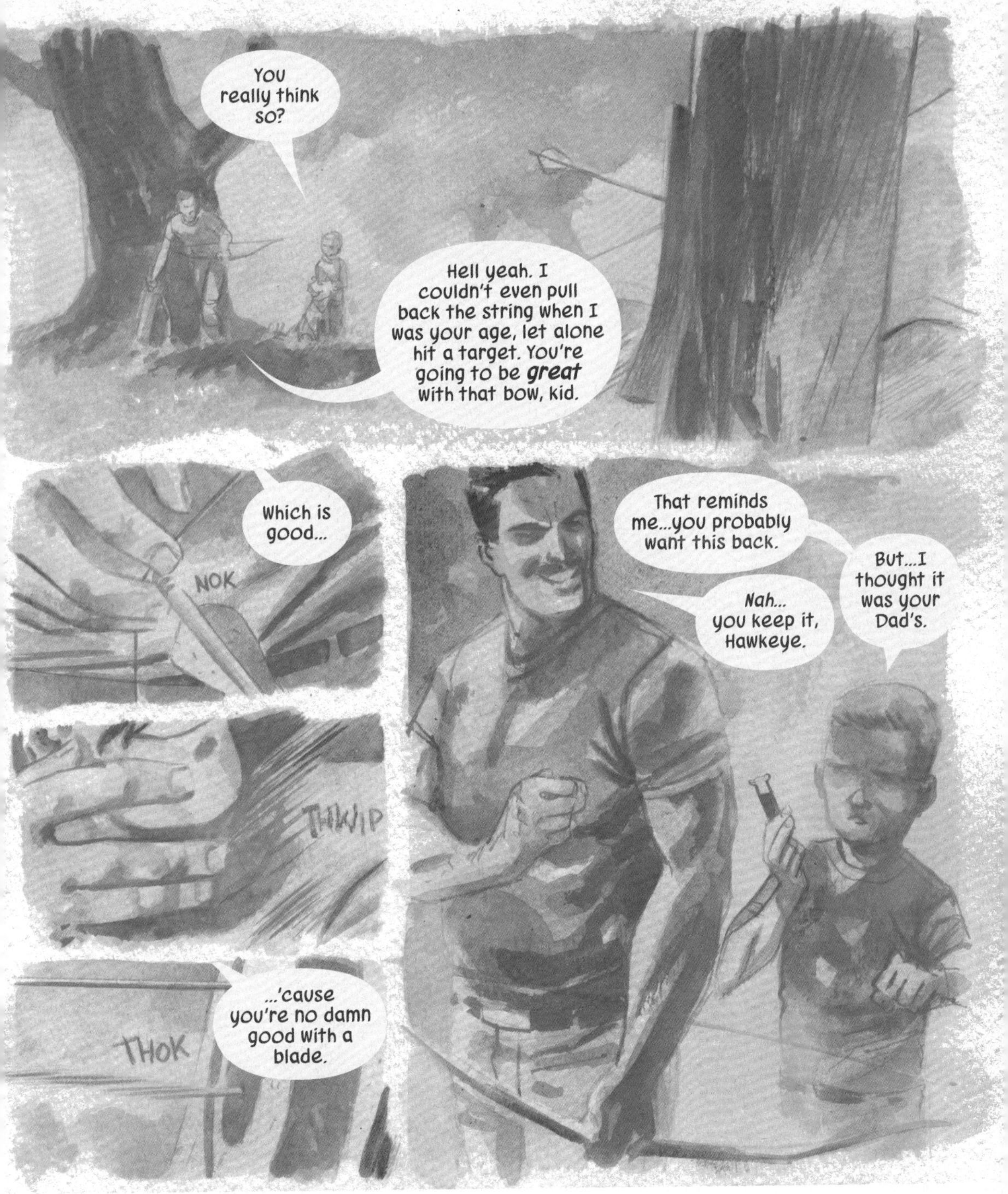
You really think so?
Hell yeah. I couldn't even pull back the string when I was your age, let alone hit a target. You're going to be **great** with that bow, kid.
Which is good...
NOK
THWIP
...'cause you're no damn good with a blade.
THOK
That reminds me...you probably want this back.
But...I thought it was your Dad's.
Nah... you keep it, Hawkeye.

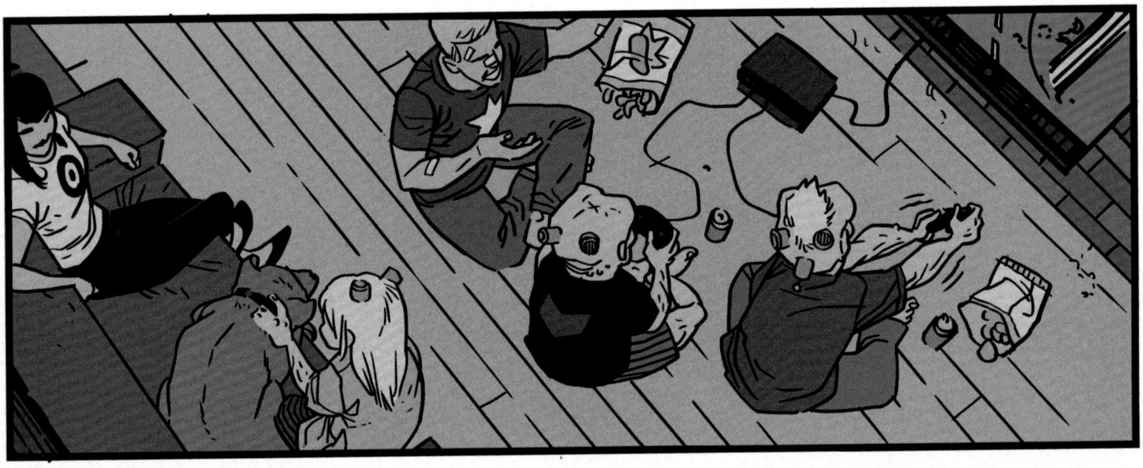

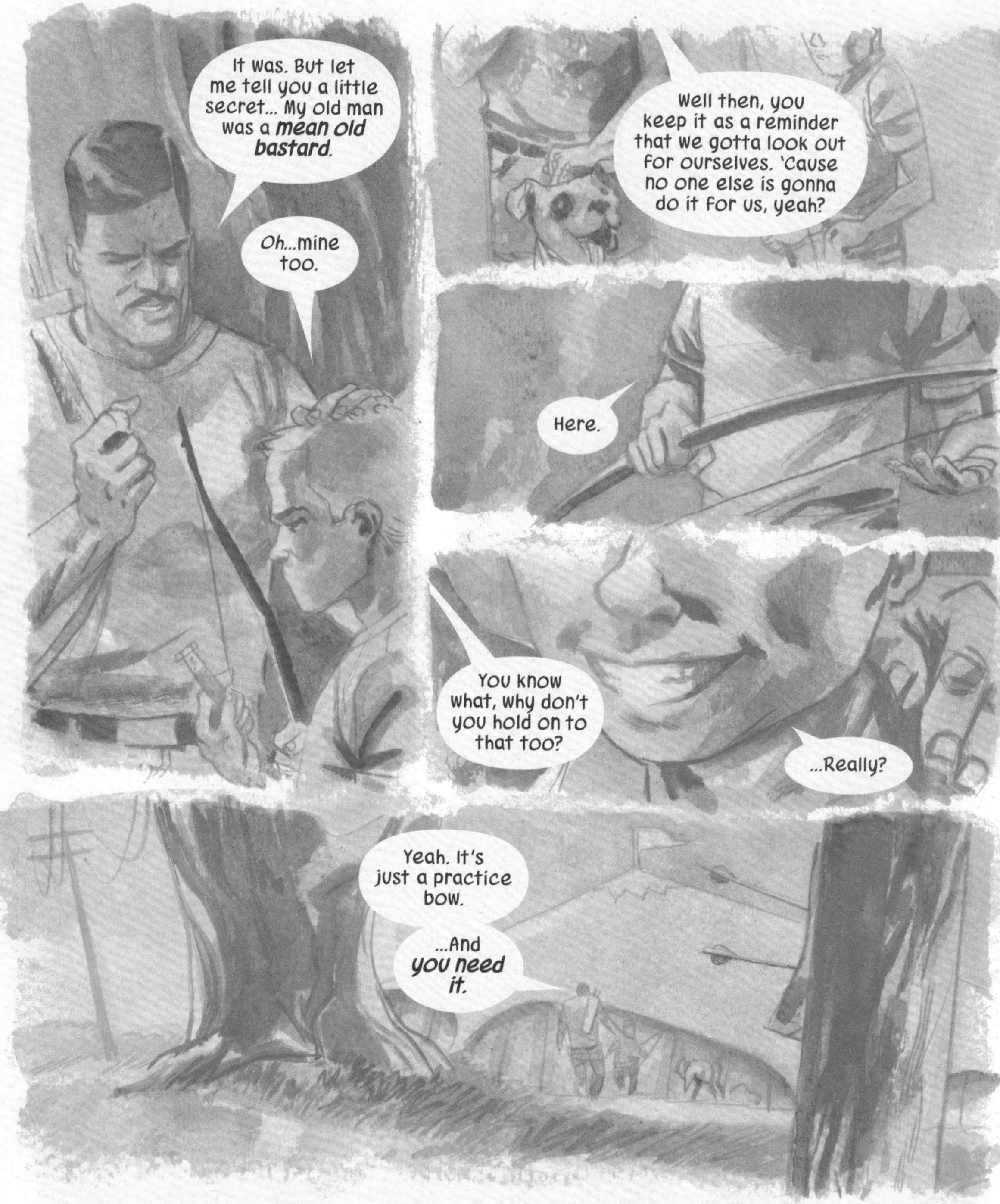
It was. But let me tell you a little secret... My old man was a ***mean old bastard***.
Oh...mine too.
Well then, you keep it as a reminder that we gotta look out for ourselves. 'Cause no one else is gonna do it for us, yeah?
Here.
You know what, why don't you hold on to that too?
...Really?
Yeah. It's just a practice bow.
...And ***you need it.***

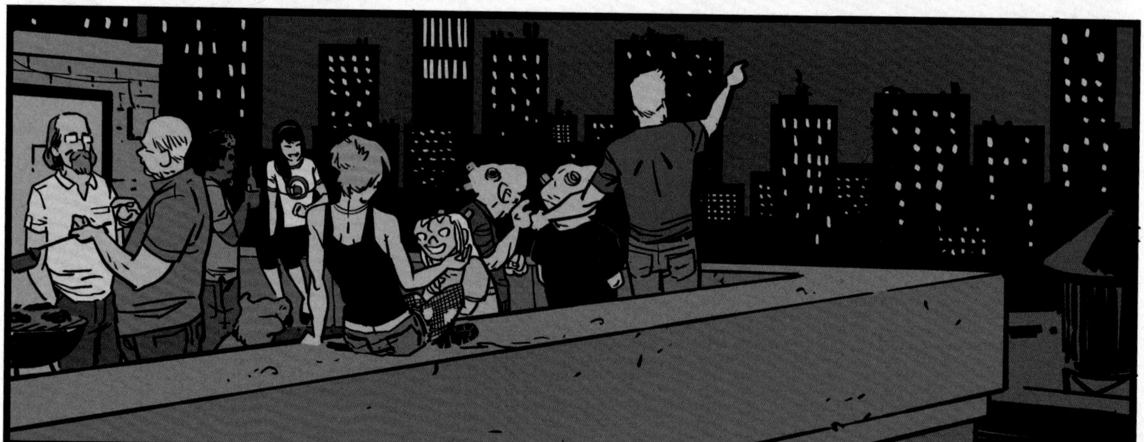

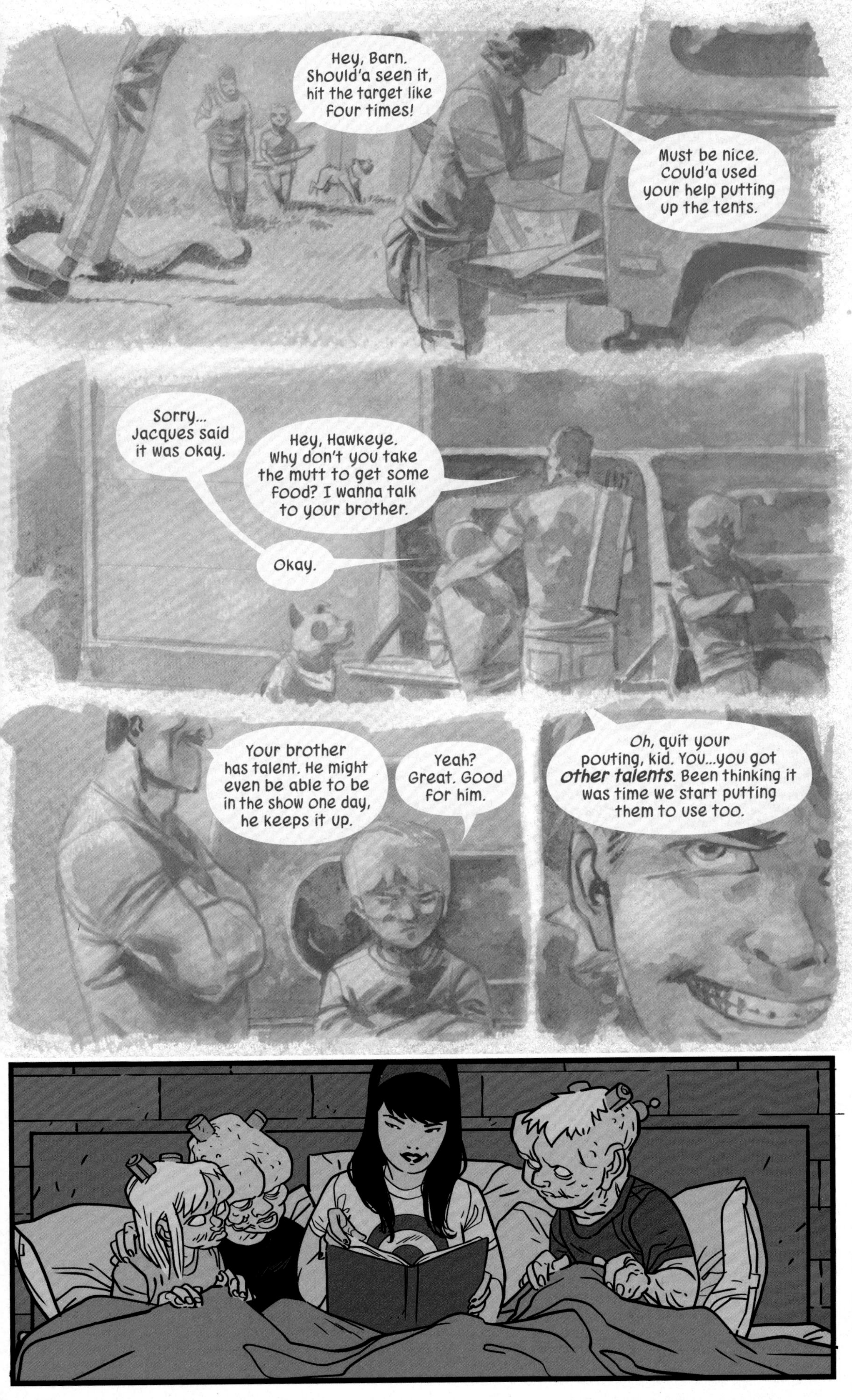
Hey, Barn. Should'a seen it, hit the target like four times!
Must be nice. Could'a used your help putting up the tents.
Sorry... Jacques said it was okay.
Hey, Hawkeye. Why don't you take the mutt to get some food? I wanna talk to your brother.
Okay.
Your brother has talent. He might even be able to be in the show one day, he keeps it up.
Yeah? Great. Good for him.
Oh, quit your pouting, kid. You...you got *other talents*. Been thinking it was time we start putting them to use too.

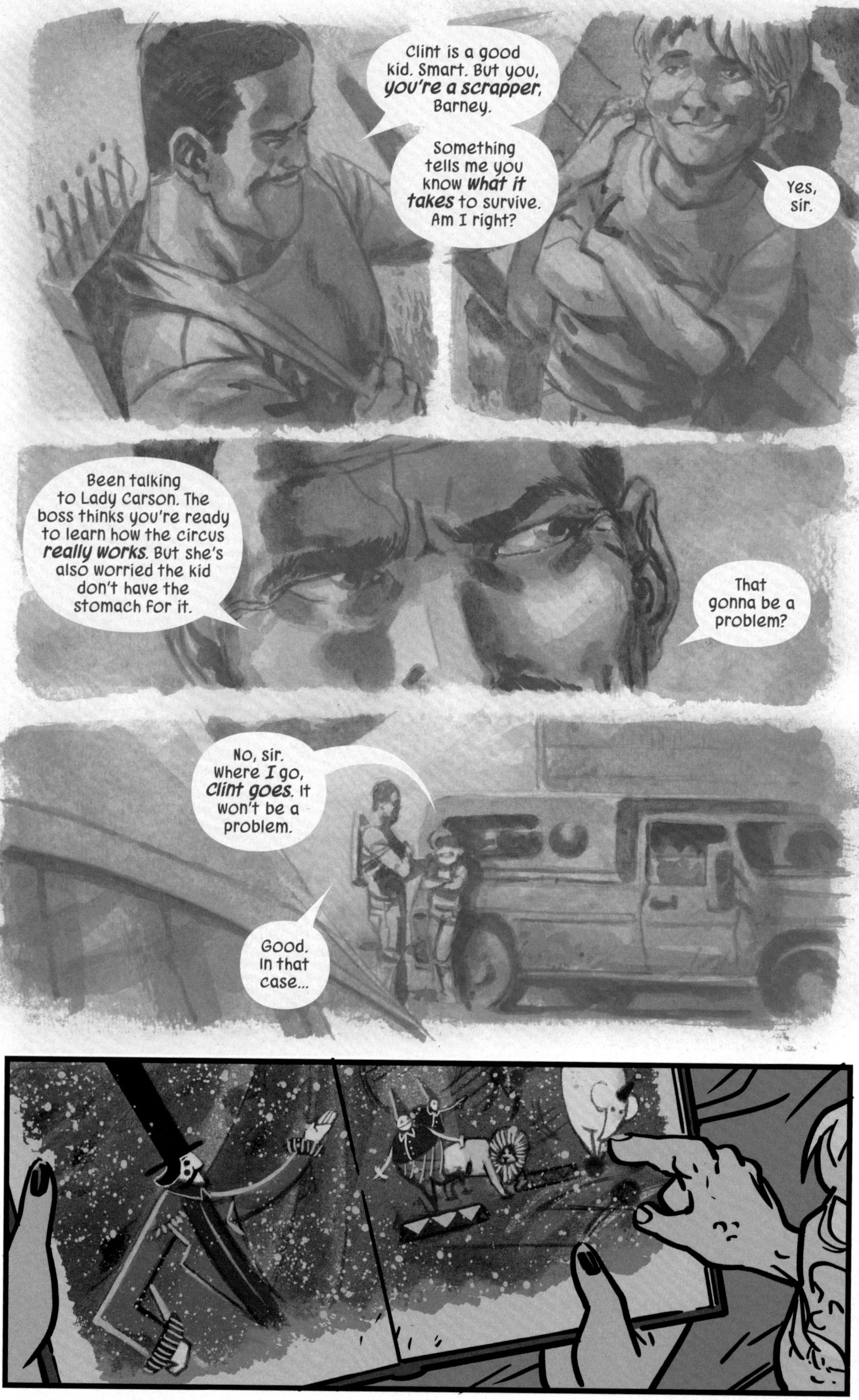
Clint is a good kid. Smart. But you, **you're a scrapper**, Barney.
Something tells me you know **what it takes** to survive. Am I right?
Yes, sir.
Been talking to Lady Carson. The boss thinks you're ready to learn how the circus **really works**. But she's also worried the kid don't have the stomach for it.
That gonna be a problem?
No, sir. Where **I** go, **Clint goes**. It won't be a problem.
Good. In that case...

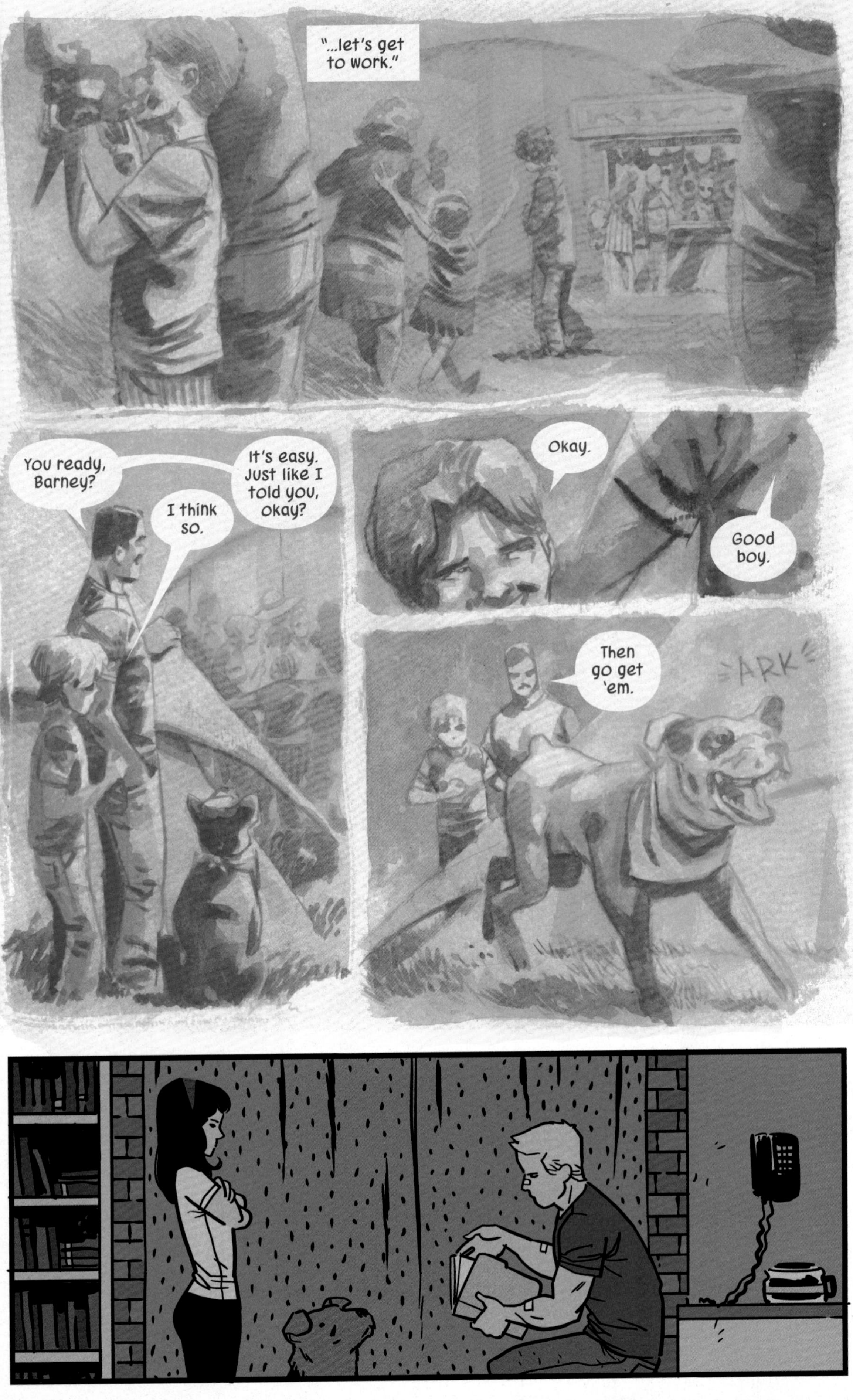
"...let's get to work."
You ready, Barney?
It's easy. Just like I told you, okay?
I think so.
Okay.
Good boy.
Then go get 'em.
ARK

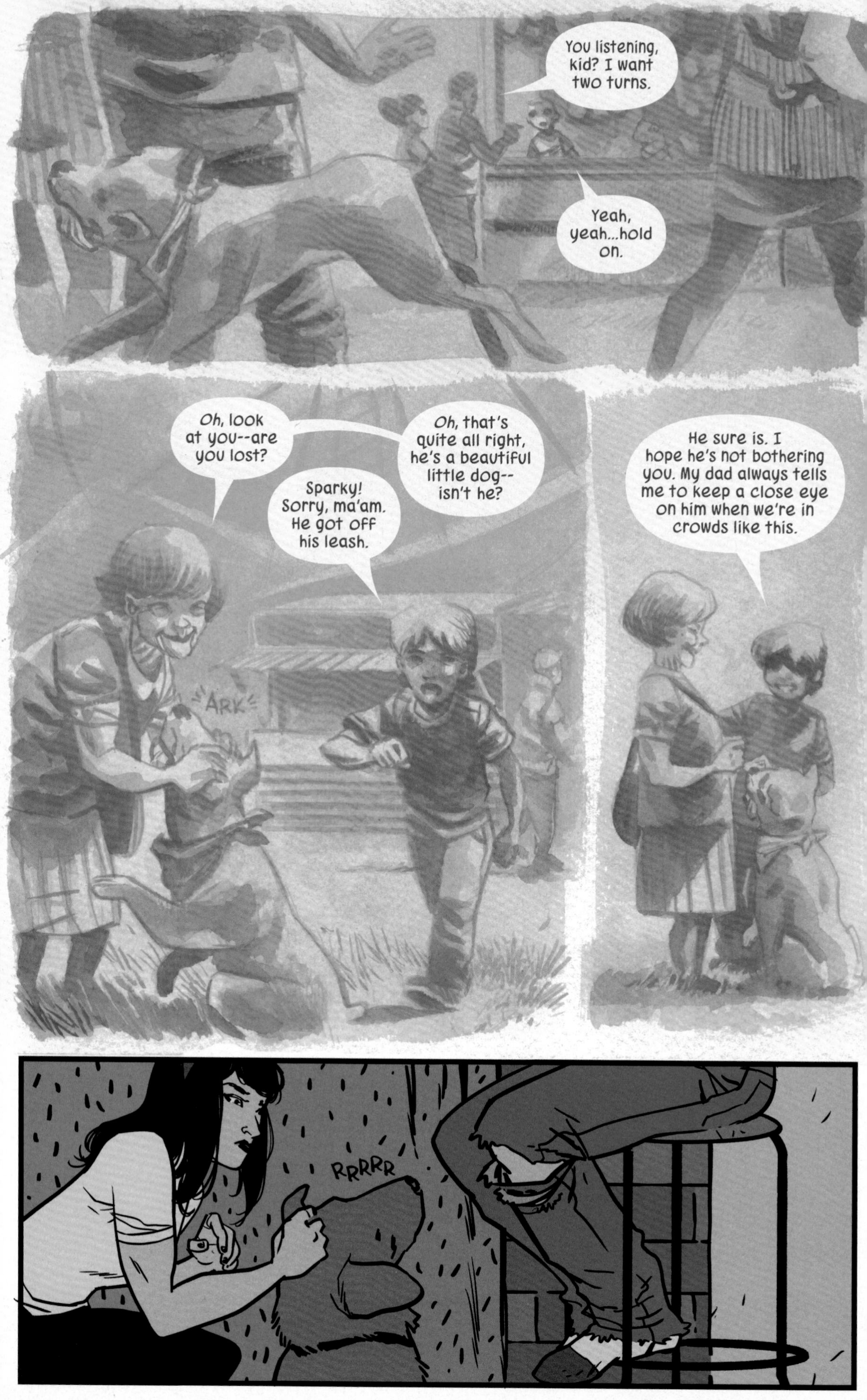
You listening, kid? I want two turns.
Yeah, yeah...hold on.
Oh, look at you--are you lost?
Sparky! Sorry, ma'am. He got off his leash.
Oh, that's quite all right, he's a beautiful little dog--isn't he?
ARK
He sure is. I hope he's not bothering you. My dad always tells me to keep a close eye on him when we're in crowds like this.
RRRRR

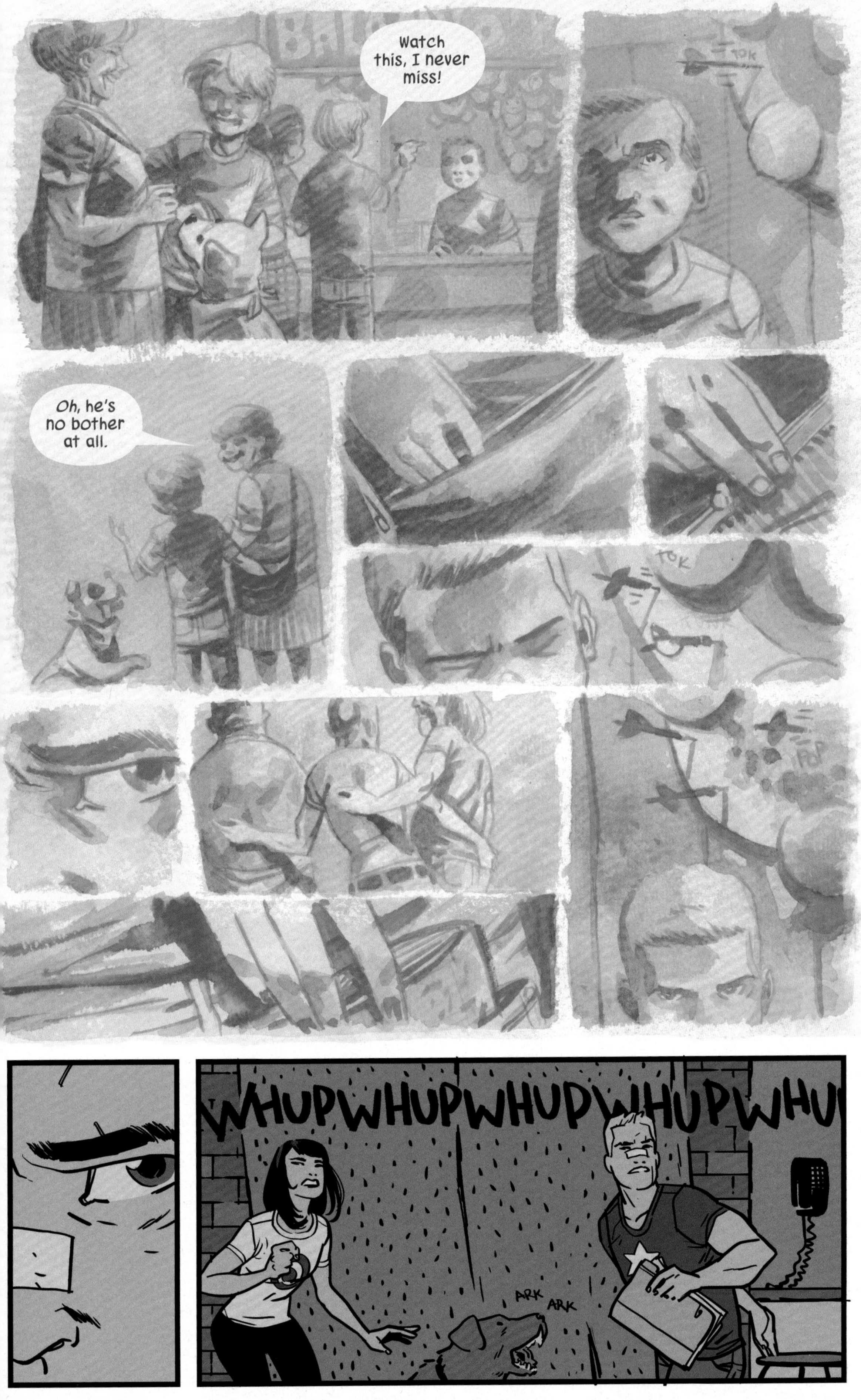
Watch this, I never miss!
TOK
Oh, he's no bother at all.
TOK
POP
WHUPWHUPWHUPWHUPWHU
ARK ARK

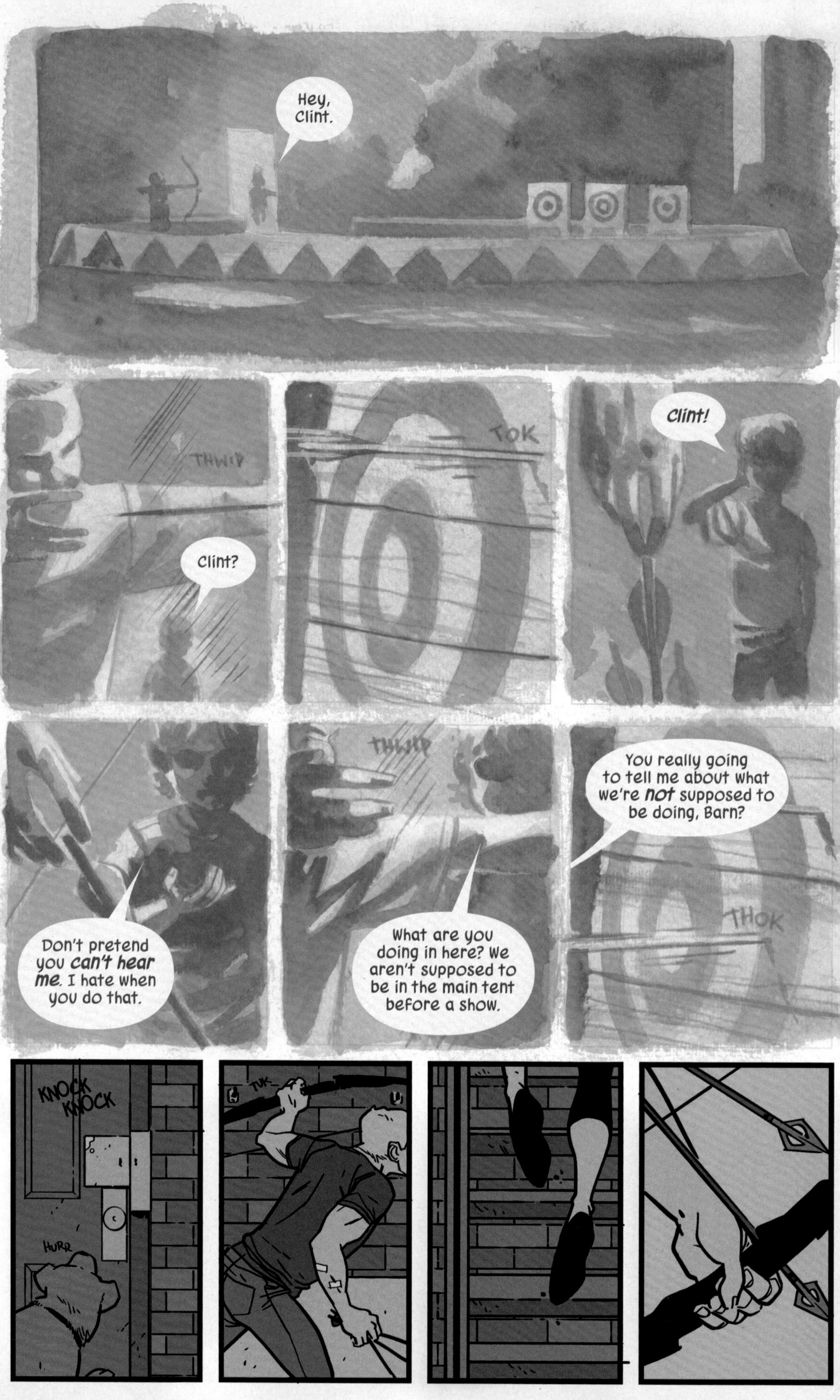
Hey, Clint.
THWIP
Clint?
TOK
Clint!
Don't pretend you can't hear me. I hate when you do that.
THWIP
What are you doing in here? We aren't supposed to be in the main tent before a show.
You really going to tell me about what we're not supposed to be doing, Barn?
THOK
KNOCK KNOCK
HURR
TUK

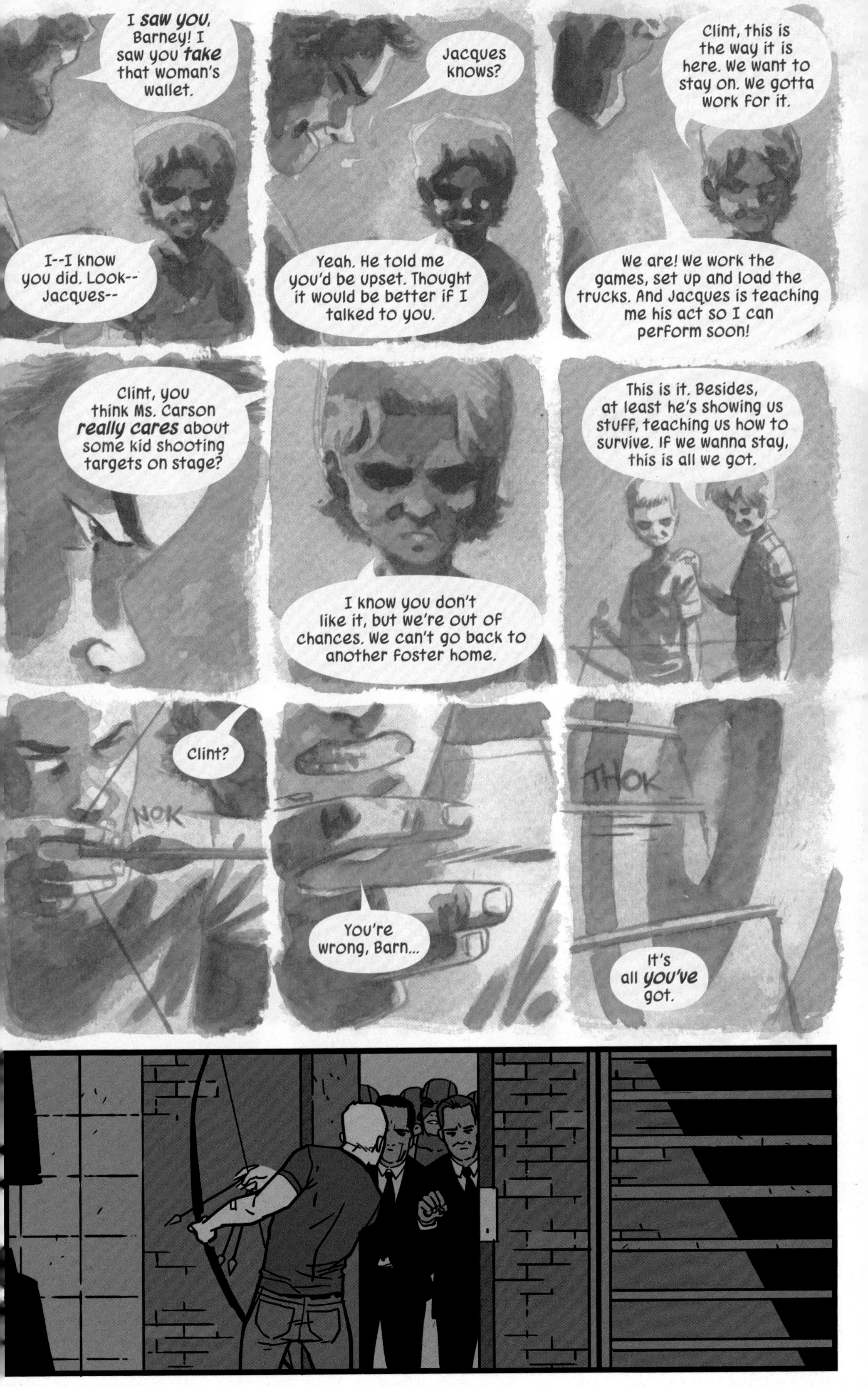
I saw you, Barney! I saw you take that woman's wallet.
I--I know you did. Look-- Jacques--
Jacques knows?
Yeah. He told me you'd be upset. Thought it would be better if I talked to you.
Clint, this is the way it is here. We want to stay on. We gotta work for it.
We are! We work the games, set up and load the trucks. And Jacques is teaching me his act so I can perform soon!
Clint, you think Ms. Carson really cares about some kid shooting targets on stage?
I know you don't like it, but we're out of chances. We can't go back to another foster home.
This is it. Besides, at least he's showing us stuff, teaching us how to survive. If we wanna stay, this is all we got.
Clint?
NOK
You're wrong, Barn...
THOK
It's all you've got.

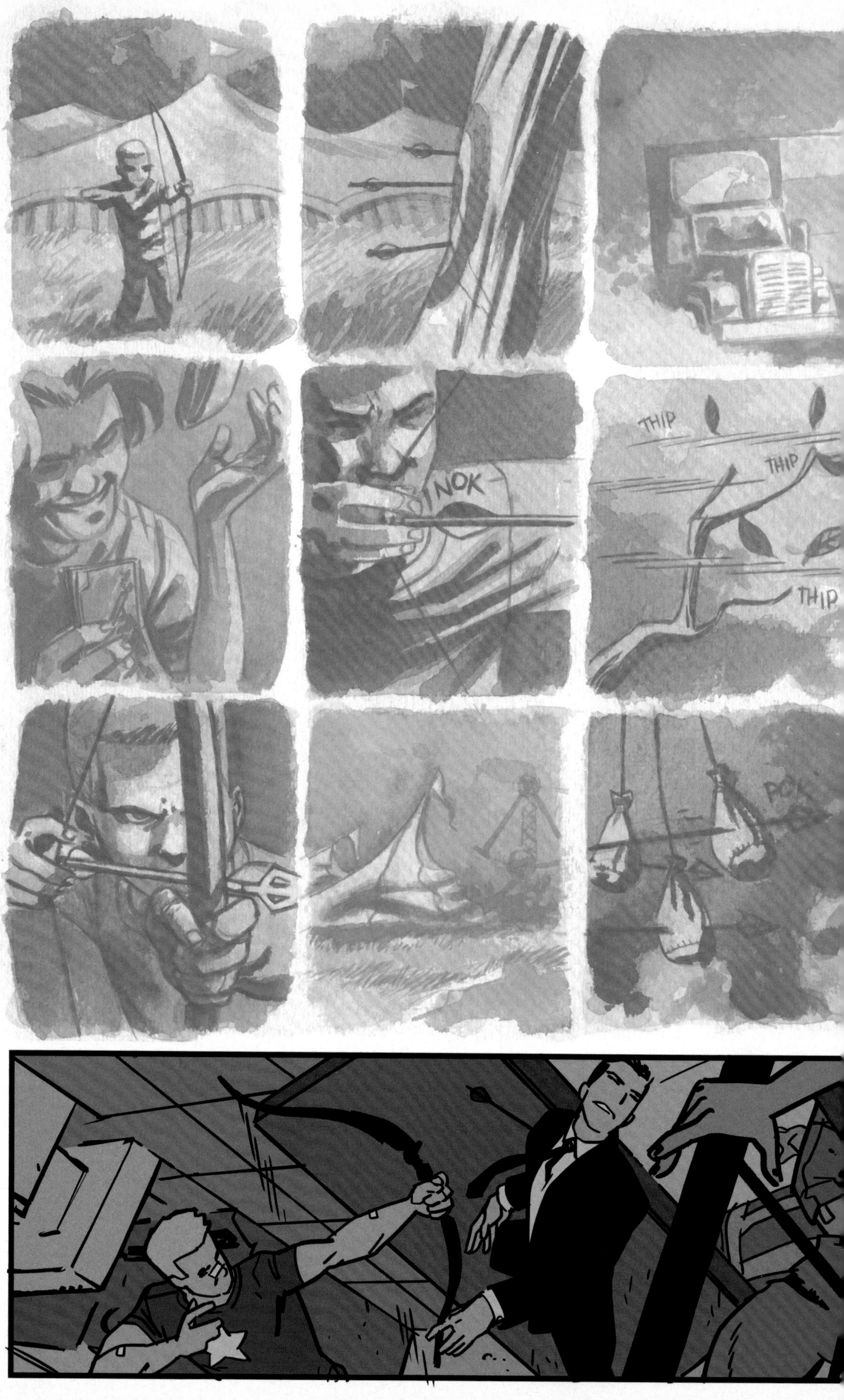
NOK
THIP
THIP
THIP

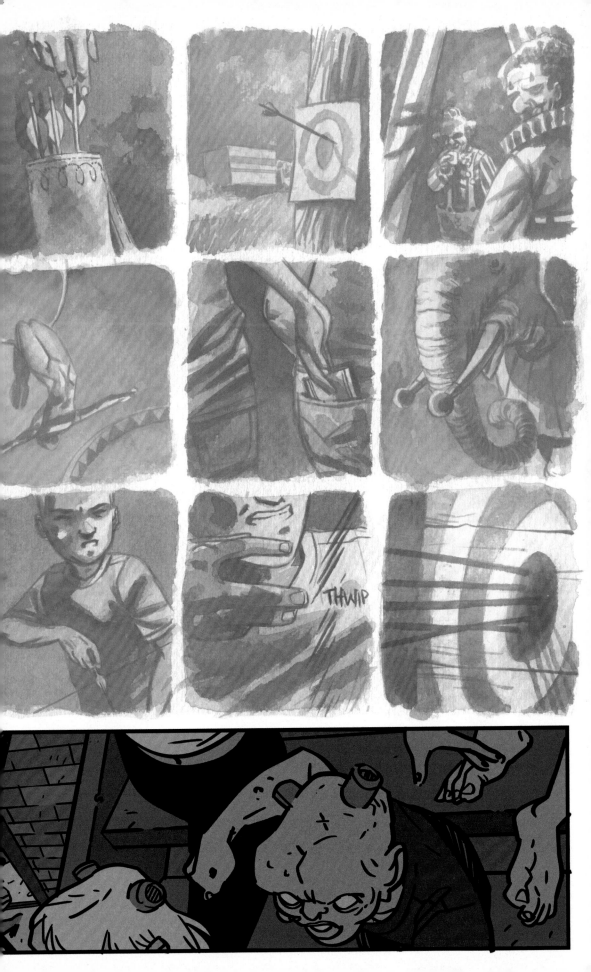

THWIP

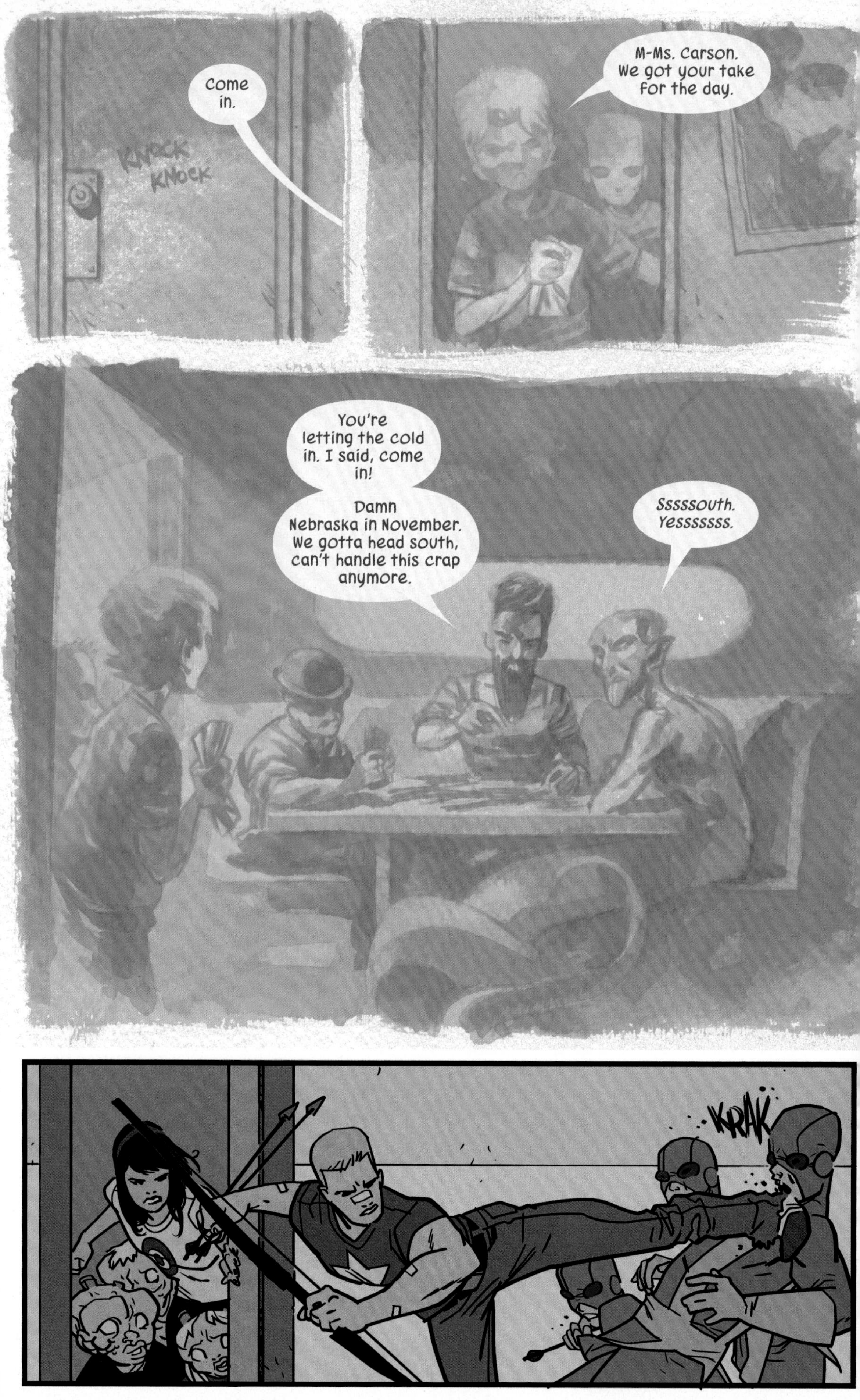
KNOCK KNOCK
Come in.
M-Ms. Carson. We got your take for the day.
You're letting the cold in. I said, come in!
Damn Nebraska in November. We gotta head south, can't handle this crap anymore.
Sssssouth. Yesssssss.
KRAK

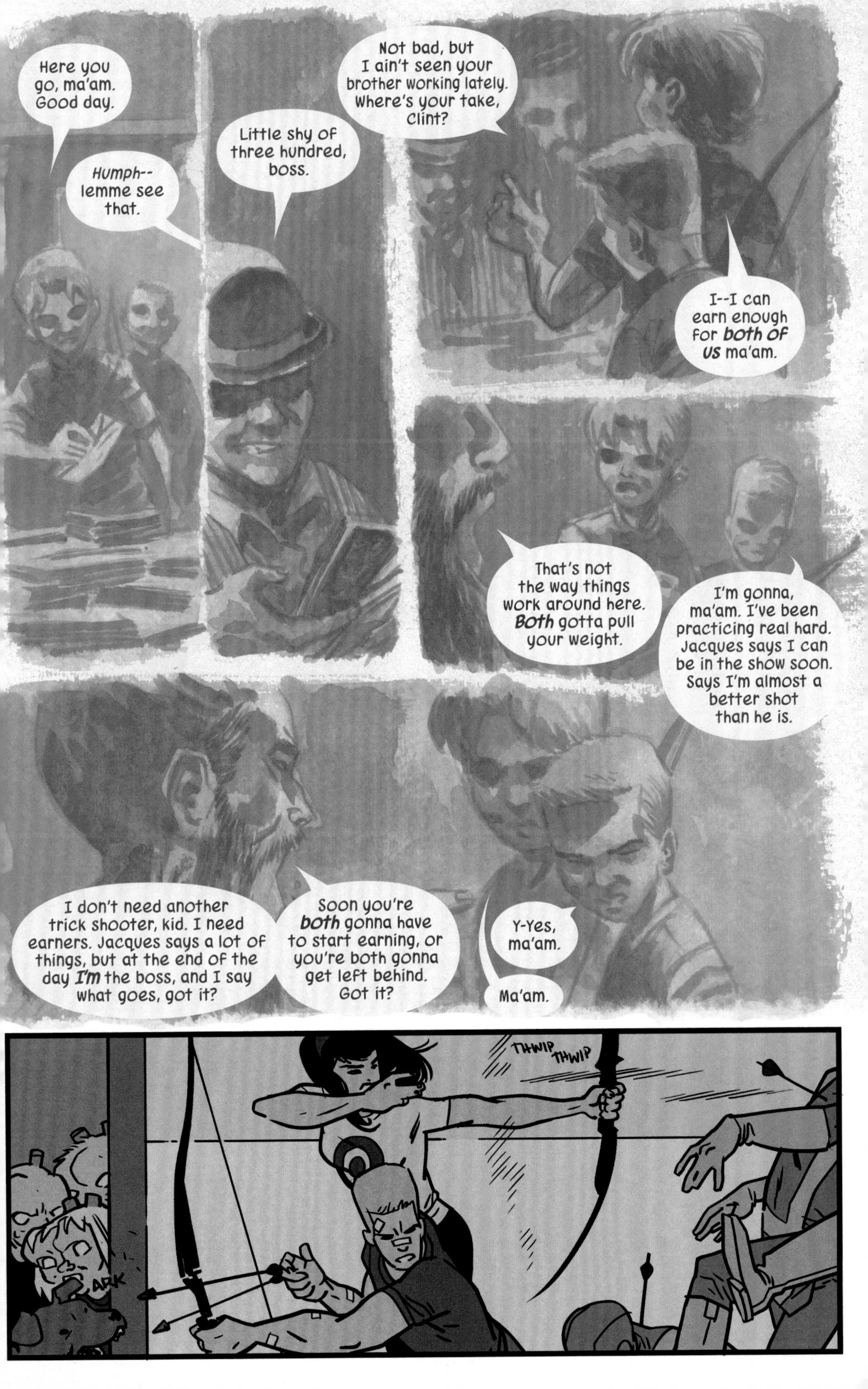
Here you go, ma'am. Good day.
Humph-- lemme see that.
Little shy of three hundred, boss.
Not bad, but I ain't seen your brother working lately. Where's your take, Clint?
I--I can earn enough for *both of us* ma'am.
That's not the way things work around here. *Both* gotta pull your weight.
I'm gonna, ma'am. I've been practicing real hard. Jacques says I can be in the show soon. Says I'm almost a better shot than he is.
I don't need another trick shooter, kid. I need earners. Jacques says a lot of things, but at the end of the day *I'm* the boss, and I say what goes, got it?
Soon you're *both* gonna have to start earning, or you're both gonna get left behind. Got it?
Y-Yes, ma'am.
Ma'am.
THWIP THWIP
ARK

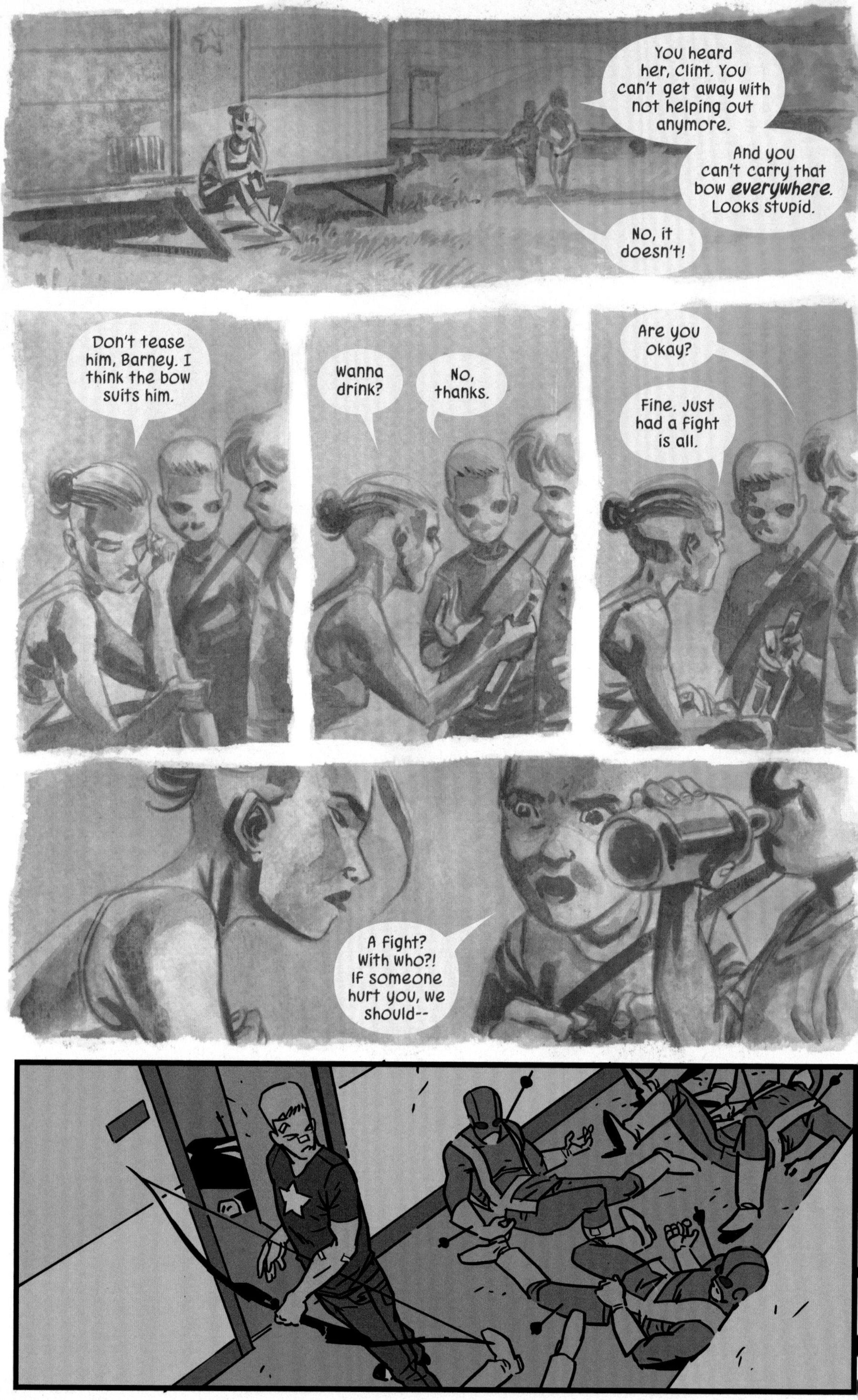

You heard her, Clint. You can't get away with not helping out anymore.
And you can't carry that bow *everywhere*. Looks stupid.
No, it doesn't!
Don't tease him, Barney. I think the bow suits him.
Wanna drink?
No, thanks.
Are you okay?
Fine. Just had a fight is all.
A fight? With who?! If someone hurt you, we should--

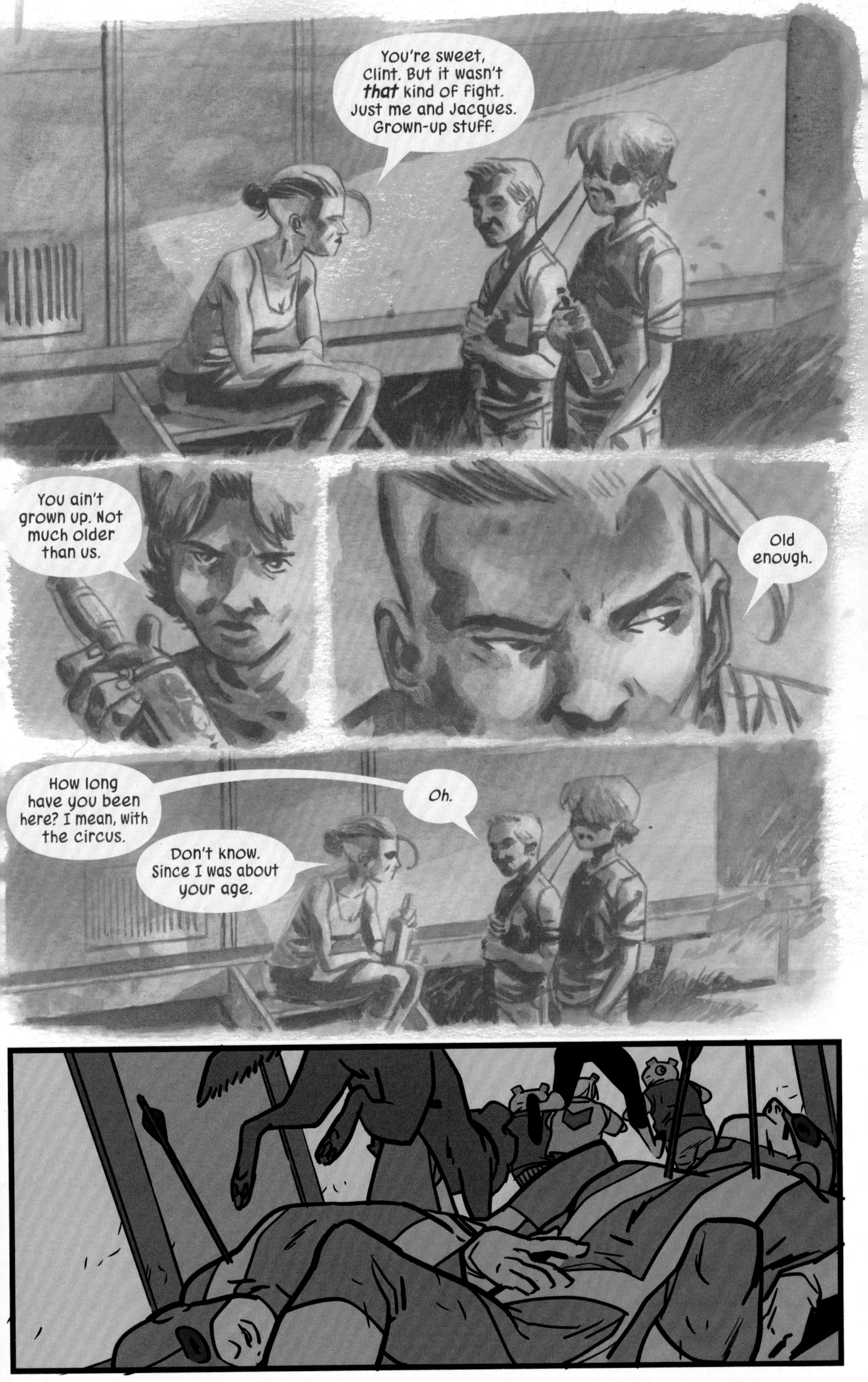
You're sweet, Clint. But it wasn't *that* kind of fight. Just me and Jacques. Grown-up stuff.
You ain't grown up. Not much older than us.
Old enough.
How long have you been here? I mean, with the circus.
Don't know. Since I was about your age.
Oh.

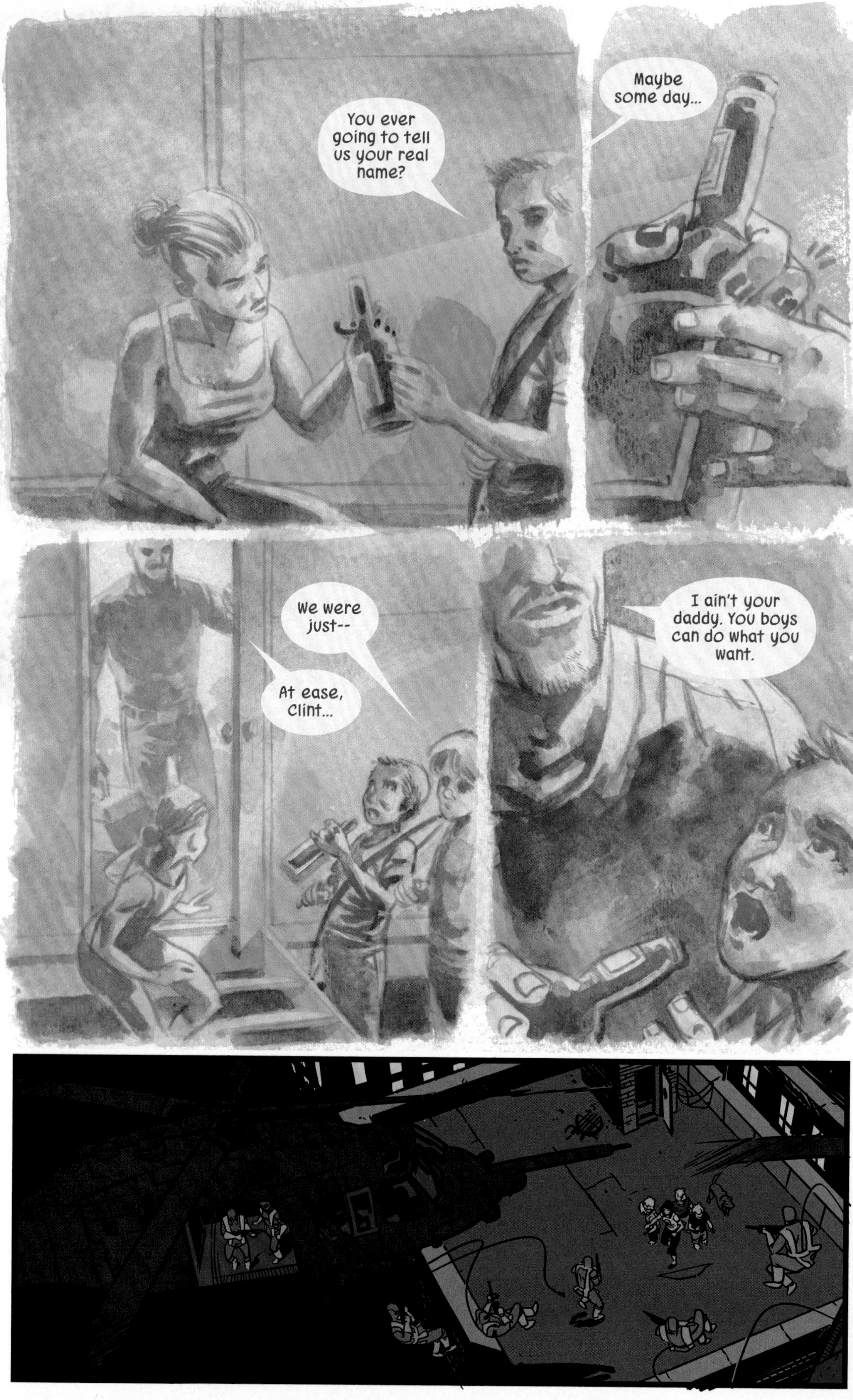
You ever going to tell us your real name?
Maybe some day...
We were just--
At ease, Clint...
I ain't your daddy. You boys can do what you want.

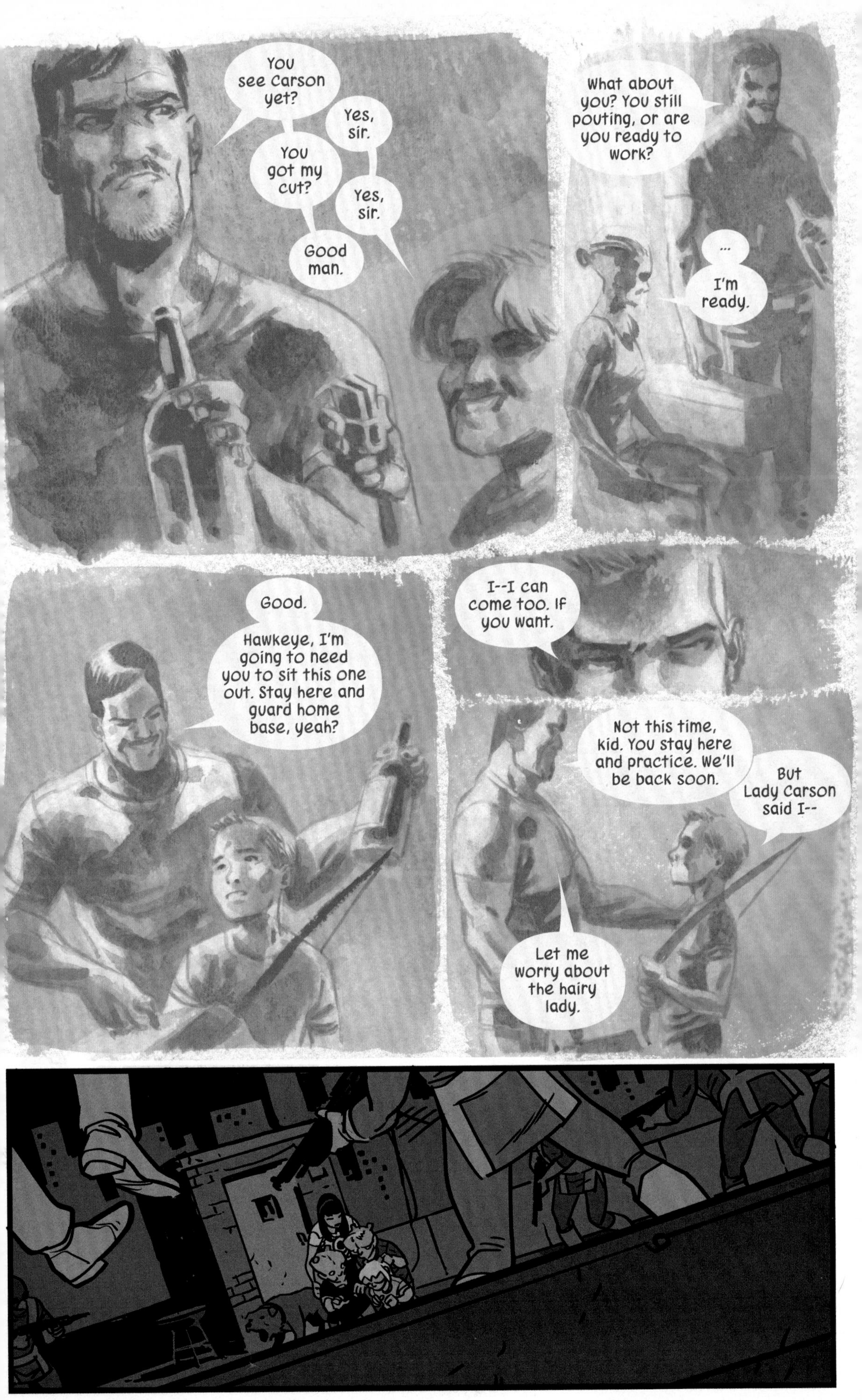
You see Carson yet?
Yes, sir.
You got my cut?
Yes, sir.
Good man.
What about you? You still pouting, or are you ready to work?
...
I'm ready.
Good.
Hawkeye, I'm going to need you to sit this one out. Stay here and guard home base, yeah?
I--I can come too. If you want.
Not this time, kid. You stay here and practice. We'll be back soon.
But Lady Carson said I--
Let me worry about the hairy lady.

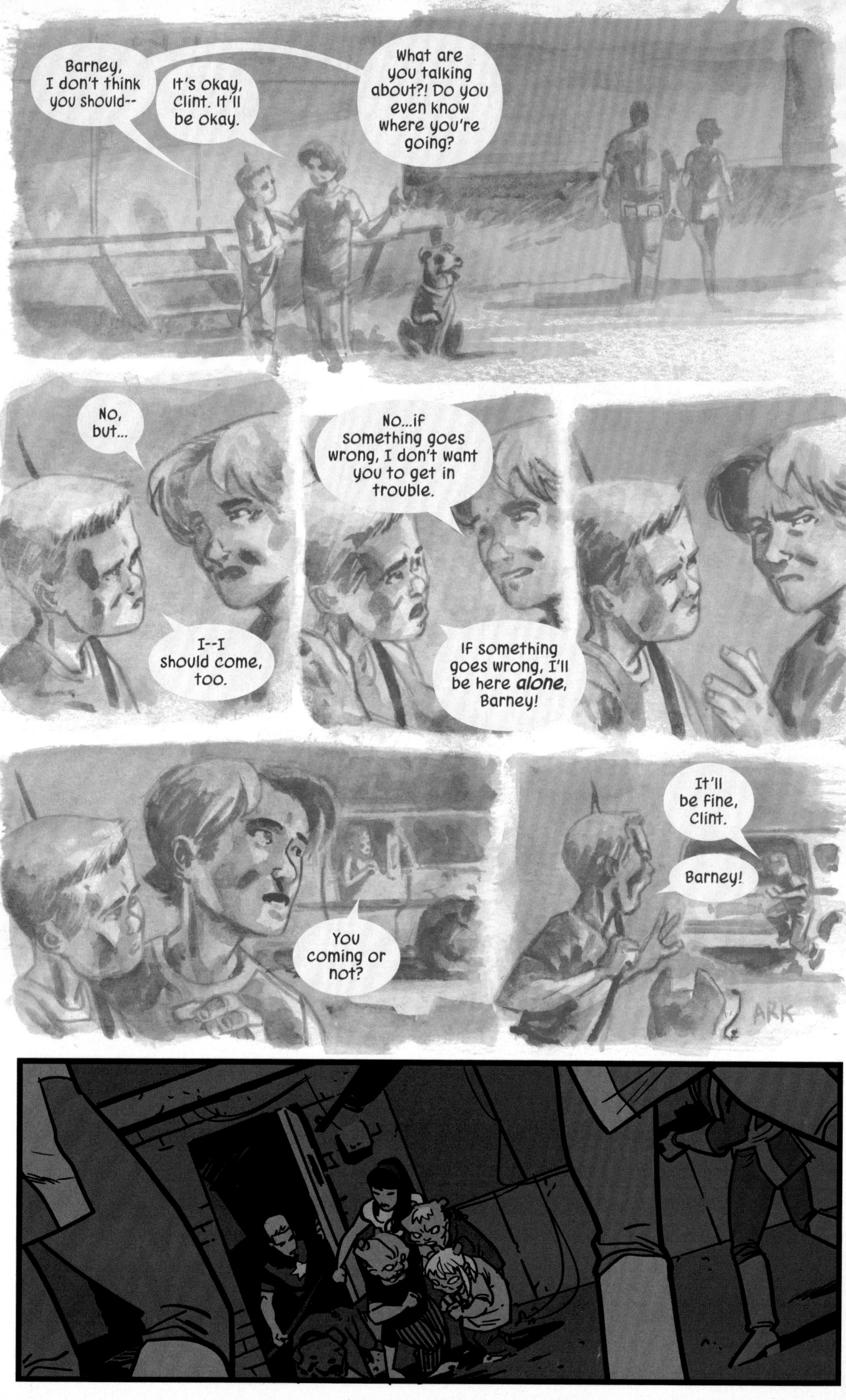
Barney, I don't think you should--
It's okay, Clint. It'll be okay.
What are you talking about?! Do you even know where you're going?
No, but...
I--I should come, too.
No...if something goes wrong, I don't want you to get in trouble.
If something goes wrong, I'll be here *alone*, Barney!
You coming or not?
It'll be fine, Clint.
Barney!
ARK

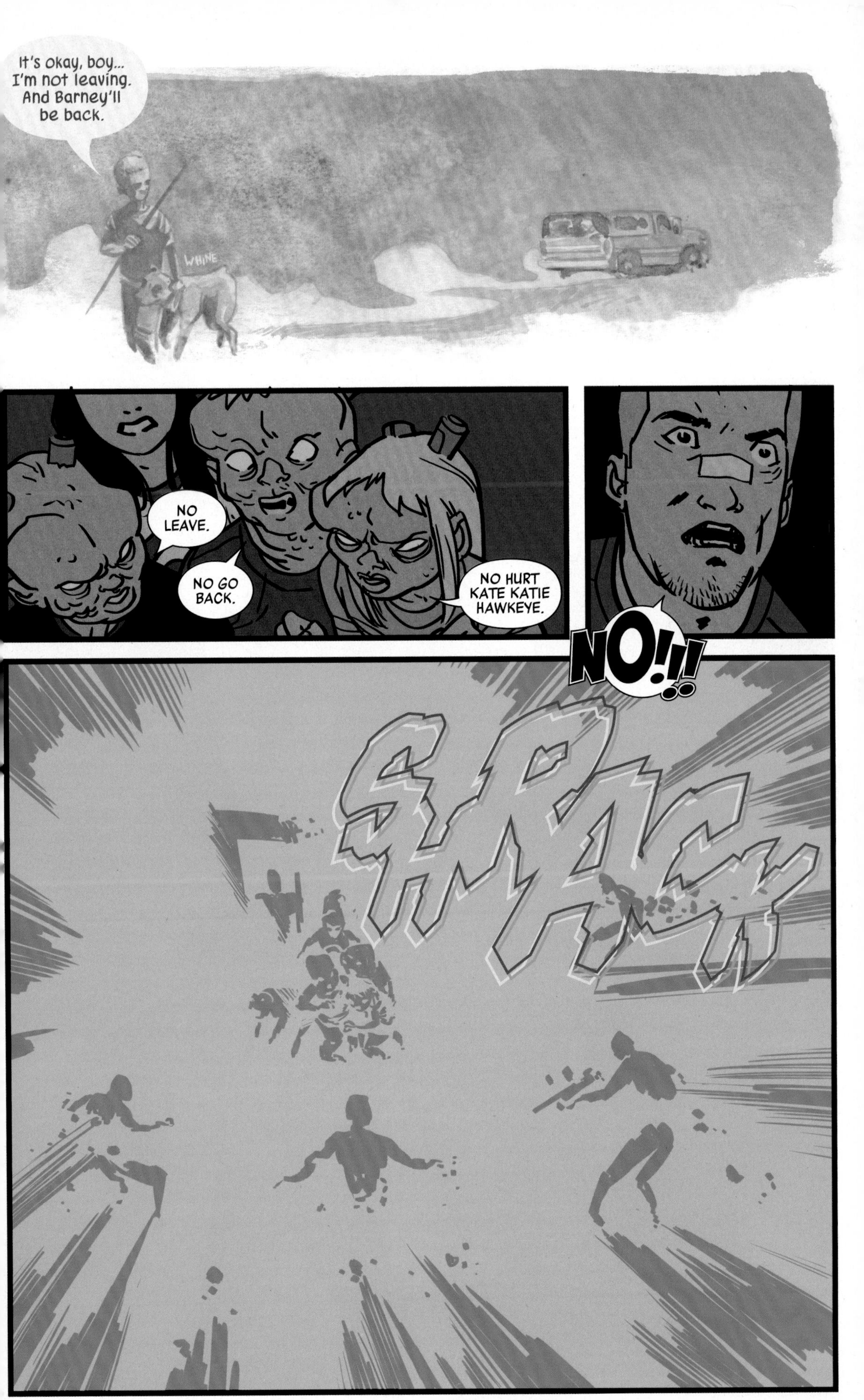
It's okay, boy... I'm not leaving. And Barney'll be back.
WHINE
NO LEAVE.
NO GO BACK.
NO HURT KATE KATIE HAWKEYE.
NO!!!

5

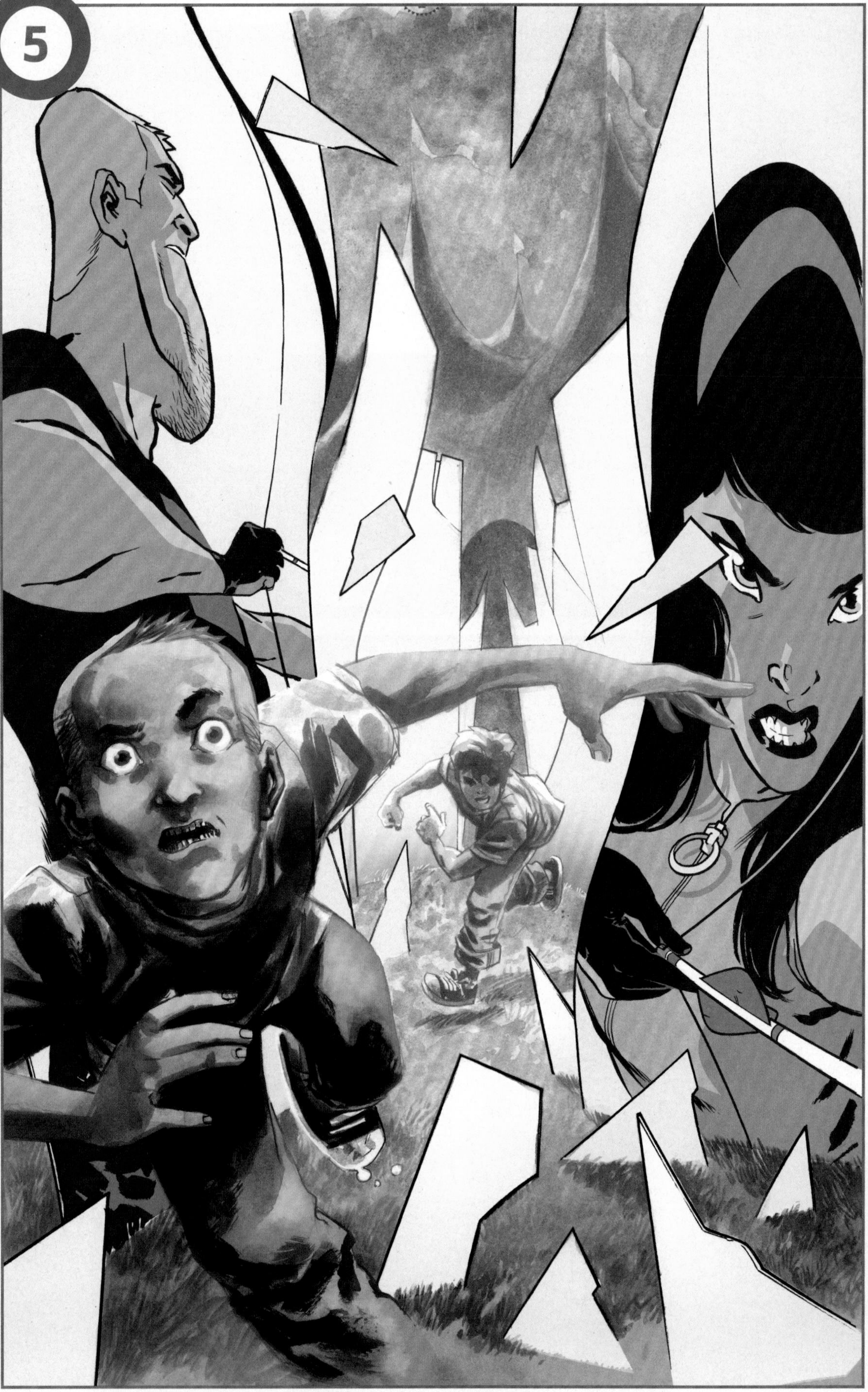

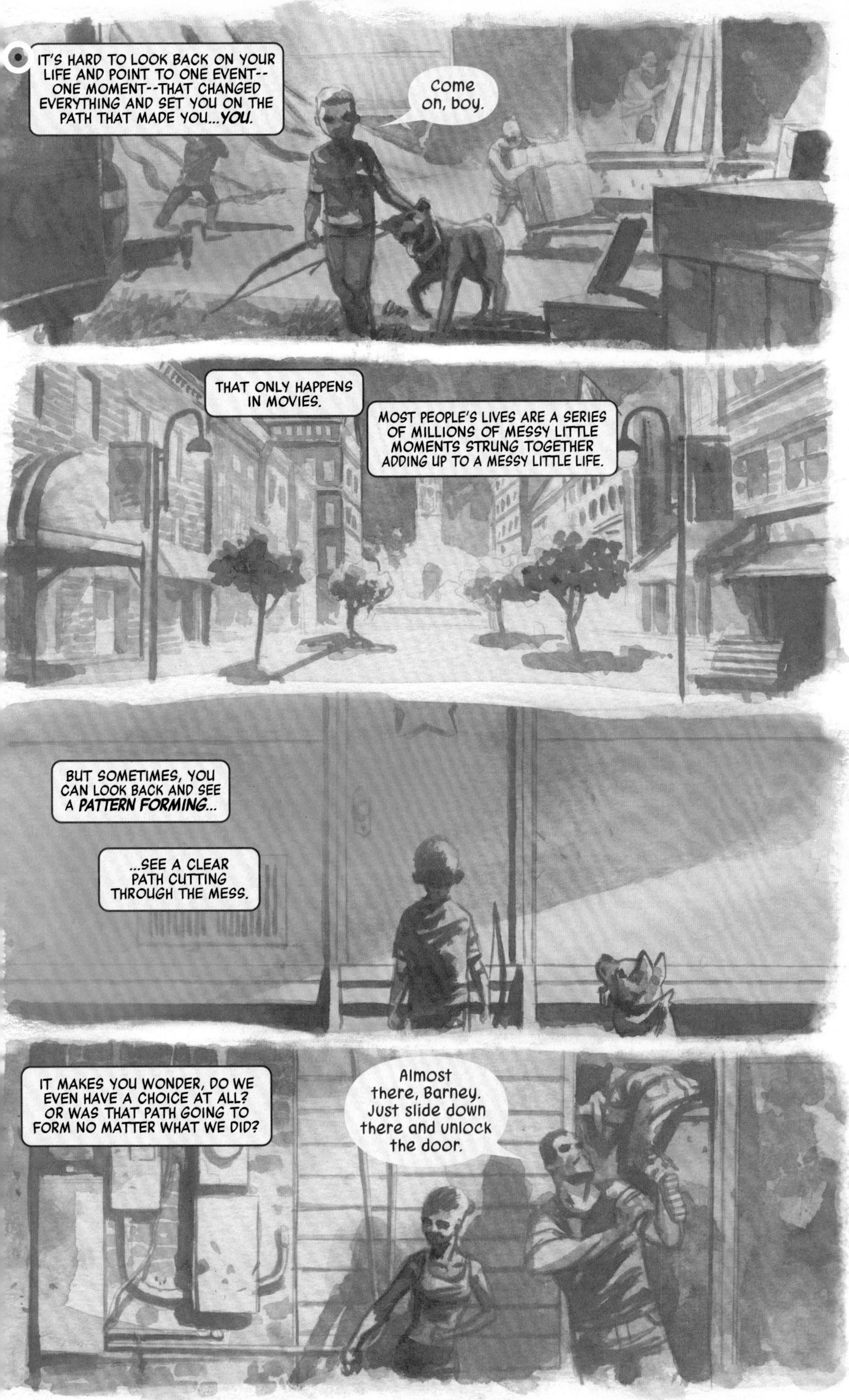

IT'S HARD TO LOOK BACK ON YOUR LIFE AND POINT TO ONE EVENT-- ONE MOMENT--THAT CHANGED EVERYTHING AND SET YOU ON THE PATH THAT MADE YOU...YOU.
Come on, boy.
THAT ONLY HAPPENS IN MOVIES.
MOST PEOPLE'S LIVES ARE A SERIES OF MILLIONS OF MESSY LITTLE MOMENTS STRUNG TOGETHER ADDING UP TO A MESSY LITTLE LIFE.
BUT SOMETIMES, YOU CAN LOOK BACK AND SEE A PATTERN FORMING...
...SEE A CLEAR PATH CUTTING THROUGH THE MESS.
IT MAKES YOU WONDER, DO WE EVEN HAVE A CHOICE AT ALL? OR WAS THAT PATH GOING TO FORM NO MATTER WHAT WE DID?
Almost there, Barney. Just slide down there and unlock the door.

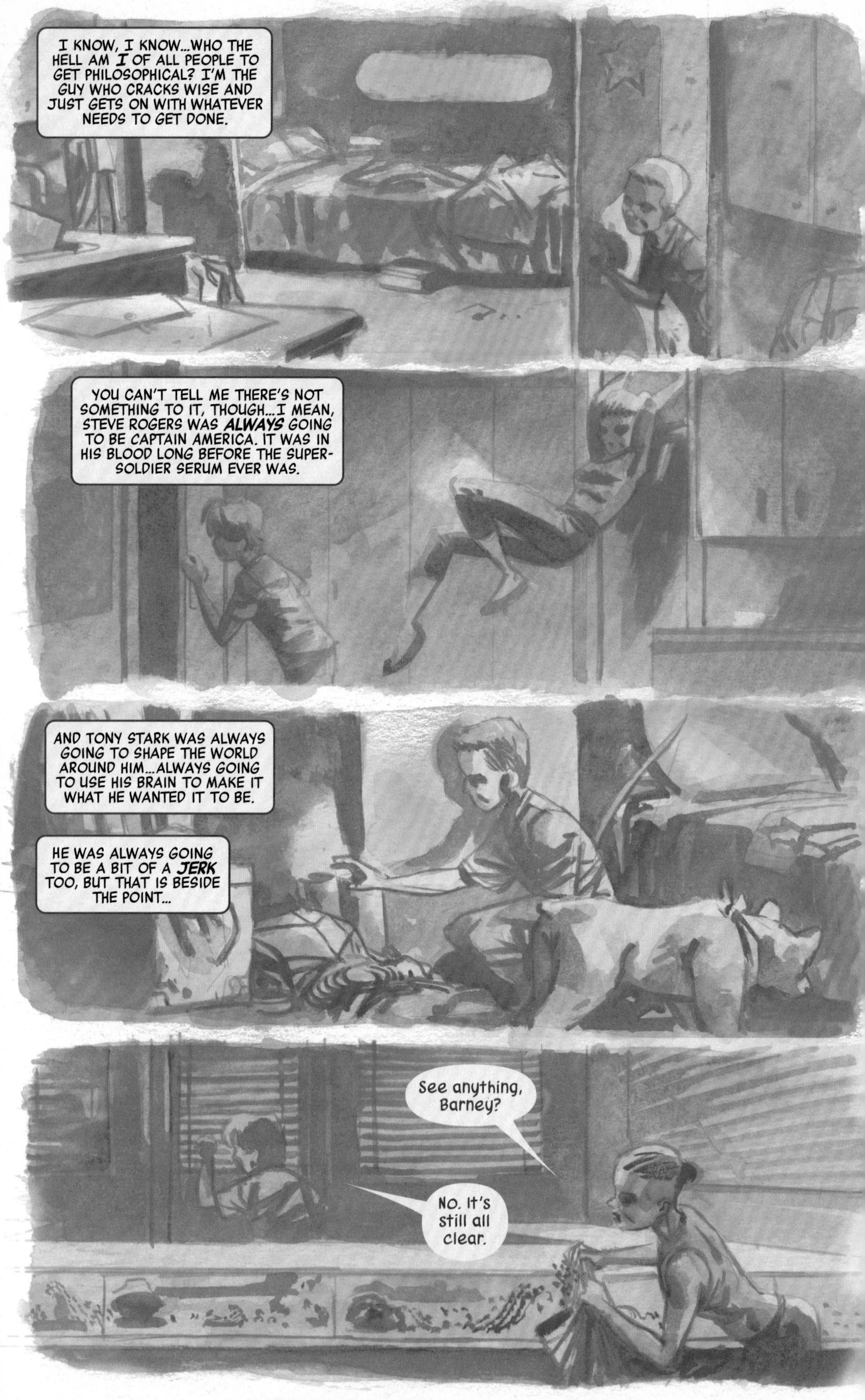
I KNOW, I KNOW...WHO THE HELL AM I OF ALL PEOPLE TO GET PHILOSOPHICAL? I'M THE GUY WHO CRACKS WISE AND JUST GETS ON WITH WHATEVER NEEDS TO GET DONE.
YOU CAN'T TELL ME THERE'S NOT SOMETHING TO IT, THOUGH...I MEAN, STEVE ROGERS WAS ALWAYS GOING TO BE CAPTAIN AMERICA. IT WAS IN HIS BLOOD LONG BEFORE THE SUPER-SOLDIER SERUM EVER WAS.
AND TONY STARK WAS ALWAYS GOING TO SHAPE THE WORLD AROUND HIM...ALWAYS GOING TO USE HIS BRAIN TO MAKE IT WHAT HE WANTED IT TO BE.
HE WAS ALWAYS GOING TO BE A BIT OF A JERK TOO, BUT THAT IS BESIDE THE POINT...
See anything, Barney?
No. It's still all clear.

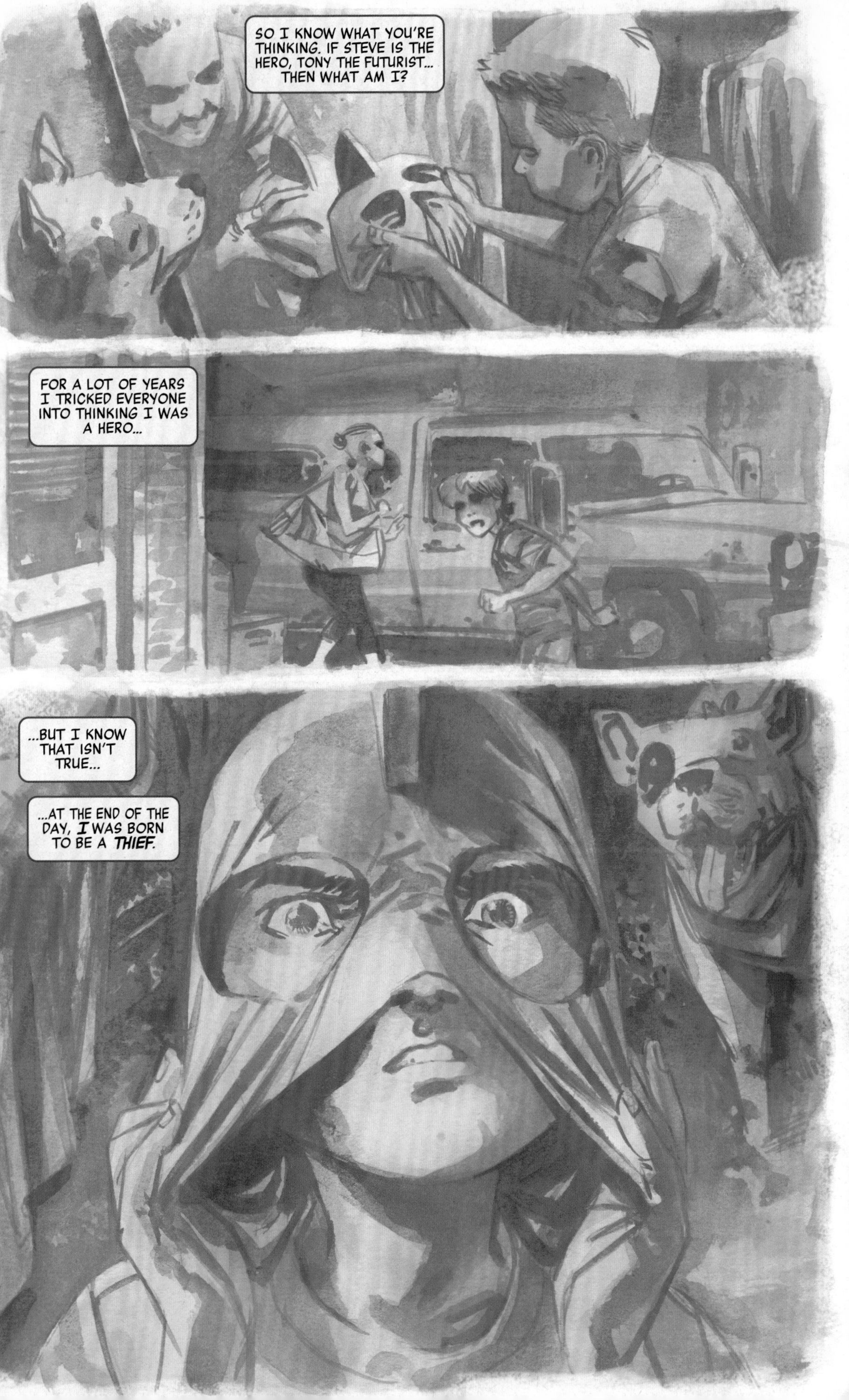

SO I KNOW WHAT YOU'RE THINKING. IF STEVE IS THE HERO, TONY THE FUTURIST... THEN WHAT AM I?
FOR A LOT OF YEARS I TRICKED EVERYONE INTO THINKING I WAS A HERO...
...BUT I KNOW THAT ISN'T TRUE...
...AT THE END OF THE DAY, *I* WAS BORN TO BE A ***THIEF***.

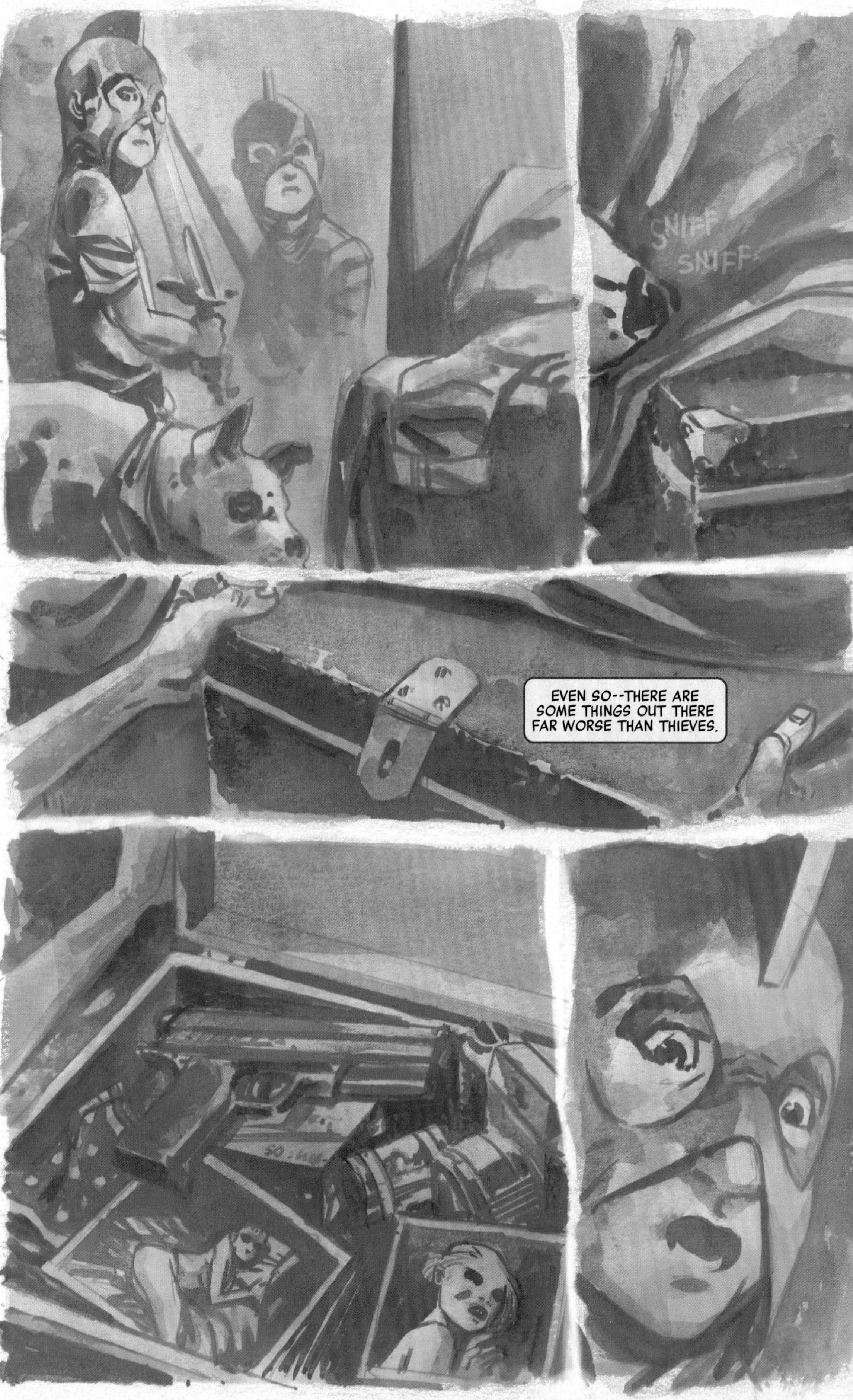
SNIFF
SNIFF
EVEN SO--THERE ARE SOME THINGS OUT THERE FAR WORSE THAN THIEVES.

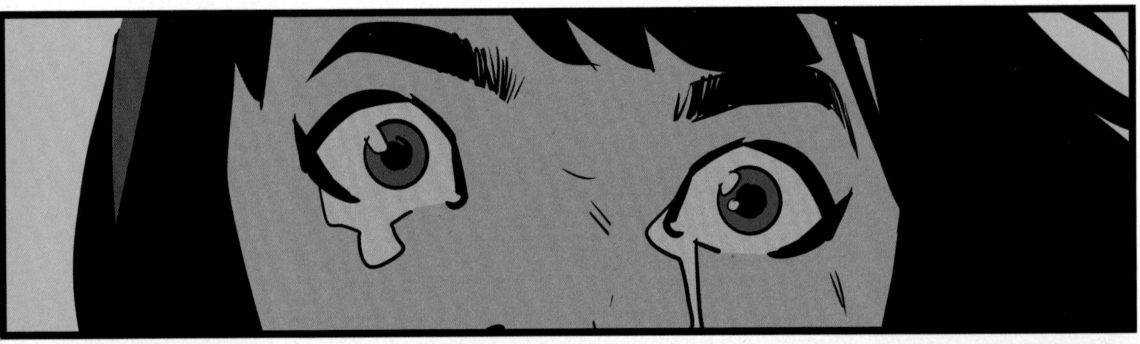

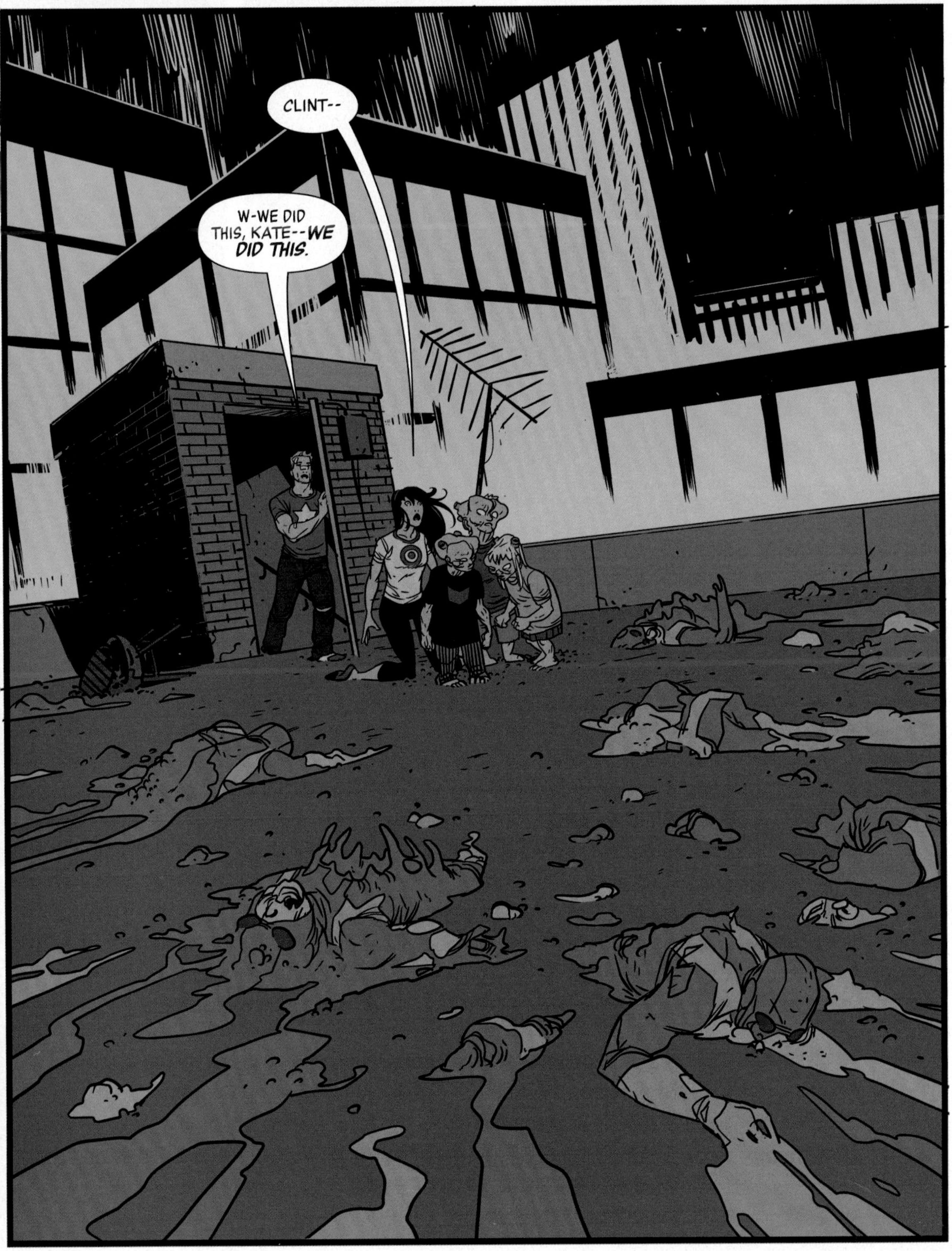
CLINT--
W-WE DID THIS, KATE--WE DID THIS.

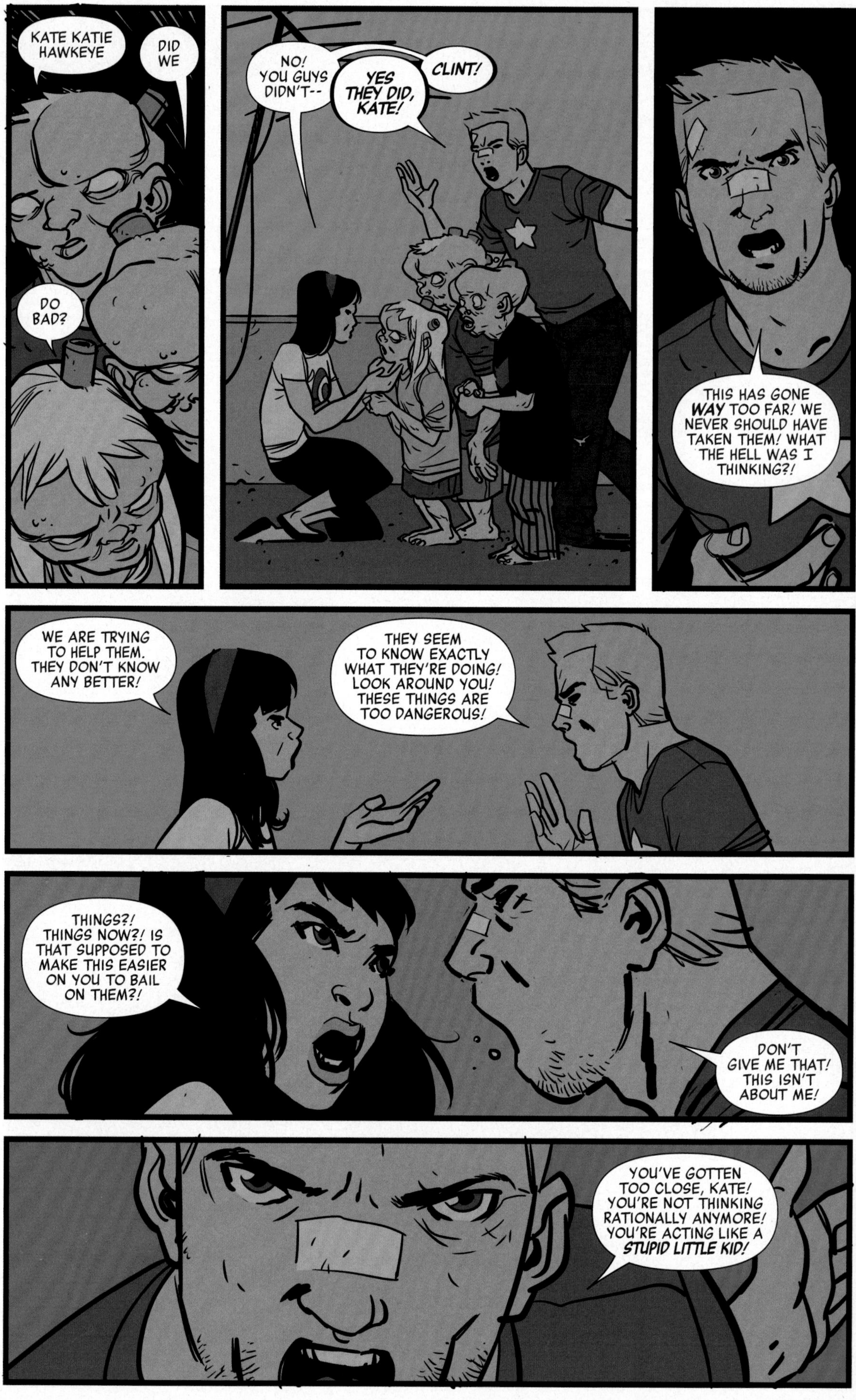
KATE KATIE HAWKEYE
DID WE
DO BAD?
NO! YOU GUYS DIDN'T--
YES THEY DID, KATE!
CLINT!
THIS HAS GONE WAY TOO FAR! WE NEVER SHOULD HAVE TAKEN THEM! WHAT THE HELL WAS I THINKING?!
WE ARE TRYING TO HELP THEM. THEY DON'T KNOW ANY BETTER!
THEY SEEM TO KNOW EXACTLY WHAT THEY'RE DOING! LOOK AROUND YOU! THESE THINGS ARE TOO DANGEROUS!
THINGS?! THINGS NOW?! IS THAT SUPPOSED TO MAKE THIS EASIER ON YOU TO BAIL ON THEM?!
DON'T GIVE ME THAT! THIS ISN'T ABOUT ME!
YOU'VE GOTTEN TOO CLOSE, KATE! YOU'RE NOT THINKING RATIONALLY ANYMORE! YOU'RE ACTING LIKE A STUPID LITTLE KID!

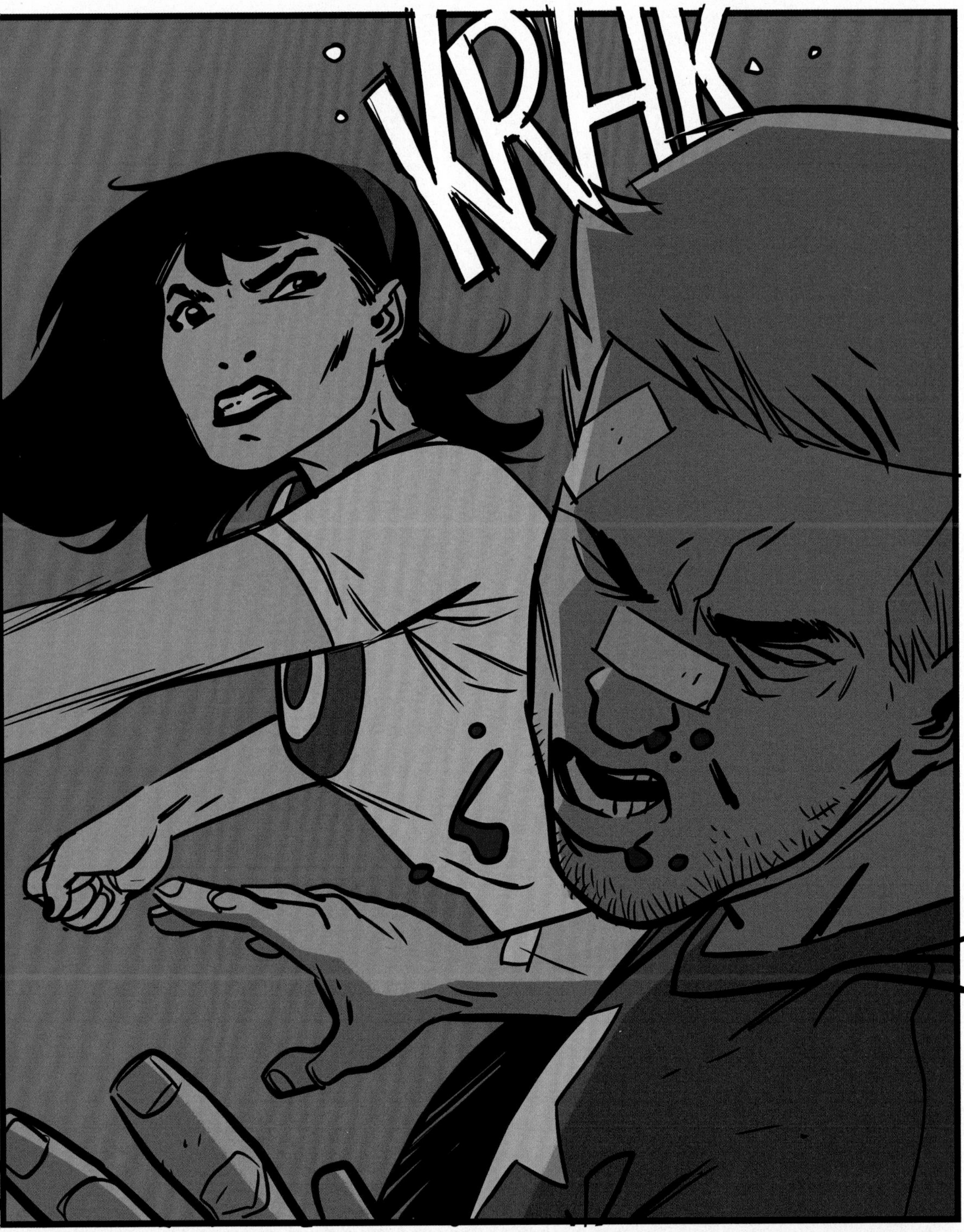
KRAK

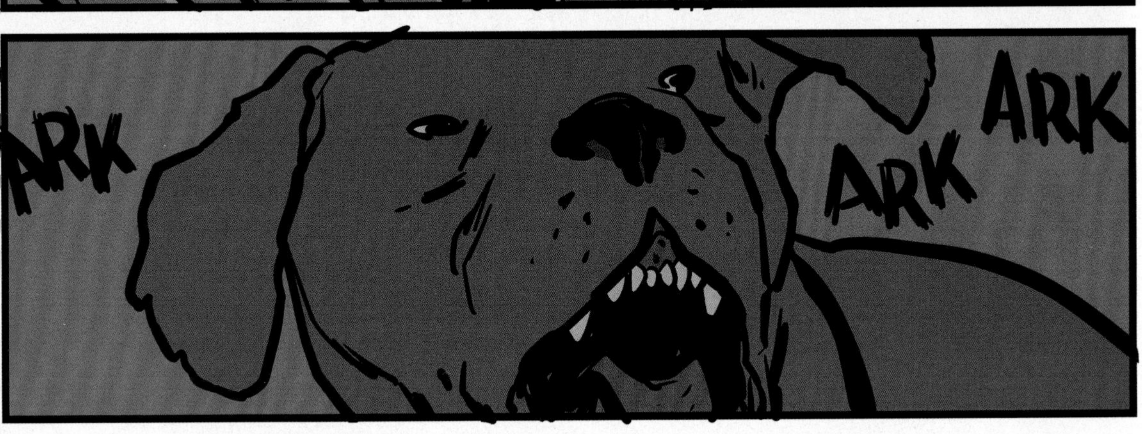
ARK
ARK
ARK

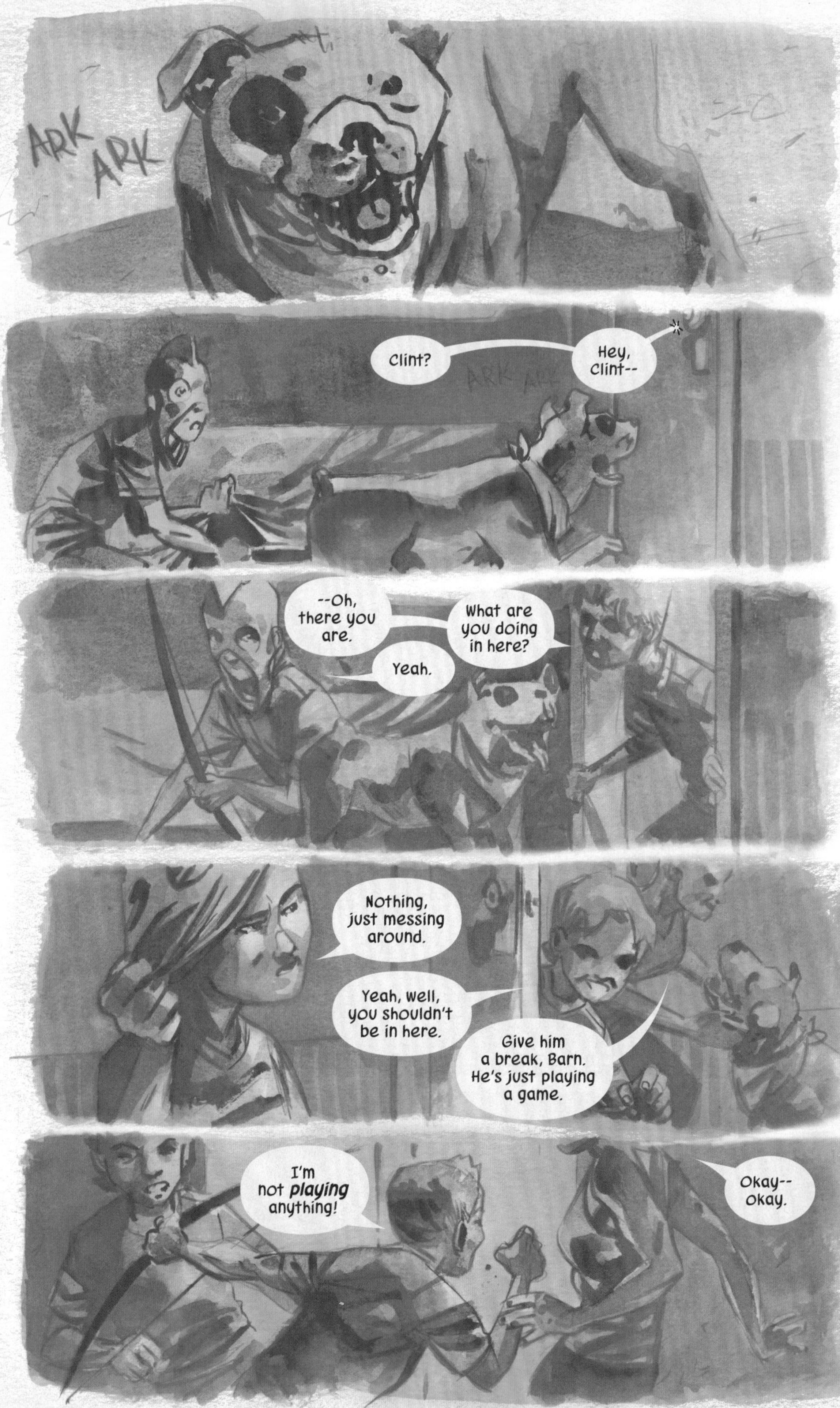
ARK ARK
Clint?
Hey, Clint--
ARK ARK
--Oh, there you are.
What are you doing in here?
Yeah.
Nothing, just messing around.
Yeah, well, you shouldn't be in here.
Give him a break, Barn. He's just playing a game.
I'm not ***playing*** anything!
Okay-- okay.

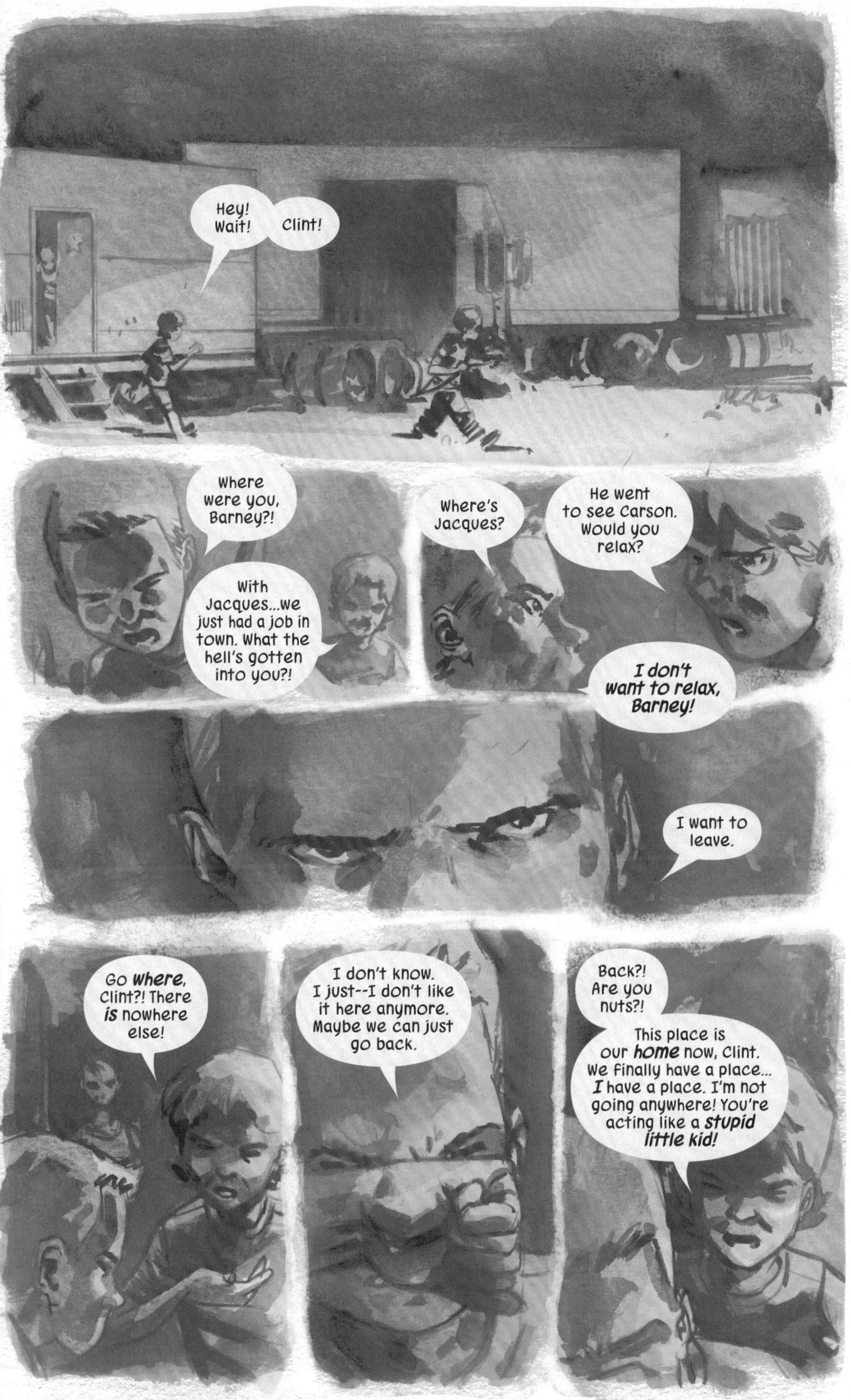

Hey! Wait!
Clint!
Where were you, Barney?!
With Jacques...we just had a job in town. What the hell's gotten into you?!
Where's Jacques?
He went to see Carson. Would you relax?
I don't want to relax, Barney!
I want to leave.
Go **where**, Clint?! There **is** nowhere else!
I don't know. I just--I don't like it here anymore. Maybe we can just go back.
Back?! Are you nuts?!
This place is our **home** now, Clint. We finally have a place... **I** have a place. I'm not going anywhere! You're acting like a ***stupid little kid!***

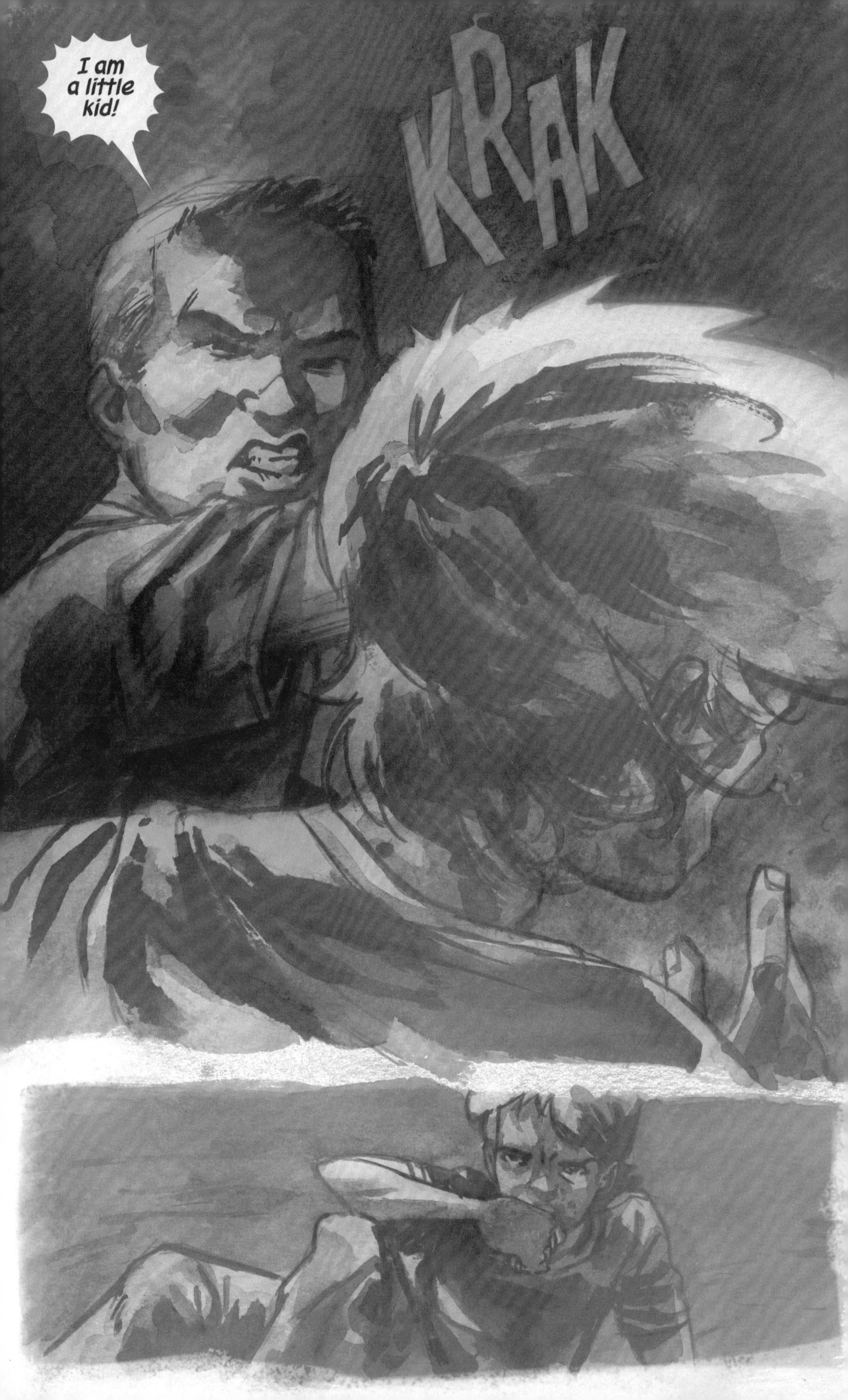
I am a little kid!
KRAK

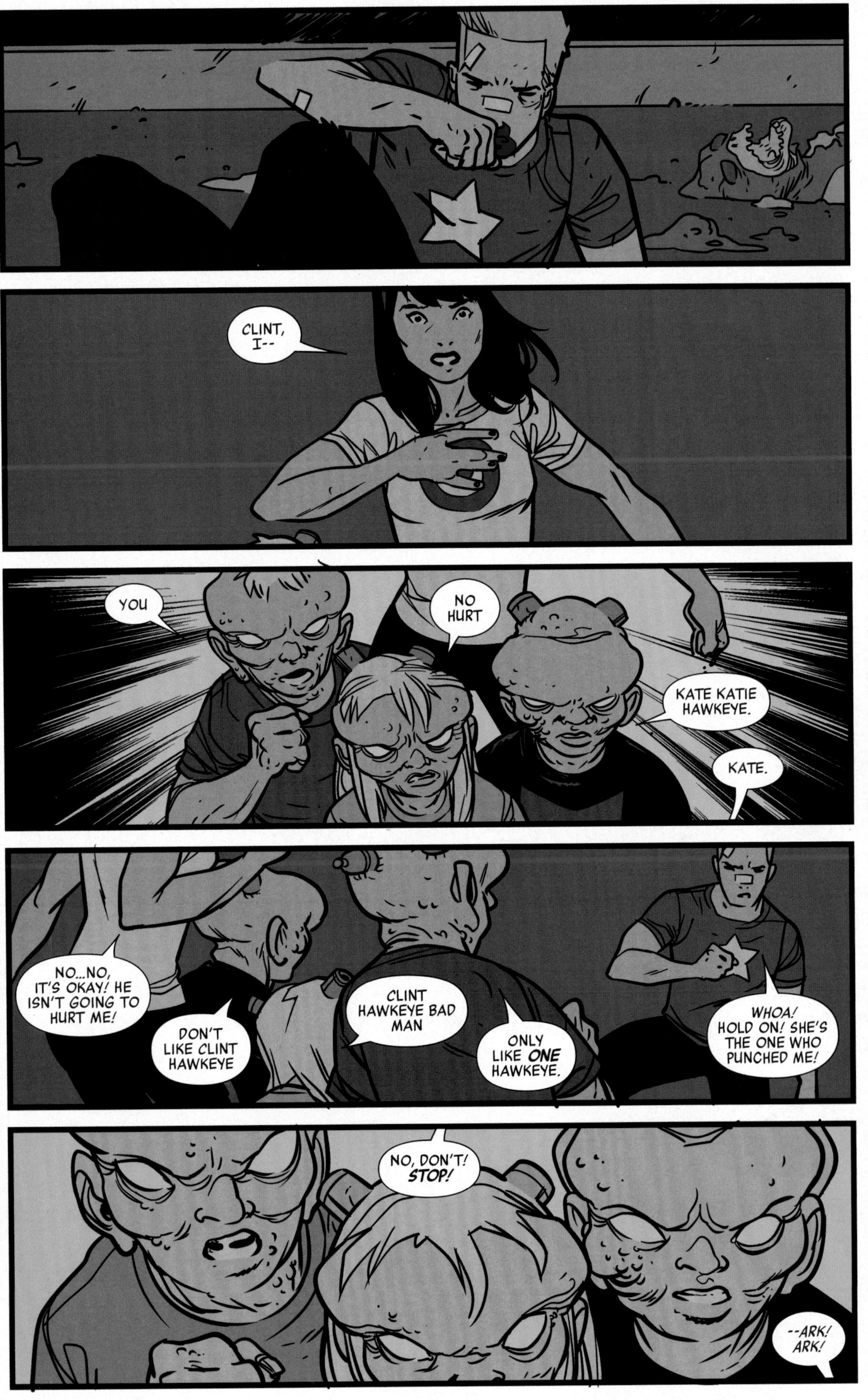
CLINT, I--
YOU
NO HURT
KATE KATIE HAWKEYE.
KATE.
NO...NO, IT'S OKAY! HE ISN'T GOING TO HURT ME!
DON'T LIKE CLINT HAWKEYE
CLINT HAWKEYE BAD MAN
ONLY LIKE *ONE* HAWKEYE.
WHOA! HOLD ON! SHE'S THE ONE WHO PUNCHED ME!
NO, DON'T! *STOP!*
--ARK! ARK!

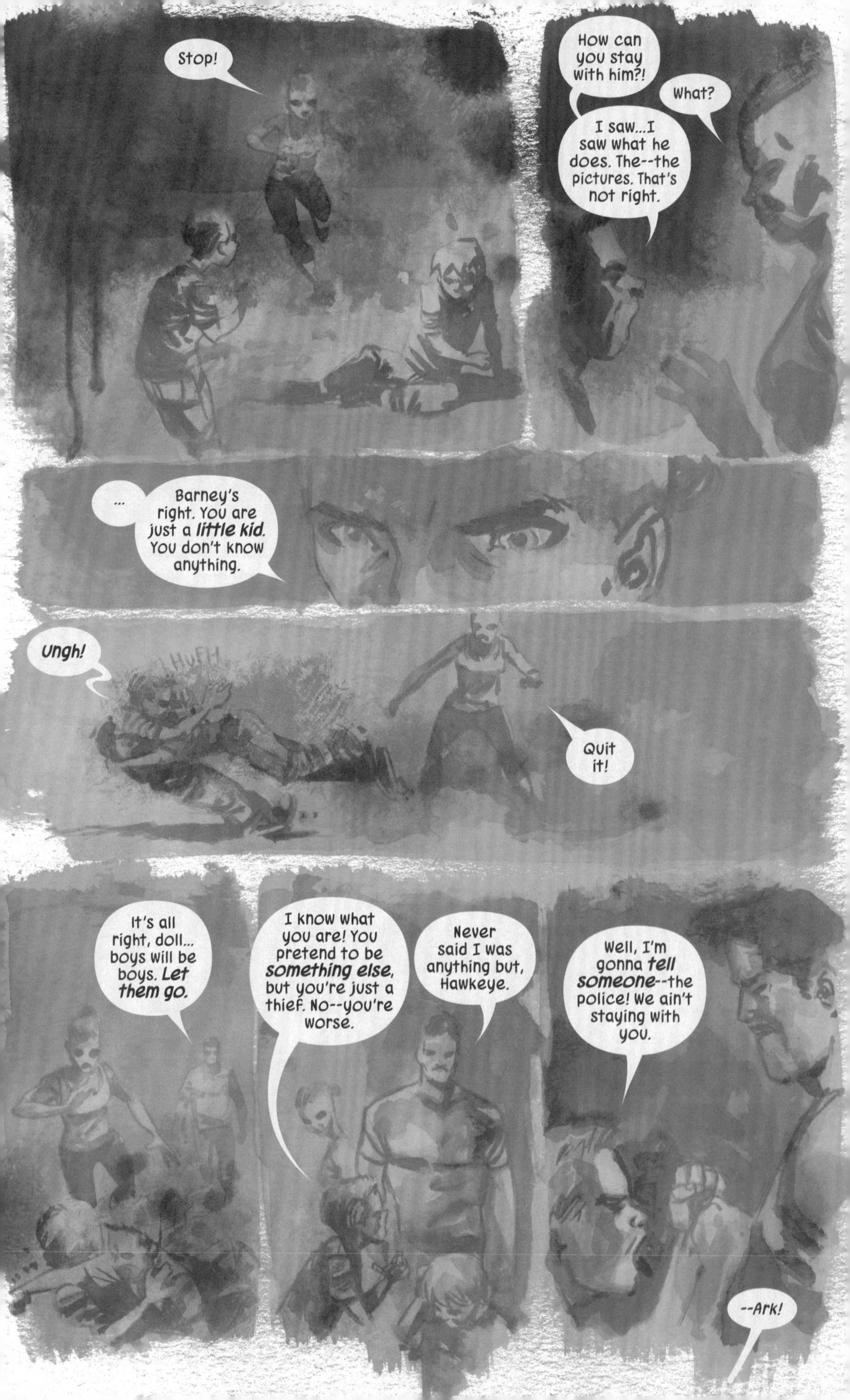
Stop!
How can you stay with him?!
What?
I saw...I saw what he does. The--the pictures. That's not right.
... Barney's right. You are just a *little kid*. You don't know anything.
Ungh!
HUFH
Quit it!
It's all right, doll... boys will be boys. *Let them go.*
I know what you are! You pretend to be *something else*, but you're just a thief. No--you're worse.
Never said I was anything but, Hawkeye.
Well, I'm gonna *tell someone*--the police! We ain't staying with you.
--Ark!

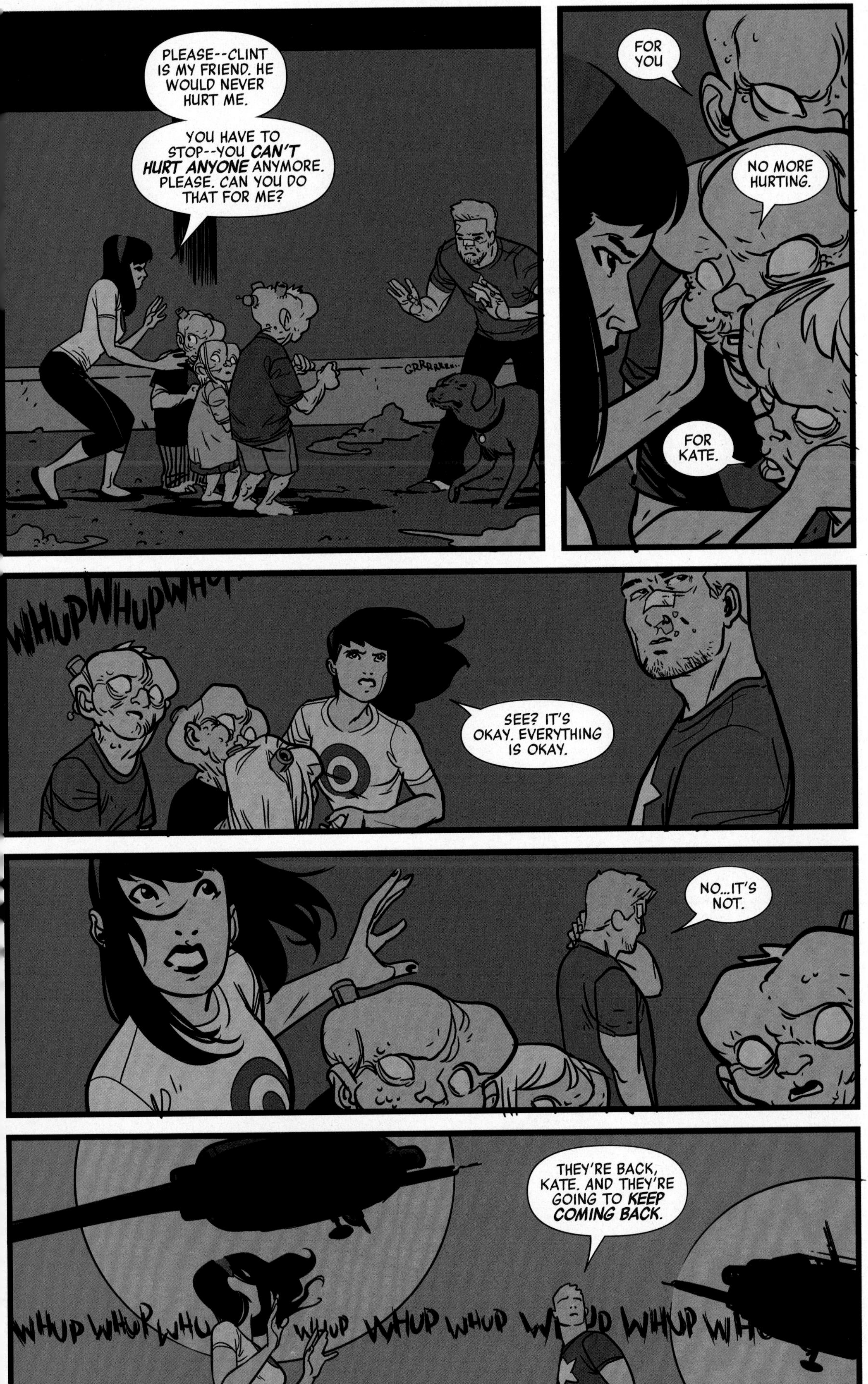
PLEASE--CLINT IS MY FRIEND. HE WOULD NEVER HURT ME.
YOU HAVE TO STOP--YOU **CAN'T HURT ANYONE** ANYMORE. PLEASE. CAN YOU DO THAT FOR ME?
GRRRRRR...
FOR YOU
NO MORE HURTING.
FOR KATE.
WHUPWHUPWHU
SEE? IT'S OKAY. EVERYTHING IS OKAY.
NO...IT'S NOT.
THEY'RE BACK, KATE. AND THEY'RE GOING TO **KEEP COMING BACK.**
WHUP WHUP WHU
WHUP WHUP WHUP
WHUP WHUP WHU

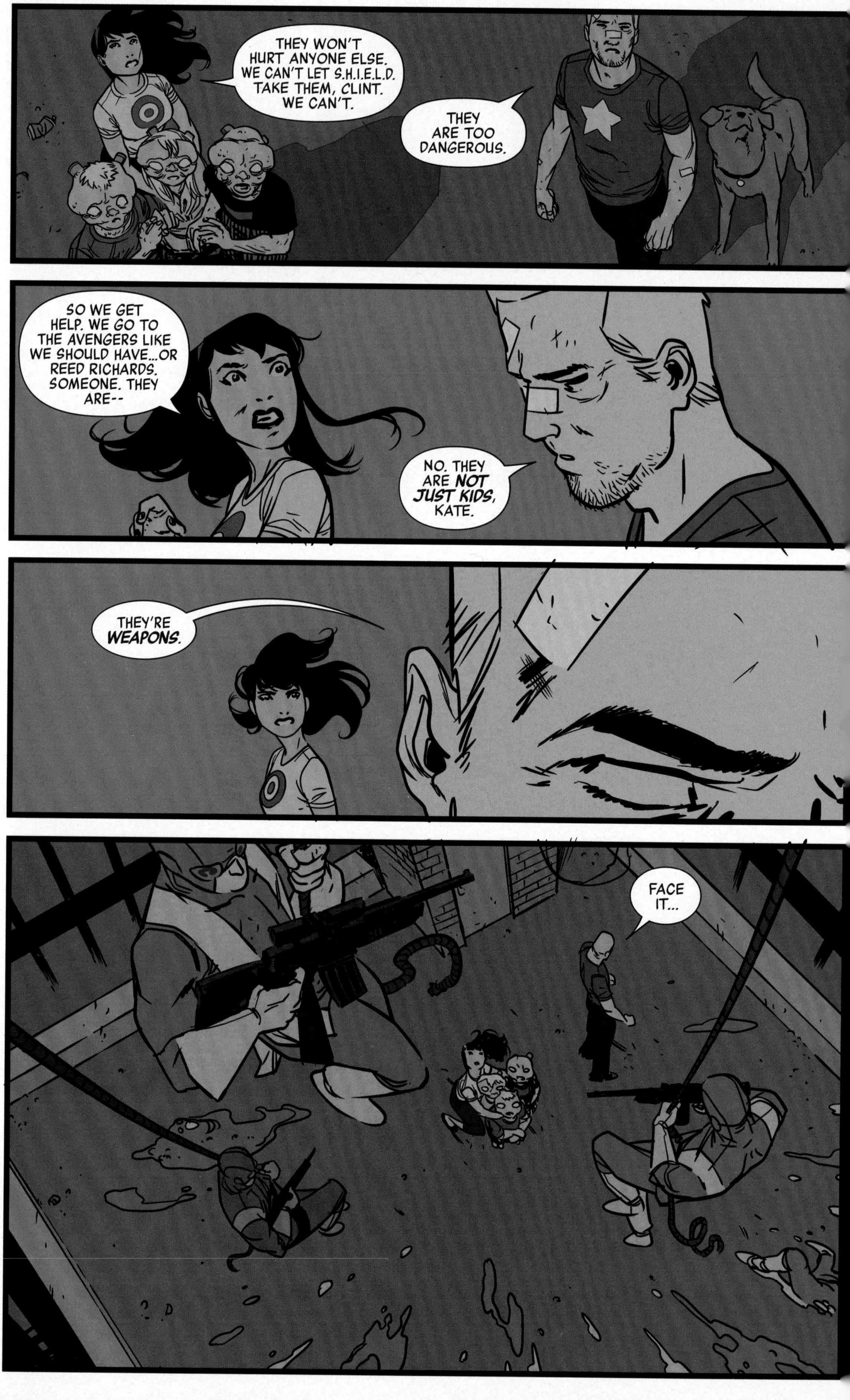
THEY WON'T HURT ANYONE ELSE. WE CAN'T LET S.H.I.E.L.D. TAKE THEM, CLINT. WE CAN'T.
THEY ARE TOO DANGEROUS.
SO WE GET HELP. WE GO TO THE AVENGERS LIKE WE SHOULD HAVE...OR REED RICHARDS. SOMEONE. THEY ARE--
NO. THEY ARE NOT JUST KIDS, KATE.
THEY'RE WEAPONS.
FACE IT...

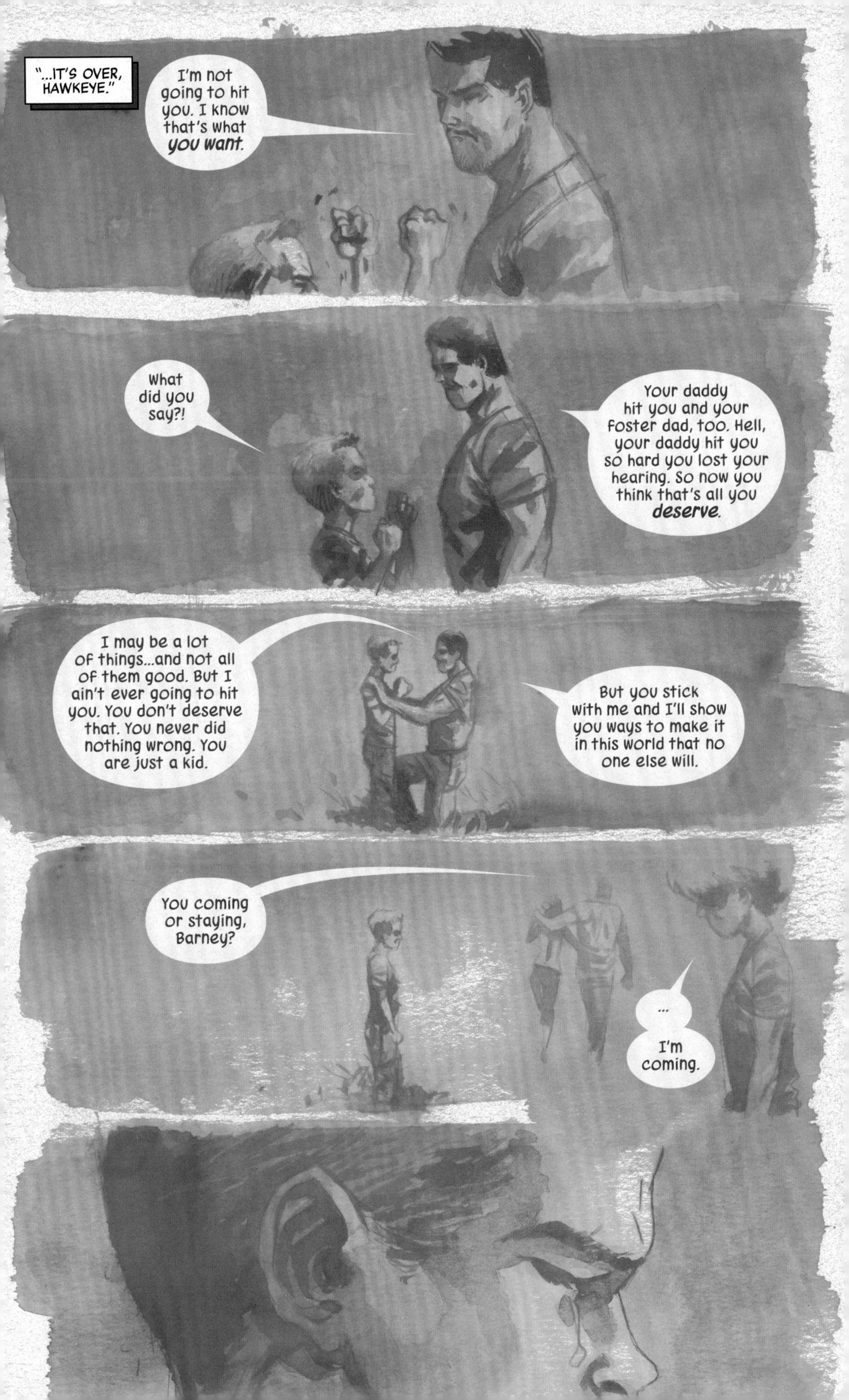
"...IT'S OVER, HAWKEYE."
I'm not going to hit you. I know that's what *you want*.
What did you say?!
Your daddy hit you and your foster dad, too. Hell, your daddy hit you so hard you lost your hearing. So now you think that's all you *deserve*.
I may be a lot of things...and not all of them good. But I ain't ever going to hit you. You don't deserve that. You never did nothing wrong. You are just a kid.
But you stick with me and I'll show you ways to make it in this world that no one else will.
You coming or staying, Barney?
...
I'm coming.

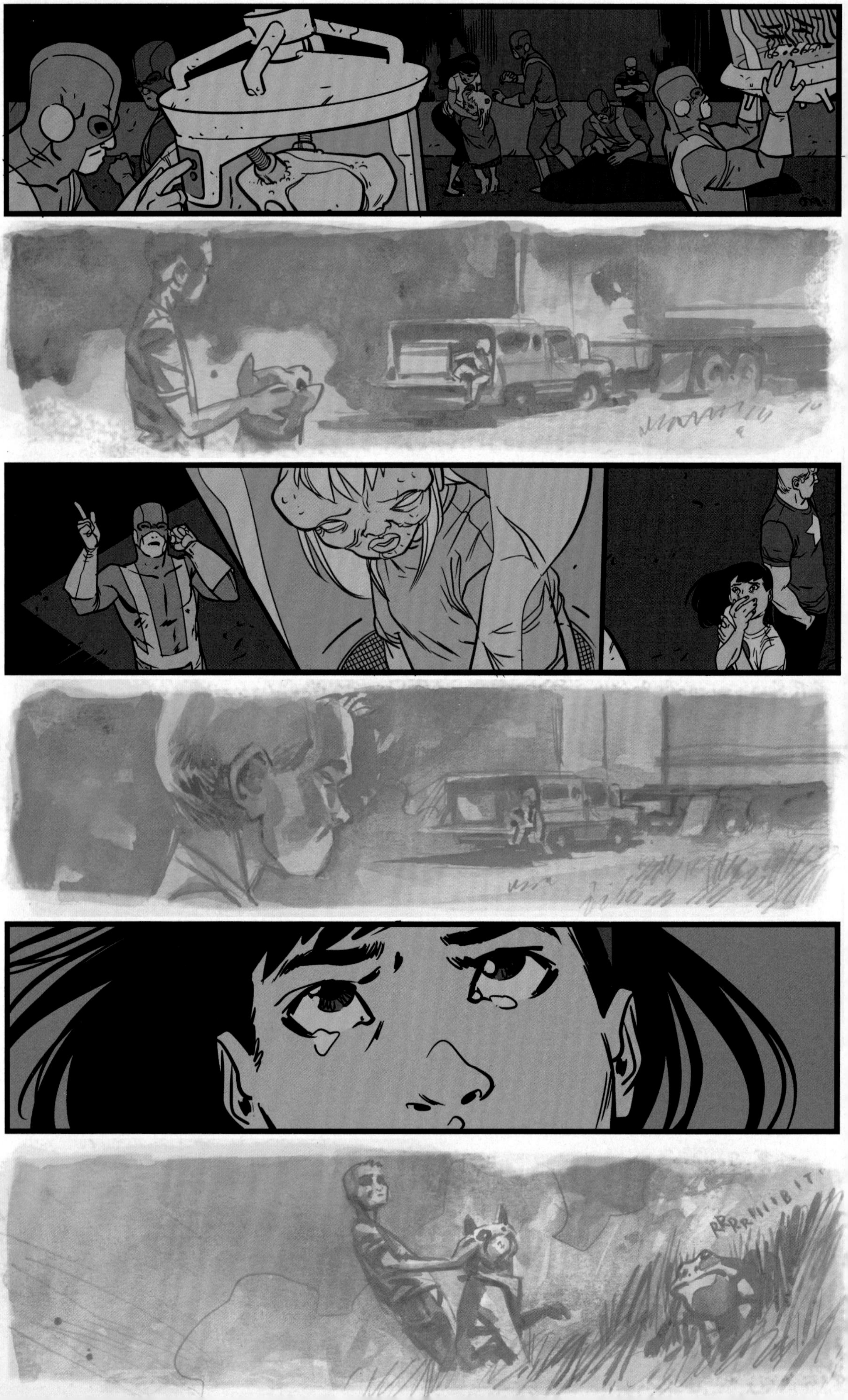
RRRRIIIBIT

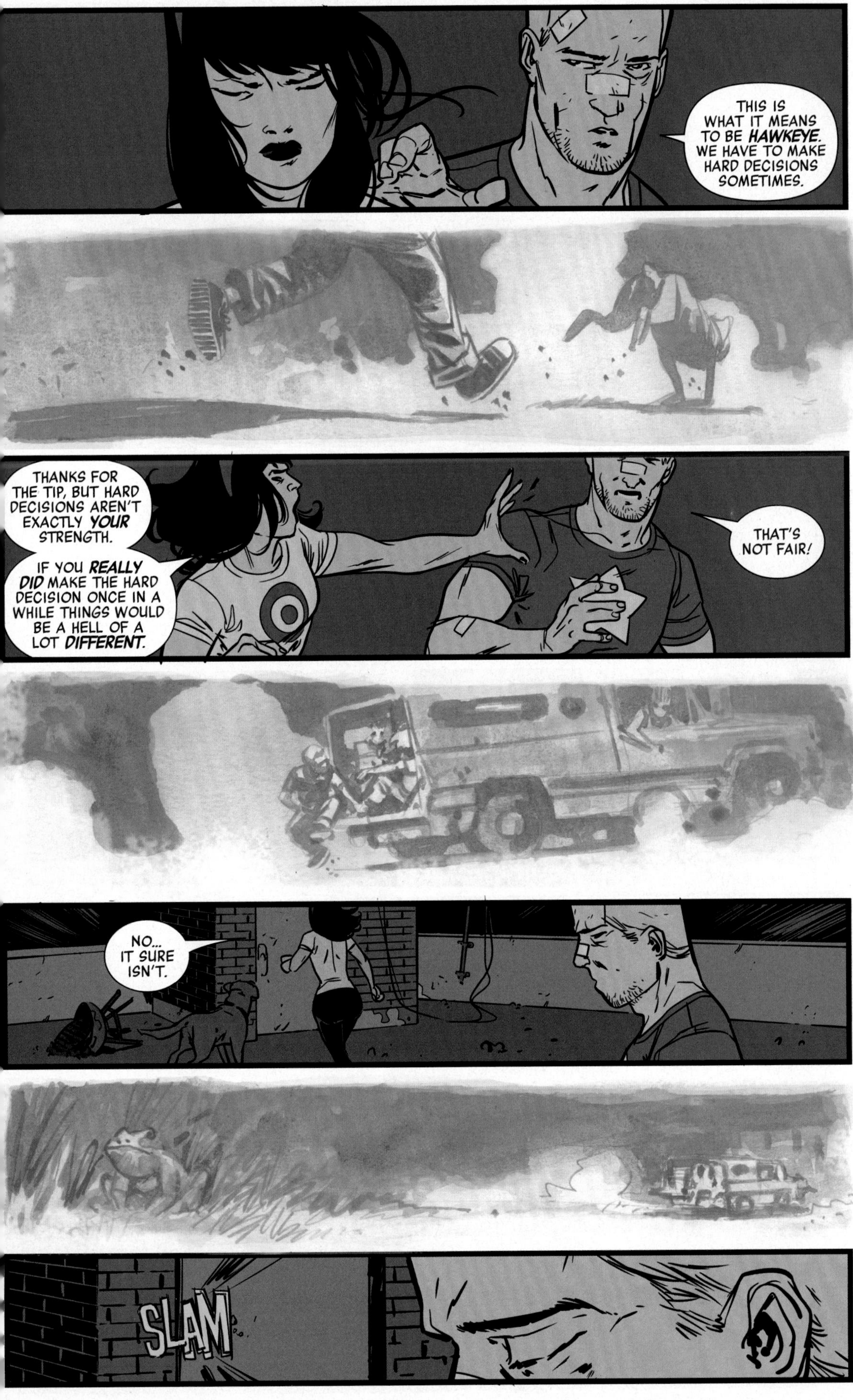
THIS IS WHAT IT MEANS TO BE HAWKEYE. WE HAVE TO MAKE HARD DECISIONS SOMETIMES.
THANKS FOR THE TIP, BUT HARD DECISIONS AREN'T EXACTLY YOUR STRENGTH.
IF YOU REALLY DID MAKE THE HARD DECISION ONCE IN A WHILE THINGS WOULD BE A HELL OF A LOT DIFFERENT.
THAT'S NOT FAIR!
NO... IT SURE ISN'T.
SLAM

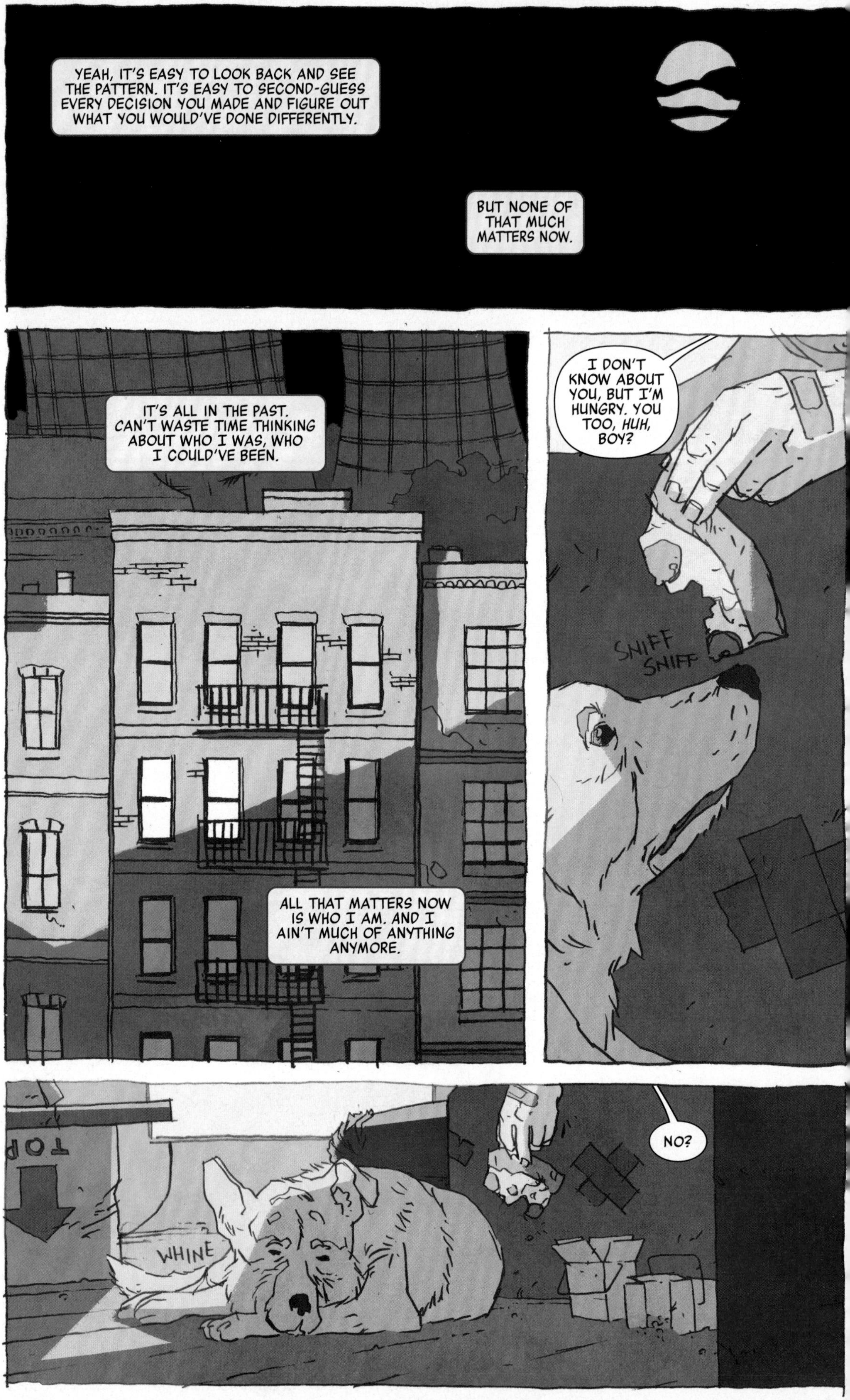
YEAH, IT'S EASY TO LOOK BACK AND SEE THE PATTERN. IT'S EASY TO SECOND-GUESS EVERY DECISION YOU MADE AND FIGURE OUT WHAT YOU WOULD'VE DONE DIFFERENTLY.
BUT NONE OF THAT MUCH MATTERS NOW.
IT'S ALL IN THE PAST. CAN'T WASTE TIME THINKING ABOUT WHO I WAS, WHO I COULD'VE BEEN.
ALL THAT MATTERS NOW IS WHO I AM. AND I AIN'T MUCH OF ANYTHING ANYMORE.
I DON'T KNOW ABOUT YOU, BUT I'M HUNGRY. YOU TOO, HUH, BOY?
SNIFF SNIFF
WHINE
NO?

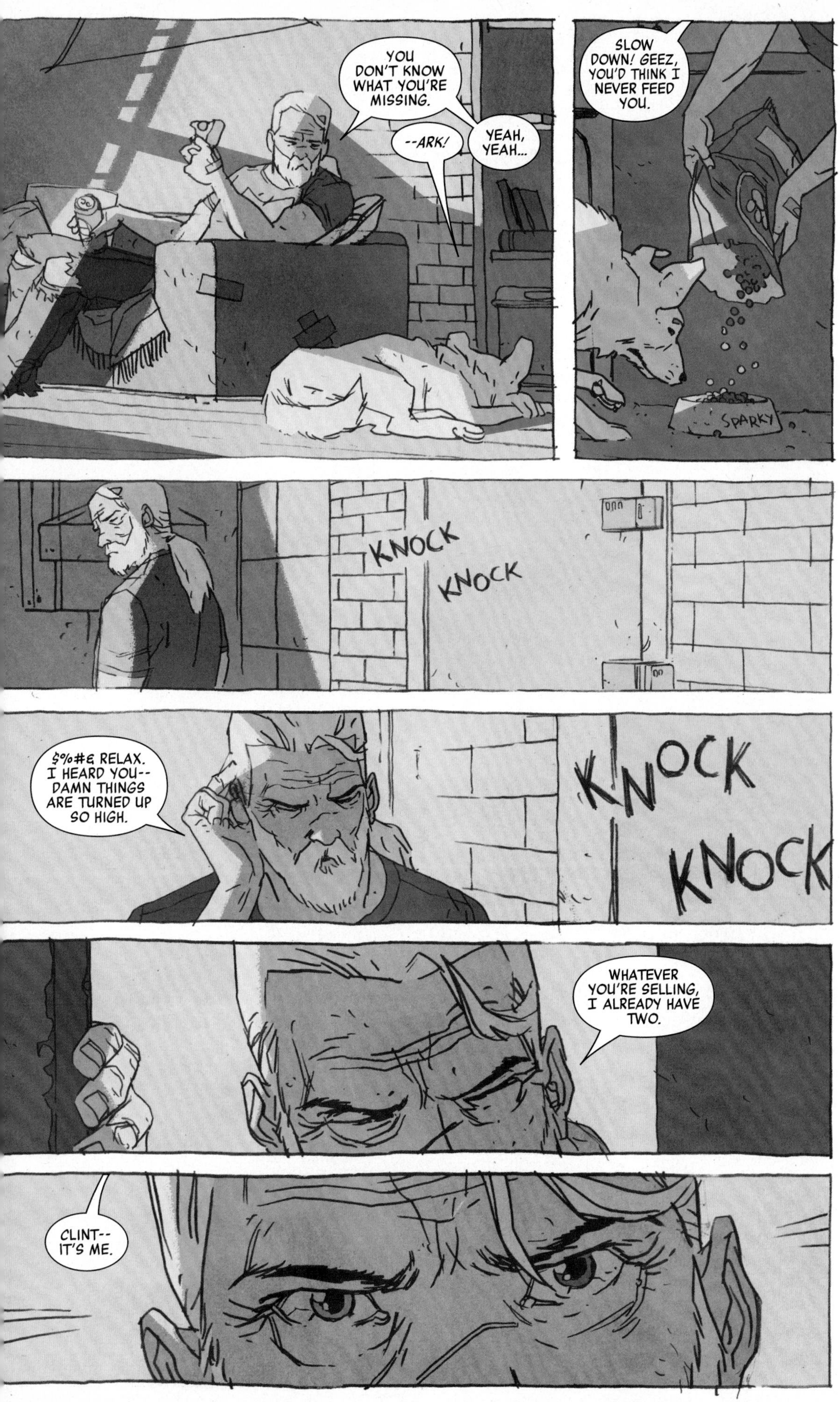
YOU DON'T KNOW WHAT YOU'RE MISSING.
--ARK!
YEAH, YEAH...
SLOW DOWN! GEEZ, YOU'D THINK I NEVER FEED YOU.
SPARKY
KNOCK
KNOCK
$%#& RELAX. I HEARD YOU-- DAMN THINGS ARE TURNED UP SO HIGH.
KNOCK
KNOCK
WHATEVER YOU'RE SELLING, I ALREADY HAVE TWO.
CLINT-- IT'S ME.

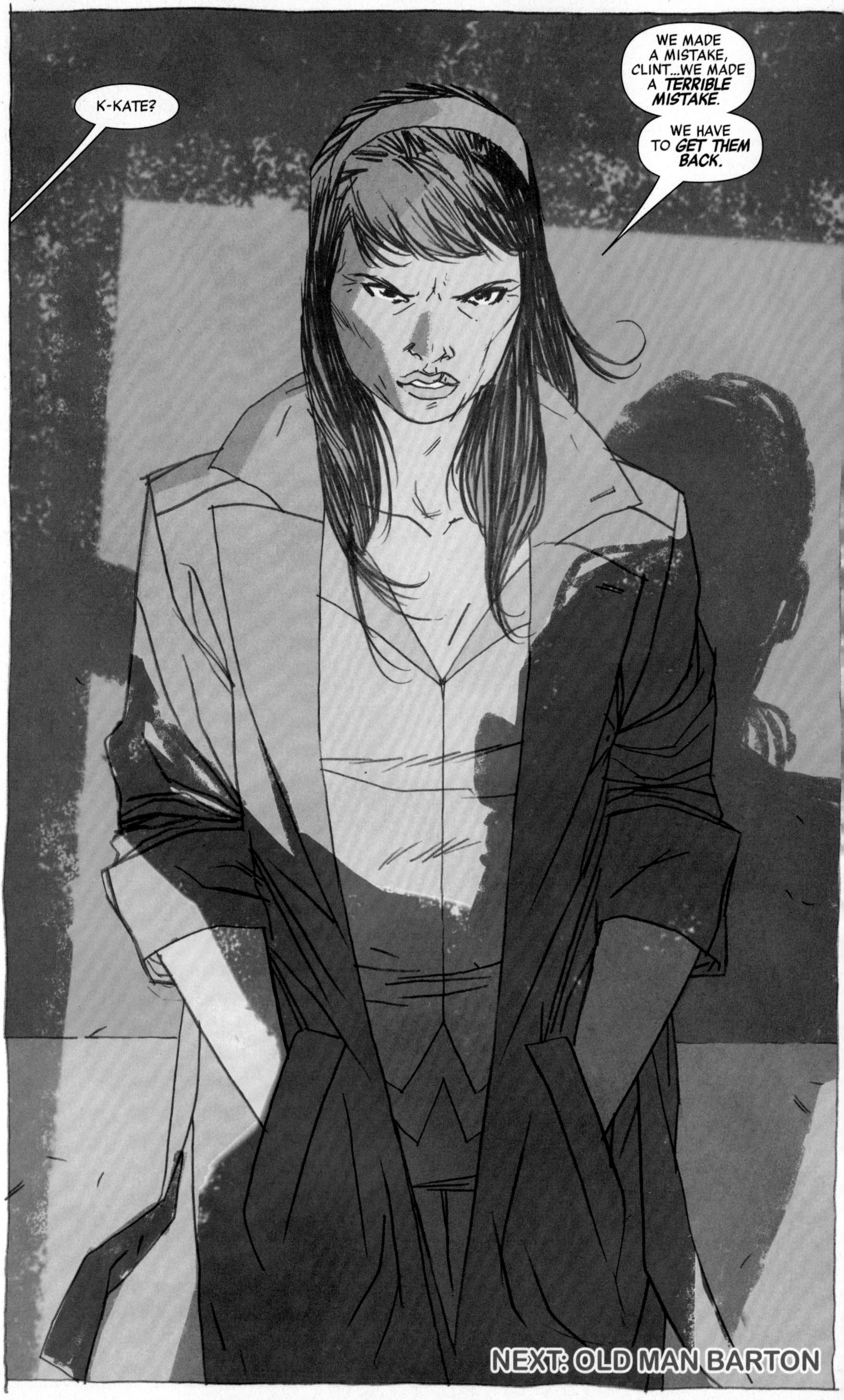
K-KATE?
WE MADE A MISTAKE, CLINT...WE MADE A TERRIBLE MISTAKE.
WE HAVE TO GET THEM BACK.
NEXT: OLD MAN BARTON

ALL-NEW HAWKEYE #1
WOMEN OF MARVEL
VARIANT BY **SHO MURASE**

ALL-NEW HAWKEYE #2
VARIANT BY **KEVIN WADA**

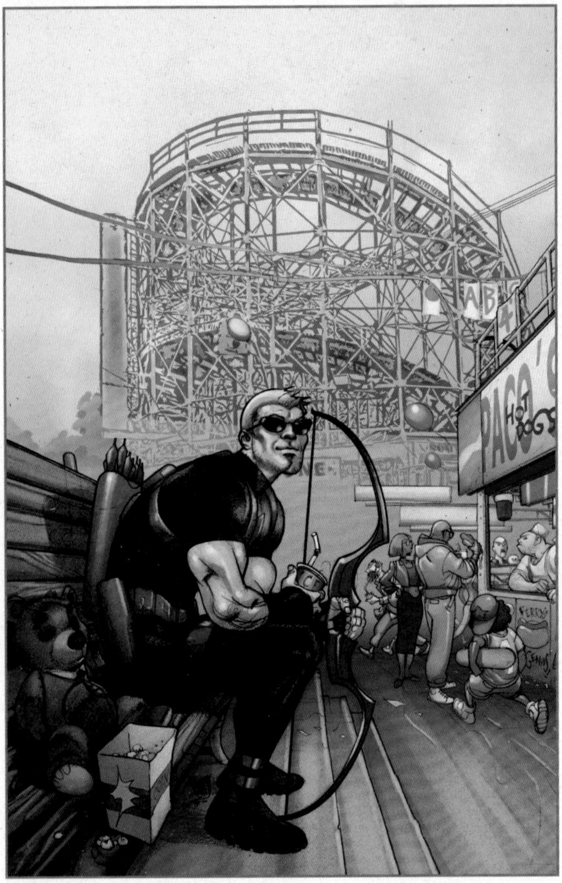

ALL-NEW HAWKEYE #3 NYC VARIANT BY
PASQUAL FERRY & **CHRIS SOTOMAYOR**

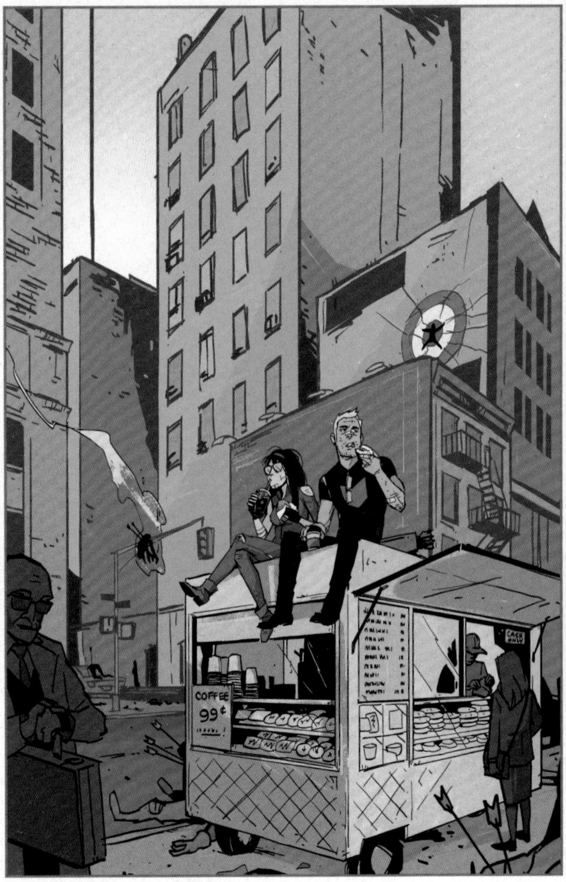
COFFEE
99¢

ALL-NEW HAWKEYE #3 VARIANT BY **ANNIE WU**

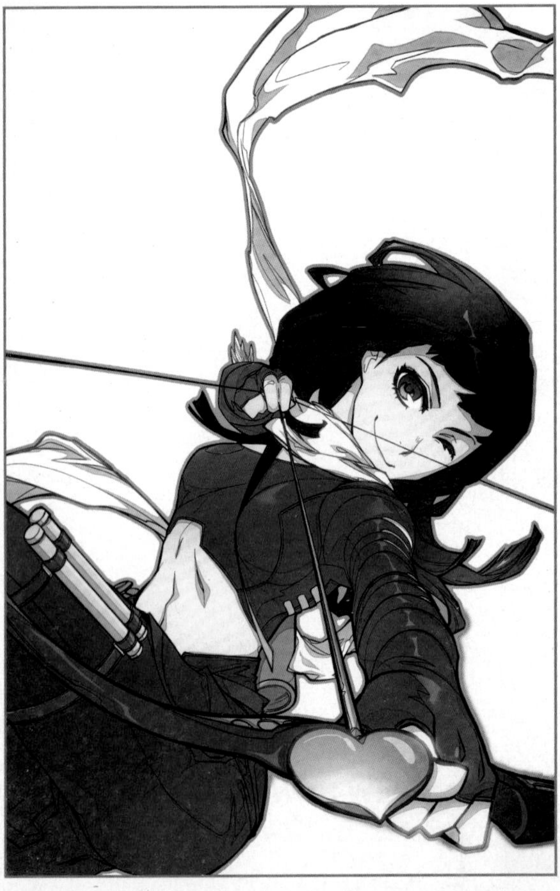

ALL-NEW HAWKEYE #5
MANGA VARIANT BY
CHIKA OGAKI